BUDDHISM

ORIGINS, TRADITIONS AND CONTEMPORARY LIFE

BUDDHISM

ORIGINS, TRADITIONS AND CONTEMPORARY LIFE

EDITED BY

JANA IGUNMA AND SAN SAN MAY

BRITISH LIBRARY

First published in 2019 by
The British Library
96 Euston Road
London NW1 2DB

British Library Cataloguing-in-Publication Data
A catalogue record for this publication is available from the British Library

ISBN 978 0 7123 52345 (hardback)
ISBN 978 0 7123 52390 (paperback)

Designed by Will Webb Design
Printed and bound in the Czech Republic by PB Tisk

FRONTISPIECE: A Buddha of the past, illustrated in a Burmese folding book providing information of their names and places of their enlightenment. Burma, 19th century. British Library, Or.14823, f. 23

CONTENTS

Preface

It was an exciting moment when, a decade ago, a small display of Southeast Asian material, including Thai and Burmese Buddhist manuscript furniture bequeathed to the Library from Doris Duke's Southeast Asian Art Collection, was opened to the public for the first time. The landing in front of the Library's Asian and African Studies reading room has since become a popular destination for many visitors: schoolchildren often sit in circles in front of the objects taking notes and making drawings, university students can be seen in lively discussions with professors or curators, some people find the gallery inspiring for yoga or meditation, families with children admire the stunning exhibits, visitor groups listen attentively to their Library tour guide, and followers of different faiths use the space for prayer, reflection and worship.

Over time, library users, visitors, students and colleagues expressed more and more frequently their interest in something bigger and asked us if we could organize a major exhibition on the theme of Buddhism. However, we saw this as too big a challenge for two curators who otherwise specialize exclusively in Southeast Asian manuscripts. We approached our colleagues within the Library who work with Buddhist material, and Sam Van Schaik, then working with the International Dunhuang Project (IDP), came back to us with an initial concept for an exhibition.

The theme of Buddhism is so broad that an exhibition of this scale could only be achieved with close co-operation between curators, academics, Buddhist practitioners and community leaders. This book aims to accompany the exhibition and to provide more insight into the religious and cultural context of the exhibits. There are too many people to mention here who have helped with the exhibition and this book – apologies, therefore, for possible omissions.

We would like to give special thanks to Sam Van Schaik, who as well as developing the initial exhibition and book concept has also been an excellent and helpful colleague throughout; and to Luisa Mengoni, who as Head of the Asian and African Collections gave us every possible support. Without the competence, experience and language skills of our colleagues neither the exhibition nor this book would have been possible. We are greatly indebted to Colin Baker, Jody Butterworth, Sara Chiesura, Sud Chonchirdsin, Eleanor Cooper, Eyob Derillo, Mélodie Doumy, Annabel Teh Gallop, Emma Harrison, Han-Lin Hsieh, Arani Ilankuberan, Pasquale Manzo, Yasuyo Ohtsuka, Burkhard Quessel, Malini Roy, Lydia Seager, Cam Sharp Jones, Ursula Sims-Williams, Ilana Tahan, Jayesh Tailor, Ching Yuet Tang, Hamish Todd and Janet Topp Fargion.

We have received invaluable advice and encouragement from the members of our advisory panel: Ajahn Amaro, Ajahn Sundara, Lama Jampa Thaye, Phra Maha Bhatsakorn Piyobhaso, Venerable Ru Chang, Jo Backus, Tim Barrett, M.R. Narisa Chakrabongse, Annabel Teh Gallop, Beth McKillop, Jerry Losty, Luisa Mengoni, Sam Van Schaik and Stanley Wong.

We gratefully acknowledge the continued support of the Royal Thai Embassy in London, especially H.E. Ambassador Pisanu Suvanajata and spouse. The World Tipitaka Foundation kindly donated to the Library a complete set of three editions of the Pali Buddhist Canon, made under His Majesty the King of Thailand's gracious patronage, which has become an indispensable resource for our research.

Other organizations and supporters we wish to thank are Amaravati Buddhist Monastery in Hemel Hempstead, Buddhapadipa Temple in London, Buddhist Heritage Project Luang Prabang, Dechen London Sakya Buddhist Centre, London Buddhist Vihara, London Fo Guang Shan Buddhist Temple, Oxford Buddhist Vihara, Soka Gakkai International UK, Venerable Mahinda Deegalle, Amal Abeyawardene, Urs App, Hans Georg Berger, John Falconer, Alexandra Green, Irving Chan Johnson, Betty Kunjara, Daravanh Nokeokouman Sananikone and David Wharton for helping with translations, identifying texts and visual material, providing information on Buddhist practices and sharing their knowledge, ideas and concerns with us. We also wish to thank Peter Holland for his generous support of the *Buddhism* exhibition.

Special recognition goes to Susan Dymond, Janet Benoy and Alex Kavanagh of the British Library's Exhibitions team, the colleagues at the Library's Conservation Centre (BLCC), as well as Abbie Day and her colleagues in the British Library Publishing team for their indispensable support throughout. Their meticulous professionalism is greatly appreciated. Some of the many others whose work was vital are the colleagues at the Library's Imaging Studio as well as textile conservator Elizabeth Rose, who had to take care of an unforeseen amount of large textile objects that needed to be prepared for photography and the exhibition.

Last but not least we would like to express our heartfelt gratitude to the authors of this book, who are listed separately with more biographical details. It is first and foremost thanks to their expertise and in-depth knowledge that this book contains a variety of contributions that reflect the great diversity of Buddhist cultures in Asia and beyond.

Jana Igunma and San San May

A note on transliteration and names

Romanization in this book follows standards of the Library of Congress, which is also used in the British Library's catalogues. Buddhist terms are spelled either in their Sanskrit or Pali form, depending on the context. Many Sanskrit and Pali terms used in the study of Buddhism have gained currency in the English language; therefore common spellings have been retained in this book. The spelling of lesser-known Sanskrit and Pali terms in the many scripts and alphabets in use in Asia is sometimes inconsistent, which subsequently leads to confusion about diacritics in the Romanized forms. For this reason, we decided to abandon the diacritics used in the Library of Congress Romanization standards, hoping that this makes reading the book easier for general audiences, while the scholarly reader will still be able to identify the term in its original form. All Sanskrit and Pali terms are searchable in the British Library catalogues without diacritics.

Place names can be problematic as they sometimes change over time, or the location changes or ceases to exist, and sometimes the same place name can be used for different locations. Generally, the most commonly known geographical names have been retained. Where this has not been possible, an explanation is given, or the more commonly known place name has been added in brackets.

INTRODUCTION

Jana Igunma

Buddhism is today one of the world's major religions, thought to have more than 500 million followers worldwide and nearly 300,000 in the UK. These numbers can only be estimates since Buddhism does not propagate conversion. Embracing Buddhism or a Buddhist lifestyle is an individual decision that is not bound to formal membership of an organization or a religious community. According to official statistics, the countries with the highest number of Buddhists in their populations are China, Thailand, Japan, Myanmar (Burma), Sri Lanka, Vietnam and Cambodia. The fact that China has recently re-embraced Buddhism accounts for a significant surge in numbers of practising Buddhists.

Beginning in north India in the sixth century BCE with the enlightenment of the historical Buddha, Buddhism was adopted in Asia, providing a unifying force across the region while at the same time being expressed in culturally specific art and rituals. The Buddhist ideal of the Middle Path, promoting awareness, compassion, tolerance and non-violence, historically helped practising Buddhists to embrace local and ethnically specific traditions. These not only helped to shape the three main schools (see page 165) of Mahayana (mainly in East and parts of Southeast Asia), Theravada (mainly parts of South and Southeast Asia) and Vajrayana

Statue of the Buddha as a healer holding in his right hand a myrobalan – a fruit with medicinal properties. The statue is thought to have been commissioned by the last king of Burma, King Thibaw (r. 1878–1885) and his family. Lacquered and gilded wood, with mirror-glass inlay, Mandalay, Burma, before 1885.
British Museum, 1923,0305.1

(mainly Central Asia), but also fostered the integration of religious elements that originated in Hinduism, ancestor worship and other pre-Buddhist faiths.

Buddhism is a religion that is well known and widely practised in the West today. However, the history of contact between the West and Buddhism is almost as old as Buddhism itself. First encounters between European and Buddhist cultures go at least as far back as the fourth century BCE, resulting in Greco-Buddhist art forms that became famous as expressions of cultural–religious syncretism. Early patrons of Buddhism like the emperors Ashoka (third century BCE), Menander (second century BCE) and Kanishka the Great (second century CE) helped to spread Buddhism to the west and south of the Indian subcontinent. Buddhism also spread along the network of trade routes known as the Silk Road and reached Southeast Asia as early as the third or fourth centuries CE and Japan around the sixth century CE.

There were extensive trade relations between Europe and Asia throughout the first millennium CE, and as a result Europeans became increasingly interested in the cultures and religions of the Near and Far East, or what they later called 'the Orient'. Buddha is mentioned in a Greek source, *Stromateis*, by Clement of Alexandria, written around 200 CE. A religious romance inspired by the life of Buddha, 'Barlaam and Josaphat', was well known in the Judaeo-Persian tradition and versions in Arabic, Georgian and Hebrew have been discovered. The name Josaphat is a corruption of the title Bodhisattva, meaning 'Buddha-to-be', and refers to Prince Siddhartha, who became Gautama Buddha with his enlightenment. An early Greek version of this story is attributed to St John of Damascus (c. 675–749). It became particularly

Scene of the renunciation of worldly life of 'Josaphat' (Christianized expression for Bodhisattva). Barlaam and Josaphat, printed in German in Augsburg, Germany, *c.* 1470–80.

British Library, IB.5919

Ethiopic version of 'Barlaam and Josaphat' (Ge'ez: Baralam and Yewasef). Translation by Habakkuk for King Claudius dated 1553 CE from an Arabic version. The present copy was made during the reign of King Iyasu II (1730–1755 CE).

British Library, Or.699, f. 4

popular throughout the Christian world after it was translated into many different languages in the Middle Ages, including Latin, French, Provençal, German, Italian, Spanish, Dutch and Swedish.[1] With the Christian tradition, the story of Barlaam and Josaphat travelled to the African continent and was translated into Ethiopic.

From the thirteenth century on, first-hand accounts like that of Marco Polo and the Flemish Franciscan friar Willem van Ruysbroeck tell of encounters with Buddhism, and early maps indicate important places of worship and Buddhist pilgrimage sites. The travels of friars who were sent to central Asia, China and Sri Lanka aroused much interest in Europe, although their knowledge was based mainly on observations and therefore very limited with regard to the Buddhist scriptures. The first Christian missionary known to have acquired a good knowledge of Tibetan was the Italian Capuchin Francesco Orazio della Penna (1680–1745), who lived in Lhasa for sixteen years and compiled a Tibetan dictionary of about 35,000 words. From the second half of the eighteenth century the Indian sources of Buddhism in the Sanskrit and Pali languages began to be studied extensively, and translations of original Buddhist scriptures helped to expand knowledge of Buddhist theory and practice in the West. In 1776 a *Kammavaca* text was translated from Pali into Italian and a translation of the life of Devadatta, Buddha's enemy, was published by Simon de la Loubère in 1691 in his *Description du Royaume de Siam*. The year 1817 saw the publication of the first comprehensive Western study of Buddhism, *Recherches sur Buddou* by Michel-Jean-François Ozeray. A Danish linguist, Rasmus Kristian Rask, visited Sri Lanka in 1821 and brought back a significant collection of Pali manuscripts, making Copenhagen one of the most important centres of Pali studies in Europe. Among the eminent scholars and translators of Buddhist scriptures in Europe were Léon Feer, Eugène Burnouf, Jean-Pierre Abel-Rémusat, Émile Senart, Viggo Fausböll, Robert C. Childers, Isaak Jakob Schmidt, Hermann Oldenberg, Max Müller, and Thomas W. Rhys Davids and his wife Caroline A.F. Rhys Davids. The Pali Text Society, which has been the major publisher of Pali text translations in Europe, was founded in 1881 by Thomas W. Rhys Davids.

The growing interest in Buddhism led to the organization of several expeditions to Buddhist countries in Asia from which large numbers of manuscripts in Sanskrit, Kuchean, Khotanese, Sogdian, Uighur, Tibetan, Chinese and other languages were brought back. These enabled the further investigation and translation of Buddhist scriptures. Among the most notable expeditions were the three led by Sir Aurel Stein at the beginning of the twentieth century, during the first of which a large Buddhist cave library containing 40,000 manuscripts and printed documents was discovered near the oasis town of Dunhuang. Thousands more manuscripts were excavated at ruined and long-forgotten Buddhist sites along the Silk Road. Research on these important manuscript collections, which were dispersed to various institutions across the world, is ongoing in the International Dunhuang Project.[2]

By the end of the nineteenth century various notable Europeans and Americans – the theosophists Henry Steel Olcott and Helena Blavatsky, U Dhammaloka and Ananda Metteyya, to mention only a few – had embraced Buddhism. The first publication making the life of Buddha and Buddhist ideas accessible to a wider audience was Sir Edwin Arnold's narrative poem 'The Light of Asia: The Great Renunciation' (1879), which after ten years

Map by Fernão Vaz Dourado indicating major cities which were also Buddhist centres and pilgrimage sites in Southeast Asia, contained in an album of seventeen maps drawn and ornamented in gold and colours, with shields of arms and flags. Portugal, 1573.
British Library, Add. MS. 31317, ff. 25v–26r

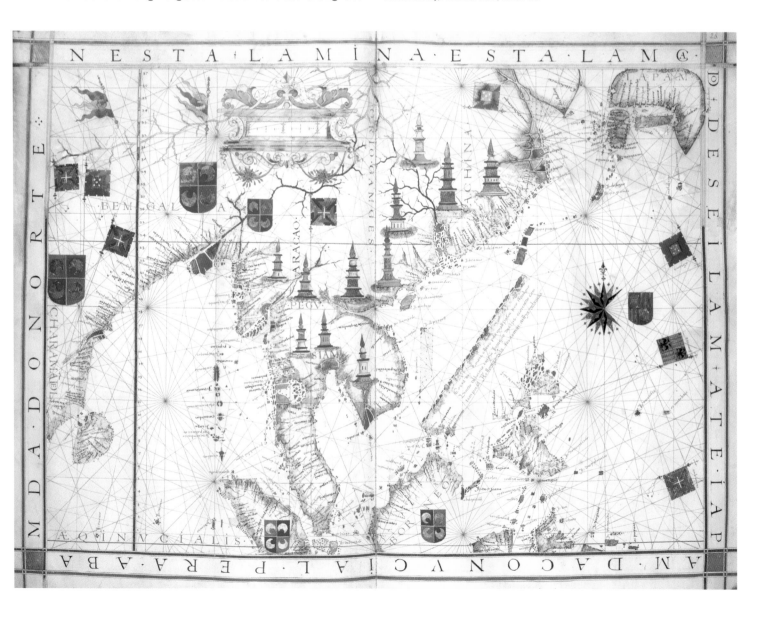

had already appeared in over one hundred editions. Dudley Buck composed an oratorio based on the very successful poem, entitled 'The Light of Asia', which was first performed in Washington DC in 1887 and in London in 1889; a German–Indian film adaptation was produced in 1928 by Franz Osten and Himanshu Rai.

Interest in Buddhist philosophy and art increased in the West during the twentieth century, also a result of the establishment of Buddhist temples and monasteries in Europe and the United States. The first Buddhist temple in Europe, Das Buddhistische Haus in Berlin, was founded by the German physician, writer and translator of Buddhist scriptures Paul Dahlke in 1924. In the same year the Buddhist Society in London was founded by the barrister Travers Christmas Humphrey. Another milestone was the English-language publication in 1927 of the Tibetan *Bar Do Thos Grol* (*Liberation through Hearing During the Intermediate State*) – in the West known as the *Tibetan Book of the Dead* – which helped to popularize Tibetan Buddhism in the West. Hermann Hesse's novel *Siddhartha* (1951), which is based on the life of Buddha (although in the book Siddhartha and Gautama Buddha are two different characters), was an influential publication during the 1950s and 1960s. Counterculture and anti-war movements during the 1960s and early 1970s fuelled a growing interest in Eastern religions, including Buddhism, and at the same time the arrival of refugees from Tibet, Vietnam, Laos and Cambodia in the West, many of whom were practising Buddhists, supported the emergence of mainstream Western Buddhism.

In modern society there are many more people who embrace a Buddhist lifestyle or certain practices, such as Buddhist meditation or Buddhist vegetarianism, without identifying themselves as Buddhists. Buddhist ideas have become inspirational within modern art, music, literature, film, architecture, design and landscape design and influence alternative ways of life and healing, environmental protection, education and so on. Buddhist themes are the subject of many contemporary literary works like Osamu Tezuka's manga series *Buddha* (1972–1983), Hikaru Nakamura's manga series *Saint Young Men* (2006–) and David Mitchell's *Cloud Atlas* (2004). Numerous contemporary artists, actors, musicians, politicians and businesspeople have embraced Buddhism or Buddhist lifestyles. Some activities that are connected with Buddhism – Zen gardening, mandala art, listening to meditation music, calligraphy and collecting Buddhist art – have found their way into mainstream Western culture and are practised by many as hobbies.

Historic and modern Buddhist sites are among the major tourist attractions of several Asian countries and are visited by tens of millions every year. Many Buddhist temples and temple ruins are pilgrimage destinations or are visited by practising Buddhists for worship and

First page of 'Part II: The Renunciation', of the oratorio 'The Light of Asia: A Cantata' by Dudley Buck, with words from the poem by Edwin Arnold, published by Novello, Ewer & Co. of London and New York, 1886.
British Library H04/2397, p. 73

The Bamiyan Valley, a UNESCO World Heritage site in Afghanistan. Monumental Buddha statues and caves represent the religious and artistic developments that characterized ancient Bakhtria from the first to the thirteenth centuries. This historic illustration shows two Buddha statues carved into the Bamiyan Cliffs between the third and fifth centuries, which were destroyed in 2001.

to make offerings. UNESCO has listed fifty-six Buddhist sites in nineteen countries as World Heritage sites, thus encouraging and actively helping the preservation and protection of Buddhist cultural heritage that is of outstanding value to humanity.

Building on the foundations laid during the nineteenth and early twentieth centuries, Buddhist Studies programmes have been developed in the past few decades at numerous universities in the UK (including Oxford, Cambridge, London's School of Oriental and African Studies [SOAS], King's College London, Bristol and Bath Spa) and in Europe (Humboldt University of Berlin, Hamburg, Munich, Heidelberg, Bonn, Vienna, Ghent, Naples 'L'Orientale', the Sorbonne and the

Centre d'Études Interdisciplinaires sur le Bouddhisme in Paris). Buddhist Studies is an academic career path that attracts much interest, which may not only be a result of a growing general interest in Buddhism and Buddhist art and literature, but also of the fact that Buddhism is now included in GCSE Religious Education specifications in the UK and those of other European countries.

The book market of the past hundred years provides a clear picture of how interest in Buddhism and Buddhism-related topics has increased. Compared to around 1920, the number of books with Buddhism-related content in the English language that are published annually has increased twentyfold, and the annual overall publication of books on Buddhism is now

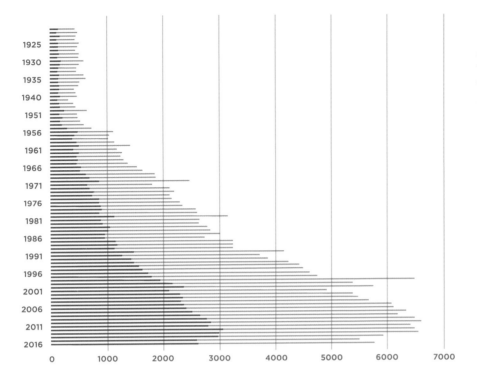

English-language publications (blue) and overall academic publications (orange) of the past 100 years on Buddhist themes that are held in libraries of the Worldcat network.

fifteen times higher than it was a hundred years ago. The Library of Congress's worldcat.org database lists more than 400,000 publications on Buddhism-related subjects, including monographs, journal articles, theses, electronic publications and audiobooks. Published film and video footage on Buddhism amounts to around 8,500 items and published music and sound recordings to more than 6,200 items. These figures only include publications recorded in electronic library catalogues, which means that the real figures are actually higher.

The British Library's collections of Buddhist manuscripts and artefacts reflect the interest that Europeans have had and continue to have in Buddhism, going back well over 1,000 years. The collections of missionaries, colonial officers, merchants, scholars and private art collectors were acquired by the British Museum and the India Office Library and subsequently these were transferred to the British Library. The uniqueness of the Library's collections of Buddhist material led to the decision to organize a major exhibition on Buddhism, which aims to showcase Buddhist treasures that have never before been displayed publicly. The provenance of most of the exhibits shows that the introduction of Buddhism in the West is not entirely a result of global migration processes of the past decades, but equally of an active interest among Europeans in Buddhist philosophy, art, lifestyles and everyday practices.

The exhibition that this book accompanies aims to show that Buddhism has a global outreach and exists across a broad range of cultures, where it has inspired diverse artistic expression and lifestyles. Despite the huge diversity of Buddhist cultures, Buddhists have shared knowledge and values that are relevant in the twenty-first century. A great variety of extant manuscripts and printed books are evidence that Buddhism was a driving force behind the advancement of manuscript production and printing techniques in Asia.

The exhibition explores the life of the historical Buddha, born Siddhartha Gautama around 2,600 years ago. Ceremonies relating to the events of his life continue to dominate the Buddhist calendar today. Buddhist philosophy is based around the word of the Buddha. Monastery libraries and Buddhist universities like the famous one at Nalanda in northeast India, now a UNESCO World Heritage site, played a key part in the spread of the faith across Asia. Scholars, Buddhist and non-Buddhist, continue to translate and to research Buddhist scriptures and their meaning in the modern world. Meditative practices and the Buddhist concepts of compassion and loving-kindness remain central to Buddhism as practitioners navigate life in the twenty-first century.

Some aspects of Buddhism that are not generally well known are highlighted: the diversity of representa-

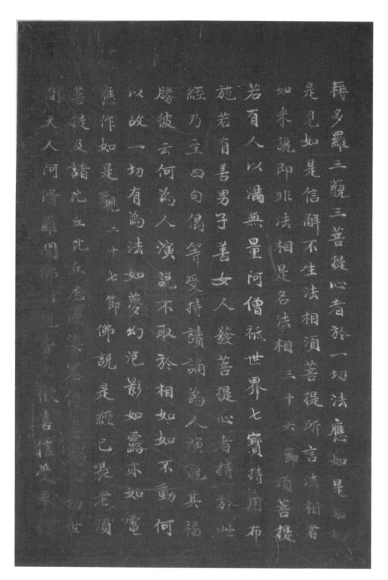

Miniature painting of Guanyin (Bodhisattva Avalokitesvara) on a leaf from a Bodhi tree (*Ficus religiosa*), in a book containing the *Heart Sutra* and the *Lotus Sutra*. China, 19th century.
British Library, Add. MS. 11746, ff. 1v–2r

tions of legendary Buddhas of the past and future as well as the historical Buddha; the variety of formats and materials of Buddhist scriptures; the outstanding art of Buddhist manuscripts and early printed works; the role of monastics in education and Buddhist scholarship; the role of women as monastics, lay practitioners and Bodhisattvas; and how Buddhism is part of people's real lives, as shown in ritual objects, amulets and meditation aids. Such objects still can play an important role for the mental health and overall wellbeing of practising Buddhists today.

Modern everyday life is becoming increasingly complex and dependent on technology with a defining overload of information and over-activity of the mind and senses. While multi-tasking is much praised as a necessary skill to succeed in professional life, the skill of mono-tasking – or mindfully concentrating on a single activity – has almost been forgotten and is being relearned in mindfulness courses and meditation sessions that are offered by an increasing number of employers and education providers. The topic of 'Buddhism' is ideal for showing ways in which individuals can liberate themselves from the emotional and mental pressures of modern life. This is a new perspective on ancient Buddhist philosophy and art, in line with the growing trend of mindfulness as a way of life that attracts interest from people with diverse religious and non-religious backgrounds.

The Life of the Buddha

The Buddha narrative and the qualities of a Buddha, or Enlightened One, play a major role in all Buddhist traditions. Although the Buddha was initially not depicted in human form but symbolically, throughout the first millennium CE a rich artistic tradition of painting and rendering in sculpture not only the Buddha but also Bodhisattvas and important monastics emerged. Painted wall hangings, temple banners and Buddhist manuscripts, which are as impressive as mural paintings in the top tourist sites of Asia, illustrate the historical Buddha's life and stories about his previous incarnations.

In addition to the historical Buddha, the Buddhas of past aeons as well as the future Buddha Maitreya and the idea of Bodhisattvas need to be considered in order to understand the concept of 'Buddhahood' that is central to Buddhist philosophy. *Stupas* – monuments where the Buddha's relics are believed to be enshrined – and also Buddha-footprints and sacred Bodhi trees related to the life of the Buddha are important Buddhist symbols and places of worship, meditation and pilgrimage. Artistic representations of Buddhas and Bodhisattvas are objects of veneration as well as aids for meditative reflection.

In the first chapter of this book, Angela Chiu explores scenes from the life of the historical Buddha, also known as Shakyamuni Buddha or Gautama Buddha. These include his birth and childhood, the Four Encounters, his renunciation of the world, defeat of Mara, enlightenment, founding of the *sangha*, meeting his former mother in Tavatimsa heaven, his later life and attainment of *pari-nirvana*. The number of scenes from the Life of Buddha varies and can reach from four or eight to up to eighty scenes, as represented, for example, at the Ananda Temple in Pagan, Myanmar (Burma). Numerous manuscripts and paintings from all geographical regions and from various periods highlight the consistency and continuity of the Buddha narrative throughout time, though represented in different cultural and artistic contexts. Whereas certain scenes from Buddha's life associated with the *mudras* (gestures) of the Buddha figure are often highlighted in mural painting and sculpture, the manuscript traditions do not always follow a particular standardization of scenes.

The concept of 'Buddhahood' (or being enlightened, being awakened) is central to Buddhist philosophy. The long path of attaining enlightenment is not only revealed through the narrative of the life of the historical Buddha, but also through stories about his 547 previous lives. These birth stories, or *jatakas*, based on belief in the cycle of rebirths (*samsara*), were used to teach lay Buddhists about moral values and ethical principles. An important text known as *Mahabuddhaguna* describes the

Printed folding book with the *Dai hannya haramita-kyo* (Sanskrit: *Mahaprajnaparamita Sutra*), a text on the Perfection of Wisdom in Chinese characters (Kanbun text without reading marks), with a frontispiece illustration of Shakyamuni Buddha teaching the *dharma* to the Chinese pilgrim monk Xuan Zang. Kofukuji temple, Japan, *c*. 1380.
British Library, Or.64.b.16, ff. 1–4

佛説大報父母恩重經

[The image above contains Japanese/Chinese text in vertical columns accompanying the illustration]

Japanese version of the *Sutra of Filial Piety* (Japanese: *Bussetsu daiho bumo onjugyo*), a text that was not part of the original Buddhist Canon but was composed in China during the Tang Dynasty (618–917 CE), incorporating Confucian ideas of filial piety. From China the *Sutra* was taken to Korea, and then to Japan where the first editions appeared at the end of the 14th century based on Korean exemplars. Japan, *c.* 17th century.

British Library, Or.16331

extraordinary qualities of a Buddha, a person who has attained Buddhahood. These qualities are often highlighted through lavish illustrations depicting scenes from the Last Ten *Jatakas* in Southeast Asian manuscripts.

Angela Chiu provides insight into the idea that there have been a number of Buddhas, or people who have achieved Buddhahood, in the past. The belief in the future Buddha Maitreya enjoys great popularity and is often depicted in funeral and commemoration books. The concept of Bodhisattvas includes persons who have attained enlightenment and are able to reach *nirvana*, but delay doing so out of compassion for all sentient beings. Initially, the term was used for Shakyamuni Buddha in his former lives. According to Mahayana teachings, throughout the history of the universe, which has no beginning and no end and is subject to permanent change, many have committed themselves to attaining Buddhahood. As a result, the universe is filled with a broad range of potential Buddhas, from those just setting out on the path of Buddhahood to those who have spent many lifetimes improving their qualities and have thereby acquired special powers. These 'celestial' Bodhisattvas are thought to be functionally equivalent to Buddha in their wisdom and compassion.

Wheel of Life: Philosophy and Ethics

In the second chapter of this book, Venerable Khammai Dhammasami provides insight into important aspects of Buddhist philosophy that developed from philosophical and cosmological concepts of ancient India. Buddhist teachings in their entirety are not restricted to the canonical word of the Buddha alone, but include the ideas, interpretations and commentaries of his followers and later scholars who have emerged over the past 2,500 years. The *Tripitaka* is regarded as the oldest collection of Buddhist scriptures and consists of three major 'baskets' of scriptures: *Sutra Pitaka* (discourses attributed to the historical Buddha), *Vinaya Pitaka* (monastic discipline) and *Abhidharma Pitaka* (higher teachings).

Buddhist cosmology highlights the concept of the Thirty-One Planes of Existence, which include the various heavens and hell, as well as the concept of four continents situated in an ocean around the sacred Mount Meru. The Buddhist pantheon, particularly that of the Mahayana and Vajrayana traditions, includes not only the idea of Bodhisattvas, but also pre-Buddhist and local gods and deities that found their way into Buddhist cosmology as protectors of the *dharma*. In Theravada Buddhism, Hindu gods are believed to be subservient to the teachings of the Buddha.

Venerable Khammai Dhammasami explains how the concept of *karma*, the principle of cause and effect, determines the cycle of *samsara*, or birth–death–rebirth, which is regarded as a continuation of suffering. The principles of *karma* and *samsara* are often visually expressed in form of the Wheel of Life, or Wheel of Rebirth, in Vajrayana Buddhism. The Buddha's words include the teachings on the Four Noble Truths about suffering and

'Chittanakhon', a Thai illustrated story by Theerabodhi Bhikkhu (Ajarn Theeraphan Lorpaiboon) explaining the Buddhist approach to psychology through the representation of thoughts and emotions by characters living in the 'City of the Mind' (Pali: 'Citta Nagara') with inspiration from a work by His Holiness Phra Nyanasamvara, the 19th Supreme Patriarch of Thailand. Bangkok, Thailand, 2013.
British Library, EMP.2017.b.11, front cover

its causes, and the Noble Eightfold Path, which describes eight practices that lead to enlightenment, and finally *nirvana*, the overcoming of the cycle of rebirths, *samsara*.

The creation of manuscripts and artworks as acts of merit helped to preserve the Buddha's wisdom and to develop further Buddhist ethical principles and aesthetic standards. Rare cosmologies and lavishly painted manuscripts and banners illustrate Buddhist ideas such as *samsara*, *karma* and the Four Noble Truths. Narratives of popular monastics, Bodhisattvas and local Buddhist heroes helped to integrate folk traditions with Buddhist ethics and to popularize Buddhism beyond urban centres of education and monasticism across Asia.

The Pali *Tipitaka*, being a large collection of texts comprising between fifty and eighty large volumes (depending on language), is thought to contain the original words of Shakyamuni Buddha. If regarded as one corpus, the *Tipitaka* is the largest book in the world, set in stone at the Kuthodaw Pagoda in Mandalay, Myanmar (Burma). In addition, the Pali *Tipitaka* has been complemented by numerous commentaries, sub-commentaries and extra-canonical texts.

The sacred scriptures of the Mahayana and Vajrayana schools include large numbers of additional texts that summarize and highlight essential teachings of the Buddha and are regarded as canonical in the Mahayana and Vajrayana traditions, although they were created after Shakyamuni Buddha's attainment of *pari-nirvana*. Many of the Mahayana texts serve important educational and devotional purposes of the lay communities.

There are numerous Buddhist texts that are not formally part of the Buddhist Canon, but are important sources in some geographical regions or among some ethnic groups that speak many different languages. These are often based on texts in the Buddhist Canon and commentaries, for example the *Pannasa jataka*, and they helped to popularize and spread Buddhism across Asia.

Finally, Venerable Khammai Dhammasami outlines the contribution of Buddhist philosophy to psychological research and new approaches to mental health care in the West. Ongoing scientific studies are exploring the effectiveness of Buddhist meditation and mindfulness and how they can be applied in modern healthcare without a religious context.

The Book: Manifestations of Knowledge and Cultural Exchange

Although the Buddha's words may have been handed down orally in the first two or three centuries after his passing, the production of manuscripts and printed books was an important religious activity in the promotion and dissemination of his teachings and ideas over the past two millennia. Beth McKillop explores in the third chapter how early Buddhist scholars adapted to local traditions and adopted methods and technologies of recording and spreading the spoken word. A great variety of scriptures were created across Asia, using tree bark, palm leaves, silk, paper, ivory, gold, silver and other metals as writing materials. Buddhism was the driving

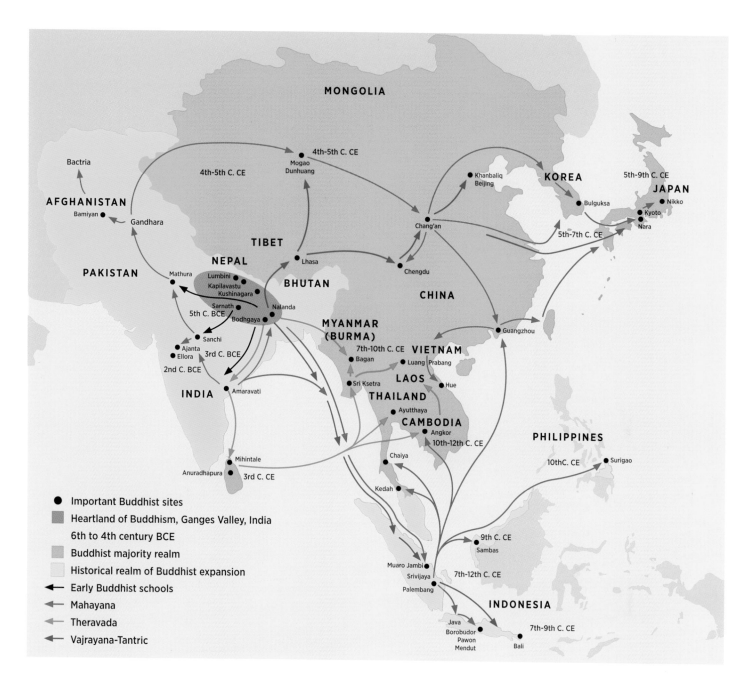

MONGOLIA

Bactria

4th-5th C. CE

Mogao
Dunhuang 4th-5th C. CE

AFGHANISTAN

Bamiyan Gandhara

Khanbaliq
Beijing **KOREA**

JAPAN 5th-9th C. CE

Bulguksa Nikko
Kyoto
Nara

Chang'an

5th-7th C. CE

PAKISTAN Mathura

NEPAL
Lumbini
Kapilavastu
Kushinagara **TIBET** Lhasa

BHUTAN

Chengdu

CHINA

Sarnath
Bodhgaya Nalanda
5th C. BCE

Sanchi

Ajanta
Ellora 3rd C. BCE

2nd C. BCE

**MYANMAR
(BURMA)** 7th-10th C. CE **VIETNAM**

Guangzhou

INDIA Amaravati

Bagan Luang Prabang

Sri Ksetra **LAOS**

THAILAND Hue

Ayutthaya

CAMBODIA

Angkor
10th-12th C. CE

PHILIPPINES

Chaiya

Mihintale

Anuradhapura 3rd C. CE

10th C. CE Surigao

Kedah

9th C. CE
Sambas

Muaro Jambi

Srivijaya 7th-12th C. CE

Palembang

INDONESIA

Java
Borobudor 7th-9th C. CE
Pawon
Mendut Bali

● Important Buddhist sites

▉ Heartland of Buddhism, Ganges Valley, India
6th to 4th century BCE

▉ Buddhist majority realm

▉ Historical realm of Buddhist expansion

← Early Buddhist schools

← Mahayana

← Theravada

← Vajrayana-Tantric

Map illustrating the spread of Buddhism and formation of the major Buddhist traditions.

Novice monks practising the art of making palm leaf folios, selecting suitable leaves from palm tree fronds. Vat Manolom, Luang Prabang, Laos, 1999.

force behind the mass production of paper and of printing technologies (stamping and block printing) to further the ethical and moral education of the general population.

Buddhists were also early adopters of emerging knowledge systems and technologies, and monasteries were the centres of the production, reproduction and preservation of Buddhist scriptures. The spread and adaptation of scripts and writing systems, innovations such as the use of wooden printing blocks, early methods of translation and interpretation, text classification,

safe storage, conservation and retrieval of scriptures in monastery libraries, as well as the advancement of visualization techniques, are among the major achievements of Buddhist scholars. Translations of Buddhist scriptures and commentaries from Sanskrit and Pali, the languages used by early Buddhists, into local languages helped to spread Buddhist philosophy across Asia and worldwide, and are exemplary works of early academic translation that form the basis of international Buddhist scholarship and research up to today.

Beth McKillop looks at methods of production of Buddhist scriptures that not only required and further developed the knowledge of scribes and translators, but also demanded creative craftsmanship and artistic talent. The earliest writing materials and bindings formed the basis for the development of new book formats on paper and metal derivatives that followed the model of natural leaves, particularly those of the palm tree. There is no rule as to which texts can be written or incised on which material, but the durability of any particular material and the purpose for which a text was written played an important role in the decision. Illumination, illustration and decoration of Buddhist scriptures always played an important role not only to add meritorious value to manuscripts, but also to simplify the identification and retrieval of certain scriptures or text passages, which could be very extensive, in monastery libraries.

Paper scrolls and folding books could be used in more diverse ways than palm leaf manuscripts. Paper as the carrier of a variety of Buddhist scriptures, which in the form of scrolls, folding books and bound books was flexible and light, was easy to store and to carry along on pilgrimages. Paper is also a material ideally suited for illustration and illumination, which helped to transmit Buddhist ideas, values and ethics in picture form, in turn facilitating reaching the general population of many different countries who had no knowledge of Sanskrit or Pali. Sometimes mural paintings were copied on paper to produce a kind of portable mural for worship, prayer and meditation. Paper was therefore crucial for the spread of Buddhism all over Asia.

The technology of block printing revolutionized knowledge transfer mainly in the Mahayana and Vajrayana traditions. Through block printing techniques it was possible for the first time to mass-produce Buddhist scriptures and images for distribution to lay communities. This technology was of particular importance along the routes of the Silk Road and in East Asia, where monastics acquired the necessary skills and established printing workshops at monasteries. These became flourishing businesses as they also mass-produced protective paper amulets and pocket chanting books, which are still popular today.

Beth McKillop also mentions Buddhist monastery libraries, which played a central role in Buddhist education and scholarship. The challenging climate in many geographical regions made special storage solutions of manuscripts and books necessary. Furniture and containers that are traditionally used to store manuscripts at temple libraries had to be designed to keep the scriptures safe from damage by water, humidity, mould, insects and rodents. To manage large monastery libraries, Buddhist monastics developed retrieval methods using title indicators, registers of scriptures, custom-made manuscript

Buddhist Practice: Mindfulness and Compassion

The fourth chapter, by Dion Peoples, investigates everyday life in Buddhist communities and explores the interrelationship between monastics and lay people in historical and contemporary perspectives. Manuscripts that are used in Buddhist ceremonies document the main Buddhist rituals, but they also illustrate important duties and responsibilities of monastics, which can include engagement in charitable activities, general education, healthcare and funeral practices as well as methods to improve mental and emotional wellbeing. Dion Peoples demonstrates how the Buddhist scriptures give advice and answers to questions that arise in people's daily lives, and how monastics provide guidance and support for lay Buddhists in all sorts of situations. In return, lay communities provide material support for the monastic communities and help with the establishment and upkeep of Buddhist temples and monasteries. Peoples also contemplates how the themes of pilgrimage, transmigration and rebirth have inspired literature and folklore in many Buddhist countries, and the ways in which this long-standing tradition is continued in contemporary media and art. At the same time, however, there have been instances of trivialization and desacralization of Buddhist symbols.

Today, Buddhism enjoys greater diversity than ever before, and new Buddhist movements can be relevant to and support people living in modern society. Socially engaged Buddhists address social, environmental and political issues in various non-violent ways, thus attracting much interest in the West. Buddhist meditation has become a widespread practice all over the world that

Scroll of the *Diamond Sutra*, the oldest reliably dated printed book. Cave 17, Mogao Caves near Dunhuang, China, Gansu Province, 868 CE.
British Library, Or.8210/P.2

Annual procession of manuscripts containing Buddhist scriptures at Gangteng Monastery. The collection was digitized 2005–2006 with the support of the British Library's Endangered Archives Programme EAP039. Bhutan, 2006. Photograph by Karma Phuntsho.

are often perceived as negative, like stress, information overload, overreliance on communication, lack of time, lack of happiness, lack of sense and so on.

Materials from the British Library's Endangered Archives Programme and the International Dunhuang Project document the rediscovery and preservation of Buddhist sites and manuscript treasures. Such activities help communities to preserve their cultural heritage, memories and identities, essential in the process of overcoming cultural clefts that once were fostered by colonial and postcolonial ideologies.

Dion Peoples discusses practical aspects of life in the *sangha* (order of monastics), which include not only the study of the *dharma* and memorizing Buddhist texts that are important in ceremonies, but also practical activities like the maintenance and conservation of monasteries, providing education and life guidance to lay followers as well as charitable tasks. Beside their scriptural studies, monastics are encouraged to work on their critical-thinking skills and to gain specialist knowledge, for example in medicine and healthcare, art, temple design and construction, foreign languages, manuscript production, publishing, information technology, computing and much more. The lives of monastics are often characterized by travelling for the purpose of study and knowledge exchange as well as the establishment of new Buddhist monasteries.

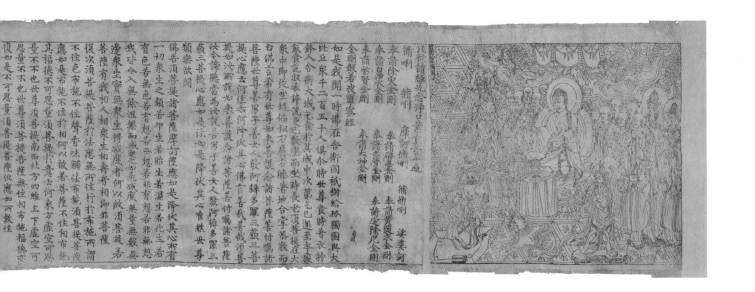

Ullambana Dharma service, a ceremony to honour parents and forefathers and to make merit on their behalf to save them from sufferings after death, held in September 2017 by nuns at the London branch of the Taiwan-based Fo Guang Shan Monastery.

The Buddhist scriptures provide answers to most questions about life in general and a right life in the Buddhist sense in particular. In his chapter, Dion Peoples gives an overview of parts of the Buddhist Canon that are important for the practising Buddhist. Most of the Buddhist scriptures have been translated into many Asian languages and many texts that deal with philosophical and ethical problems are available in Western languages. However, one significant problem is that translations of scriptures that are important for the practising Buddhist are still lacking in the latter.

Making merit is the aim of many regular activities of lay Buddhists. Such activities include the provision of food, clothes and items of everyday use for monastics, support with the maintenance of the monasteries and decoration of temple buildings for Buddhist ceremonies, participation and attendance at Buddhist festivals and temple fairs, and commission of copies of Buddhist scriptures for wider distribution and educational purposes. Monarchs or political leaders who claim to be followers of Buddhism are expected to play an active and outstanding role in such activities, which are thought to be meritorious in the context of *karma* and rebirth. Lay people receive from the monastic community spiritual and practical support in challenging life situations, in addition to other benefits like education, health and mental health care, care of the elderly and support in bereavement.

Dion Peoples also discusses the role of women in Buddhism today. Women are regarded as relatively equal to men in the Buddha's teachings. Important scriptures were composed by female Buddhists, like the *Therigatha* and the *Ittivuttaka*. Ordination as monastics is open to women who are prepared to follow 311 rules specified in the *Bhukkhuni Patimokkha* (code of monastic discipline for nuns). *Bhikkhuni sangha* (the formal order of female monastics) are well established in the Mahayana and some Vajrayana traditions. All-female monasteries thrive in most East Asian countries.

The picture of women as monastics has been distorted by the fact that a *bhikkhuni sangha* has not been officially existent for centuries in the Theravada tradition in Southeast Asia. In some countries where Theravada Buddhism is the major religion the ordination of nuns is not officially recognized or is even forbidden, although a growing number of women nowadays seek ordination in Sri Lanka, where *bhikkhuni* ordination has been revived.

Compassion and loving-kindness are at the centre of everyday Buddhist practice. There are countless examples of compassionate acts, behaviours and gifts that aim to reduce the suffering of others. The *Vessantara jataka* illustrates the Buddhist understanding of compassion, which is based on generosity and selflessness. Active compassion requires the overcoming of egoism and self-centeredness, part of human nature. Awareness, mindfulness and meditation are important techniques that aid the overcoming of selfishness to enable a compassionate Buddhist lifestyle.

'No Mud, No Lotus'

Thich Nhat Hanh's short but concise aphorism 'No mud, no lotus' reveals one of the core aspects of Buddhism. The Buddha did not present himself as a saviour of the world, but accepted the existence of suffering as a universal, objective truth. He offered a path that can lead to the cessation of individual suffering by showing the causes of suffering and how to overcome them. Buddhism does not encourage the belief in a deity and does not look for a relationship between humanity and God, or for a perfect world. It is a more philosophical–spiritual tradition in search of enlightenment through the practice and development of morality, meditation and wisdom. It promotes a 'middle way' through life's challenges, rejecting all forms of extremism. Compassion and a regard for the interconnected nature of life are central to Buddhist practice.

Buddhism has always faced challenges, though. The story of the Life of Buddha mentions heretics who doubted and challenged the Buddha to exercise supernatural powers, which was against his will. Devadatta,

Illustrations of heretics opposing Buddha's teachings in a Burmese folding book with scenes from the *Life of Buddha*. Burma, 19th century.
British Library, Or.14405, ff. 57–58

Buddha's cousin and brother-in-law and formerly a disciple of Buddha wearing the monk's robe, became known as the greatest personal enemy of the Buddha, whom he attacked and attempted to kill several times. After Buddha's physical passing, the support that Emperor Ashoka gave to the Buddhist monastic order – building monasteries and the provision of robes and food – is said to have attracted people who posed as 'monks' for their own personal gain. Fake 'monks' and heretics can still be found today.

The persecution of Buddhists is as old as Buddhism itself. Controversies, however, have arisen, especially in the past decades, as Buddhists have become embroiled in violent political conflicts, for example in Tibet/China, Japan, Sri Lanka and Thailand. The most recent political controversy is related to the persecution of Muslims, and in particular of the Rohingya ethnic group in Myanmar (Burma), in which Buddhists, even monks, were involved.

One may argue that the persecution of Rohingya in Myanmar (Burma) is only one in a series of violent events that have been happening since the 1962 coup d'état that are not least rooted in divisive colonial and postcolonial policies. Members of other ethnic groups like the Karen, Kachin, Chin, Mon and Shan – the majority of the latter two follow the same Theravada Buddhism as the ethnic Burmese – have been exposed to similar hostile and violent treatments as a result of postcolonial political processes that were partially inspired by Stalinist–nationalist ideologies.[3]

However, according to the *Patimokkha* (monastic code of discipline), the intentional deprivation of a human being of life, or incitement of others to deprive a human being of life, or the praise and glorification of death entail the immediate expulsion from the monastic order. Wearing the monastic robe does not make a person a member of the *sangha* – this is the following

Press photograph by William L. Ryan showing Buddhist nuns in Saigon on a hunger strike to oppose the persecution of Buddhists under the South Vietnamese military government in the 1960s. Photograph dated 11 June 1963, the day of the self-immolation of Venerable Thich Quang Duc.
British Library, ORB.30/9528

Buddhist monks in Thailand ordaining a tree that is hundreds of years old to protect it from being destroyed.

of the precepts laid out in the *Patimokkha* code. Hate speech and violence are not permitted under any circumstances and must result in expulsion from the *sangha*.

Modern media have played a role in some controversies and should not be underestimated. When Buddhist monks and nuns in South Vietnam actively opposed – by way of hunger strike and self-immolation – the oppression and persecution of Buddhists by the anti-communist and pro-Catholic Diem regime in the early 1960s, some national Western media that ideologically supported the Diem government strongly condemned the actions of Buddhists. Self-immolation, it was argued, was an act of violence and in support of the communist north of the country. On the other side, photographs of the self-immolation of the monk Thich Quang Duc, taken by the US journalist Malcolm Browne, that were published around the world helped lead to the overthrow of the Diem regime in South Vietnam in November 1963 and subsequent changes in public opinion against the American-backed South Vietnamese government. The Second Vietnam War eventually became one of the worst conflicts that humankind has seen, with more bombs dropped on Vietnam and neighbouring Laos than on all of Europe during the Second World War.

In response to the conflict that Buddhists faced in South Vietnam in the 1960s, the Buddhist monk Thich Nhat Hanh developed guidelines for an Engaged Buddhism that abstains from any involvement in violent actions while at the same time combating social and political injustice. Engaged Buddhism is a socio-politically active form of Buddhism that analyses social structures as possible causes of suffering and identifies certain political, economic and social institutions as manifestations of greed, hatred and delusion.

> When I was in Vietnam, so many of our villages were being bombed. Along with my monastic brothers and sisters, I had to decide what to do. Should we continue to practice in our monasteries, or should we leave the meditation halls in order to help the people who were suffering under the bombs? After careful reflection, we decided to do both – to go out and help people and to do so in mindfulness. We called it Engaged Buddhism. Mindfulness must be engaged. Once there is seeing, there must be acting ...[4]

Due to its world-renouncing philosophy, Buddhism has sometimes been (mis)interpreted as passive and escapist. However, many of the Buddha's discourses laid out in the *Sutra Pitaka* demonstrate how to identify injustices and how to solve and prevent conflicts. The precepts that Buddhists follow voluntarily aim at preventing conflicts and therefore reducing suffering. With just six fellow monks and nuns, Thich Nhat Hanh founded the Order of Interbeing (*Tiep Hien*) in 1964, a group that initially cared for war victims, organized an underground for draft resisters and ran social services projects.

In 1993 Thich Nhat Hanh formulated Fourteen Precepts of Engaged Buddhism that aim to develop peace and serenity through thoughtful ethical and compassionate living. These Fourteen Precepts are thought of as guidelines for anyone wishing to live mindfully and emphasize, among other factors, the importance of speech, for example not engaging in speech that can create discord or division in the community/society and instead making every effort to reconcile and resolve conflicts as well as to discourage people from fanatic and extremist views by means of compassionate dialogue and action.

Thich Nhat Hanh's concept of Engaged Buddhism has inspired many other movements and organizations across the world. International organizations that are committed to socially engaged Buddhism include the Buddhist Peace Fellowship, Zen Peacemaker Order, Soka Gakkai International, Buddhist Global Relief, International Network of Engaged Buddhists, Network of Buddhist Organisations, Fo Guang Shan, Buddha's Light International Association and Tsu Chi Foundation, to mention only a few.

The focus of socially engaged Buddhists is not on social or political injustices alone, but also concerns the protection of the natural environment. The Buddha's Light International Association, for example, promotes Humanistic Buddhism: in this context, awareness of the environment based on the deep connection between Buddhism and nature. Harmony between humans and the natural world plays an important role in the Buddhist scriptures, and the belief that the 'Buddha nature' is extant in all beings and things is reflected in the *jatakas*. Venerable Master Hsing Yun, founder of Buddha's Light International Association, argues against discrimination towards the natural world and for the need to look at nature as an equal partner, not servant, of humankind.[5]

In Thailand, the Buddhist ecology movement was started by a small number of Buddhist monks who engaged in ecological conservation projects in the 1990s. They address problems of deforestation, pollution of air and water, and general ecological destruction motivated by industrialization and consumerism. The Buddhist ritual of 'tree ordination' is used to raise awareness about the problem of deforestation and to build villagers' commitment to ecological conservation. The movement promotes sustainable solutions to everyday

Miniature scroll containing the *Daihannya rishubun omamori* (Sanskrit: *Prajnaparamita-naya-satapancasatika*) for use as a protective amulet. Japan, *c.* 1960.
British Library, ORB.Misc/95

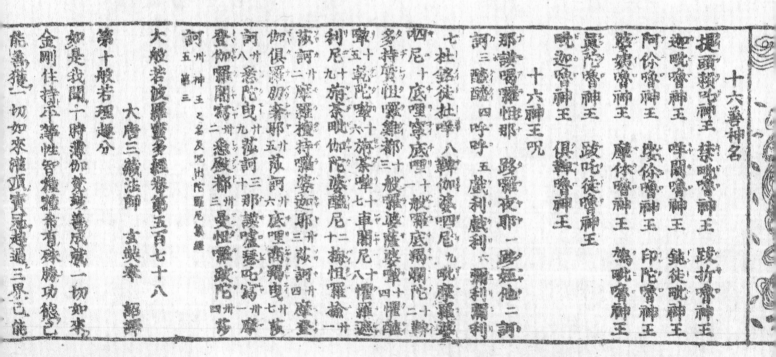

problems, seeks consultation with government officials on environment initiatives and helps rural farmers to improve their skills through education programmes. Sulak Sivaraksa, a leading Thai Buddhist activist, social critic and co-founder of the International Network of Engaged Buddhists, initiated a number of ecological, social and humanitarian non-governmental projects in Thailand, such as the 'Spirit in Education' movement and 'Alternatives to Consumerism'. Sivaraksa emphasized the significance of religion for social change and described a vision of 'Buddhism with a small "b"' in which the Five Precepts for lay Buddhists, the role of women and non-violence are of particular importance. His vision of a socially engaged Buddhism rejects consumption-based economics (consumerism) and aims for a more equitable, compassionate human society:

> Today, greed is clearly personified in capitalism and consumerism. Human beings are taught to worship money, worldly sciences and technological advance, at the expense of human development and the spiritual dimension of men and women.

> Descartes said *cogito ergo sum* – 'I think therefore I am'. I feel that he started the Western dilemma that has now come to the core concept of consumerism, which says 'I buy therefore I am'. Without the power of purchasing, modern people become nobodies.[6]

Philosophically, Buddhism is opposed to materialism, whether of the Western capitalist or the Stalinist communist variety. However, there is a trend of 'commercialization of Buddhism', which is partly caused by the increasing monetarization of society. Whereas traditionally the laity provided material support 'in kind' to monastic communities, in modern society this support becomes more and more money-based, which raises ethical questions. Every now and then 'billionaire monks' who live a lavish lifestyle in offence against the precepts laid out in the *Patimokkha* are exposed. Related to the commercialization of Buddhism is its trivialization. Buddhist symbols are often robbed of their meaning when they are used in a non-religious context, for example as cheap fashion objects, tourist souvenirs or in room decoration.

Glenn Wallis in his *A Critique of Western Buddhism: Ruins of the Buddhist Real* (2019) points out that Western Buddhism is the result of an articulation and self-understanding that initially took shape in Asia, but has been adapted to Western ways of thinking and values, which were eventually adopted among Eastern Buddhists and Buddhist scholars. The European mindset altered the self-understanding of Eastern Buddhists, which led to changes to and modernization of Buddhism in the

East. Wallis criticizes the 'scientification' of Buddhism in the West, the abandonment of transcendental cosmic wisdom and the rejection of the concept of Buddha being a *mahapurusa* (person with thirty-two characteristics of a Great Man) with superhuman powers. The perception of the Buddha changed to that of a rational, empirically minded individual, which is significantly different from the early perceptions of the Buddha in Asia.

Wallis argues that in the West Buddhism is seen as a predominantly lay, not monastic, activity; there is a new articulation of Buddhism in the privatized and internalized sphere of the individual's mind and soul. Communal Buddhist festivals and rituals are often regarded as superstitious folk Buddhism. In Western Buddhism, elements are adopted that are convenient and comprehensible for the practitioner in the West, and in line with the values of Western civilization. Other elements that are at the core of traditional Eastern Buddhism, like the belief in Buddhist cosmology, which in the West is considered as superstition, or the practice of making merit by giving material or financial offerings to the monastic community, are frowned upon as expressions of materialist attitudes.

After such a critique, one must ask whether Western Buddhism is a form of Buddhism at all. Is it non-Buddhism, or Buddhism in ruins, as Wallis suggests?

The exhibition that this book accompanies gives us a clear answer by revealing what theoreticians may sometimes overlook: as one can see from the huge diversity of scriptural, artistic and cultural expression, Buddhism has always embraced diversity of thought and practice. Tolerance is at the core of Buddhism, and this has allowed a large number of schools and local traditions to develop. Every single object in the exhibition is a real-life artefact and has a story to tell; many reveal an entire history, or indeed a herstory.

Arther E. Imhof highlights the fact that objects and artefacts held in museum, archival or library collections have been separated from the context in which they came into existence and for which they were of real-life importance; thus they have lost their original function.[7] It is an important task for curators and scholars to work together to re-tell and translate into modern terms the stories that come alive through those artefacts.

Western Buddhism is just one addition to the many schools and traditions of Buddhist thought and practice that have developed over the past 2,500 years. In each of the Buddhist traditions, core teachings and principles contained in the *Tripitaka* have been retained; practices have been adjusted in order for them to make sense within the context of the civilizations where Buddhism was adopted. The same accounts for Western Buddhism. Nonetheless, there is an amazing continuity of the Buddha narrative and of core concepts like *samsara*, *karma*, *nirvana*, the Four Noble Truths and the Noble Eightfold Path that are essential for the Buddhist practitioner. The aim of Buddhism is not to create an imagined 'perfect' world, but to support individuals to live mindful and meaningful lives, whatever the environment. The purpose of Buddhism is not to eliminate the mud, but, like the sunlight, to help the lotus grow out of it.

Buddha seated on a lotus flower with the teaching gesture (Sanskrit: *vitarka mudra*). The lotus is one of the most recognizable symbols of all Buddhist traditions and represents the Buddha's achievement of enlightenment and purity of mind. Woodblock-printed book with hand-coloured illustrations. China, 1808.
British Library, Or.13217, vol. 4, f. 23

Notes

1 See Constanza Cordoni and Matthias Meyer, eds, with Nina Hable, *Barlaam und Josaphat: Neue Perspektiven auf ein europäisches Phänomen* (Berlin and Boston: De Gruyter, 2015).

2 http://idp.bl.uk/

3 Graham Field, 'Market Stalinism: Burma, China, Laos, North Korea and Vietnam' in *Economic Growth and Political Change in Asia* (London: Palgrave Macmillan, 1995), p. 128.

4 Thich Nhat Hanh. Source: https://upliftconnect.com/thich-nhat-hanhs-14-principles-of-engaged-buddhism/

5 Hsing Yun, *Venerable Master: Ecology from a Buddhist Perspective* (Los Angeles: Buddha's Light, 2016).

6 Sulak Sivaraksa. Source: https://www.schumachercollege.org.uk/learning-resources/a-buddhist-response-to-global-development)

7 Arthur E. Imhof, *Geschichte sehen. Fünf Erzählungen nach historischen Bildern* (Munich: Beck, 1990).

THE LIFE OF THE BUDDHA
Angela S. Chiu

For over 2,000 years, every generation of Buddhists has retold the story of the Buddha's life in its own forms. The story has been depicted in rock-cut reliefs, painted murals, palm leaf, comic books and film; the Buddha is arguably one of the individuals most frequently depicted in art and literature. For his followers, the Buddha's life story is a source of doctrinal and ethical values, and it inspires the devotional experiences through which they seek advancement towards insight and freedom from suffering.

The Buddha, called Gotama (Sanskrit: Gautama) or Sakyamuni (Sanskrit: Shakyamuni),[1] is estimated to have lived some time between the sixth and fourth centuries BCE, in what is today Nepal and northeastern India, expounding his teachings (Pali: *dhamma*). These provide a path to enlightenment or awakening (Pali/Sanskrit: *bodhi*), by which one achieves *nirvana*, or extinguishing (Pali: *nibbana*), liberation from the repeating cycle of birth and death.

In Buddhist tradition, the biography of the Buddha not only focuses attention on the lifetime of one individual but also expresses a broader vision situating that lifetime in a whole network of lifetimes. The journey to Buddhahood entailed efforts over many previous lives not only of the Buddha himself, but also of his family members and followers, people of all walks of life whose lives were *karmically* interwoven with his through the ages. This broader dimension of the Buddha's biography integrates Buddhists as they make their individual paths towards liberation into a wider cosmic history and space of Buddhism. Below, we will review the life story of the Buddha as it is told in canonical sources and consider the social and *karmic* lines that frame the story. Finally, we will consider the ways in which the Buddha's biography is considered not yet finished, but ongoing through to the present.

The Story of the Buddha

The Buddha's disciples gathered to recollect and organize his teachings shortly after his passing. For at least the first couple of centuries, they recorded his teachings largely in memory and transmitted them orally. The Theravada Canon was not established as it is now known in written form until the fifth century CE.[2] There is no full, birth-to-death biography of the Buddha recounted in a continuous narrative in this Canon, though episodes of the Buddha's life appear in a number of texts, often cited by the Buddha to frame or illustrate particular ideas. Some longer segments of the Buddha's life are embedded in various scriptures such as the *Ariyapariyesana Sutta*. A couple of centuries after his passing, accounts of the Buddha's biography were compiled that included discussion of his previous lives, in which he performed meritorious actions that contributed to his eventual attainment of Buddhahood. Examples of these

Queen Maha Maya's dream and the birth of Prince Siddhartha at Lumbini Grove. Second in a series of 10 classic Tibetan block prints from Derge (East Tibet) depicting events in the life of the Buddha. Printed on paper in 1971 from an older wooden printing block.
British Library, Or.16921/17

Chinese version of the *Life of Buddha* in four volumes, with
scenes depicting two of Prince Siddhartha's four encounters.
Woodblock-printed book with hand-coloured illustrations.
China, 1808.

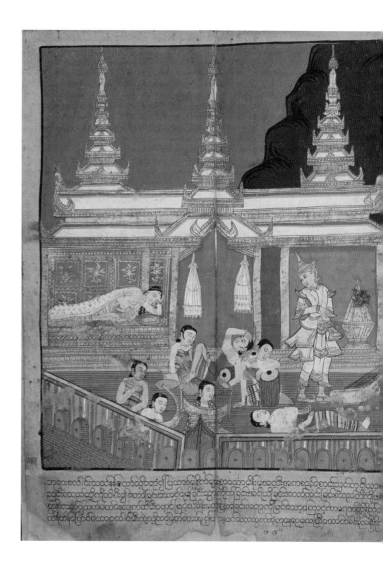

texts are the *Mahavastu* (*c.* second century BCE); the *Lalitavistara,* an important text for Mahayana traditions; the *Abhiniskramana Sutra,* a popular text in China; and, perhaps most famous of these, the *Buddhacarita* (first century CE), attributed to the monastic author Asvaghosa.[3]

The *Nidanakatha* (*c.* fifth century CE) is the introduction to the *Jataka atthavannana*, a collection of stories of the Buddha's past lives in the Theravada Canon. The *Nidanakatha* provides an extended account of the life of the Buddha up to his receipt of a significant donation, Jeta's Grove. Later authors drew on this text and other non-canonical sources to compose continuous narrative accounts of the Buddha's life. For instance, in Southeast Asia, the *Pathamasambodhi* recounts the Buddha's life through to his funeral. It is dated to at least the sixteenth century and found in Pali and at least eight vernacular languages in Southeast Asia.[4] Its popularity is reflected in the fact that some of its passages have been found to resemble the narratives found in murals, manuscript illustrations and other artworks.

Let us take a look at the life of the Buddha, particularly as it is recounted in the *Nidanakatha*, which recounts the early part of his biography, and another canonical scripture, the *Mahaparinibbana Sutta*, which relates his final months. Many of the episodes described in these texts have also been popular subjects for visual art. The significance of artistic presentations in Buddhism should not be underestimated. Such works have communicated Buddhist concepts and values while serving as objects of devotion; the sponsorship of artistic works is also viewed as a virtuous deed supporting the spiritual progress of the donors. Here follows a summary of the Buddha's biography, with reference to examples of items illustrated in this book.

In N.A. Jayawickrama's translation, the *Nidanakatha*[5] begins 'four *asankheyyas* [incalculable periods] and a hundred thousand aeons ago', that is, a time so long ago it is virtually beyond reckoning. At that time, the Buddha was in a previous life as an ascetic named Sumedha. When a Buddha called Dipamkara was visiting his city, Sumedha lay down in the road, spreading out his matted locks of

hair as a bridge for Dipamkara to cross over a patch of mud. Beholding Dipamkara, Sumedha resolved that he himself would some day become a Buddha and help humans and gods towards enlightenment. Dipamkara then predicted that Sumedha in a future lifetime would indeed become a Buddha named Gotama. He also made other predictions, including the names of Gotama's parents and chief disciples and the kind of tree under which he would achieve enlightenment. Sumedha then considered that in order to become a Buddha he would need to fulfil the Ten Perfections, that is, perfect his practice of ten virtues: generosity, morality, renunciation, wisdom, effort, patience, truth, resolution, amity and equanimity.

In subsequent lifetimes, the Bodhisatta or Buddha-to-be (Sanskrit: *Bodhisattva*) encountered twenty-four other Buddhas who appeared at intervals through the numerous aeons and also made predictions of his future Buddhahood. During his many rebirths, the Bodhisatta also practised the virtues.

When the Bodhisatta was living an existence as a god in heaven, the deities proclaimed that the time for

a Buddha to appear in the world was approaching. The Bodhisatta then identified the woman endowed with the necessary qualities to be the mother of a Buddha: Queen Maya, a scion of the clan of the Sakyas and wife of King Suddhodana of the city of Kapilavatthu (Sanskrit: Kapilavastu). The Queen's pregnancy began when she dreamt that the Bodhisatta, in the form of a white elephant, entered her right side. Ten months later, Queen Maya was on a leisurely visit to Lumbini Grove (in present-day Nepal) when she gave birth to Prince Siddhattha (Sanskrit: Siddhartha). He stood up straight upon being born, walked seven steps and declared 'I am the chief of the world.'

A Tibetan woodblock print depicting the birth (see page 32) indicates the importance of a mother of a Buddha: Maya is the central and largest figure. Her energy suggested by her flowing robes, she stands on a lotus blossom, like a goddess; she seems to extend to both heaven and earth. The just-born Bodhisatta is a small figure below her. Maya, like the mother of all other Buddhas, died seven days after giving birth.

Mara's temptation illustrated in a Sanskrit manuscript of the *Life of Buddha* (Sanskrit: *Lalitavistara Sutra*), copied in Devanagari script by the scribe Amritananda and commissioned by Captain William Douglas Knox, British Resident Minister in Nepal (1802–1803). Patan, Nepal, 1803.
British Library, IO.San.688, f. 112

The king invited learned Brahmins to examine the infant to predict his future. They stated that if he led the life of a householder then he would become a Universal Monarch (Pali: *cakkavattin*; Sanskrit: *cakravartin*), ruling the four continents surrounded by two thousand islands. If he renounced the worldly life, however, he would become a Buddha. He would decide to renounce should he see Four Omens: a feeble old person, a sick man, a corpse and a religious mendicant. Suddhodana wished his son to become a Universal Monarch and therefore raised him in a luxurious palace cosseted from those sights. However, one day, while on a ride in his chariot, the Bodhisatta encountered the Four Omens, as deities deliberately placed them in his path to prompt his journey towards enlightenment. Agitated by the images of suffering while inspired by that of the religious mendicant, the Bodhisatta indeed decided to renounce worldly life. That evening, after the rest of the household had gone to bed, the Bodhisatta mounted his white horse, Kanthaka.

His last moments in the palace have been often depicted artistically. A Burmese illustrated biography of the Buddha in the form of a paper folding book (*parabaik*) dated to the nineteenth century shows the Bodhisatta taking a last look at his sleeping family. The sleeping palace women appear dishevelled and unattractive. The scene suggests the transience of sensual pleasures and limits of domestic life that the Bodhisatta was about to renounce, literally by moving onwards and upwards on his white horse at the upper right of the composition.

As the Bodhisatta rode towards the city gates, the deities held the horse's hooves with the palms of their hands to prevent their making noise that would awaken the city to the Bodhisatta's departure. When they had ridden to the bank of the river Anoma, the Bodhisatta, wielding his sword, sliced off the topknot of his hair and tossed it into the sky. The king of the gods, Sakka, scooped up the topknot mid-air and deposited it in the Crest-gem (Culamani) shrine in the heaven of the Thirty-

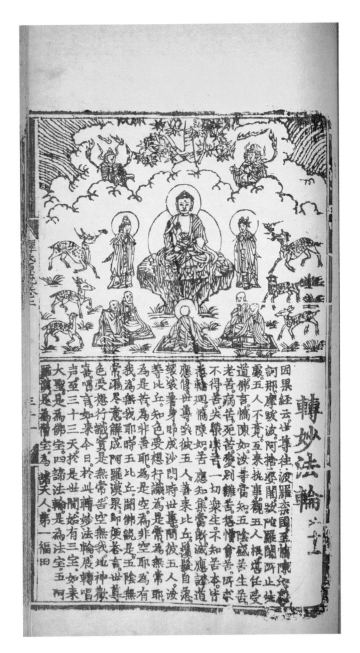

Excerpt from *Shishi Yuanliu* (*Origins and Transmissions of Sakya's House*), compiled by Baocheng with illustrations of events in the life of the Buddha. China, 1422–1436.

Three Gods (Tavatimsa) so that the gods could worship it. A deity brought a monk's robe and bowl to replace the Bodhisatta's princely finery.

The Bodhisatta then became a wandering mendicant. Under different teachers, he tried techniques such as extreme starvation, but found these were not the way to enlightenment. At Uruvela, he sat down under a tree and was given a bowl of milk-rice by Sujata, a local woman who mistook the radiant young man for a tree deity. This meal was his last intake of food through the enlightenment and for seven weeks afterwards. When the Bodhisatta had finished it, he deposited the empty bowl in the river, where it settled on the riverbed beneath the bowls of previous Buddhas. The Buddha then walked to the Tree of Awakening (Bodhi). On the way, a grass-seller named Sottiya, impressed by the Bodhisatta's appearance, gifted him eight handfuls of grass. The Bodhisatta spread the grass on the eastern side of the tree. Settling cross-legged, he vowed to achieve enlightenment.

The evil god called Mara wanted to prevent the arising of a new Buddha. He sent his army to attack the Bodhisatta. However, the Bodhisatta remained undisturbed under the tree. He called the earth to testify as a witness to the generous acts of giving he had made in

Buddha in Tavatimsa heaven where he taught his former mother about his insights when she was reborn as a deity, illustrated in a Burmese folding book on the *Life of Buddha*. Burma, 19th century.

British Library, Or.5757, ff. 17–18

his previous existences. The great earth 'resounded with a hundred, a thousand or a hundred thousand echoes', causing Mara's army to scatter. The Bodhisatta continued to meditate and attained enlightenment.

Now a Buddha, an Awakened One, he taught the insights he attained at the Deer Park at Baranasi to five religious mendicants who had been his former companions. They then became his followers. This scene is depicted in a block-printed book from China (opposite); deer and gods are shown reverencing the Buddha, as not only humans but all sentient beings are able to benefit from the path to happiness he taught.

The Buddha travelled to other places, teaching and drawing many followers. King Bimbisara of Rajagaha donated his royal park, Bamboo Grove (Veluvana), as a monastery. The Buddha visited his family at Kapilavatthu; many of his relatives, including his father, his wife and his son, became his followers. At Savatthi, a householder named Anathapindika purchased a park, Jeta's Grove (Jetavana), and built a monastery for the Buddha there.

The *Nidanakatha* ends here. Other scriptures indicate that the Buddha then continued to travel, living temporarily in various places in what are today the Indian states of Bihar and Uttar Pradesh. He even spent

၁၈ အကြောင်းကိုကျ၍လျှင်။ စည်စောင်ကြွင်မောင်ကြေနင်စ်သေ၊၊ ၁ဘတိသိံ၊ဘဖွတ်တတတ်လေသာသူတို့နှင့်တကွပုသိုအငုံ၁၅ဝ
ကုံသေ၊လျုနတ်ပ၀ုိဝတ်သတ်အ ကြောင့်တို့နင့်ဘပ်လေ၊ရသုံလျုအ ထွုန၁သုာ၁သင်ပ၀ုိနှုဟ္ဘန်စံ၁တ်မျုလေသာ၁အခြင်၁ရင်၁ျ၊တွ
ဘဝ၁ဘ္ဘုပြင်ဝ္ဘုိ၁ကြွၚခြက်ကုိပြုပြီသ၁ပနု်အနုသ၁ဝ၁ဟသသ္ဘု၊ ၊ရွ၁ခြၚ်ကုိပြ၍ခုနုစ်ရက်ပတ်လပ်ုၚ၁သ၁င်ဘ်ုတ်ရွ

time in the heaven of the Thirty-Three Gods, where his mother, after her death, had been reborn as a divinity. He preached to her and other gods for three months. The Buddha travelled from place to place for twenty years and, for twenty-five more after that, he mostly resided at either Jeta's Grove or the Bamboo Grove.

The final months of the Buddha's life are recounted in the *Mahaparinibbana Sutta*.[6] He was then travelling accompanied by a large group of monks. After a meal, the Buddha fell seriously ill. At the village of Kusinara, he lay down on a bed his disciples prepared for him in a grove of trees. Among his final words, the Buddha told his chief attendant, 'Ananda, there are four places the sight of which should arouse emotion in the faithful': Lumbini (today Rupandehi in Nepal), where he was born; Uruvela (Bodh Gaya, in the state of Bihar), where he attained enlightenment; the Deer Park at Isipatana (Sarnath, Uttar Pradesh), where he delivered his First Sermon; and the place of his death and final *nirvana*, Kusinara (Kushinagar, Uttar Pradesh). 'And, Ananda,' he continued, 'the faithful monks and nuns, male and female lay-followers will visit those places. And any who die while making the pilgrimage to these shrines with a devout heart will, at the breaking-up of the body after death, be reborn in a heavenly world.'[7]

After addressing his disciples and receiving visitors, the Buddha entered meditation, reaching more and more advanced states until he finally passed away. The funeral was conducted by princes following the Buddha's instruction that he be treated as if he were a universal monarch: the body was cremated and the relics – the ashes – enshrined. 'A stupa [a funerary mound] should be erected at the crossroads for the Tathagata [Thus-gone One],' the Buddha informed Ananda. 'And whoever lays wreaths or puts sweet perfumes and colours there with a devout heart, will reap benefit and happiness for a long time.' The Buddha's eminent disciple Kassapa, who had been travelling when the Buddha died, arrived at the funeral pyre before it was lit and paid homage with his head to the Blessed One's feet, which emerged from the coffin. After the cremation was completed, the Buddha's relics were divided among eight princely families and the gods, who all enshrined them in *stupas*.[8] The *Mahaparinibbana Sutta* ends here.

The degree of alignment between the canonical narrative and the life of the Buddha as a historical person is an open question. Data we might consider essential, such as the dates of his birth and death, were apparently unimportant in the eyes of his early followers. After all,

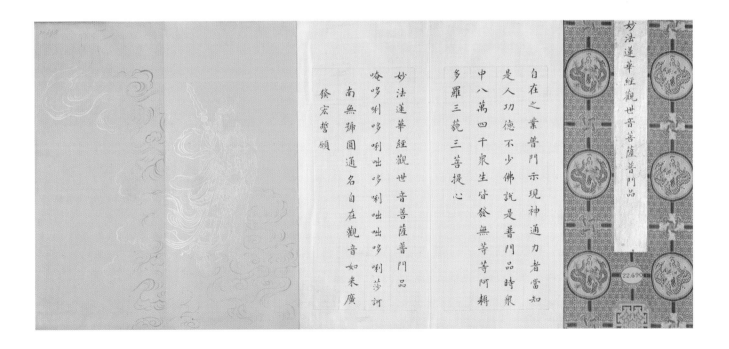

The Buddha's passing away illustrated in a Burmese folding book. Burma, 19th century.
British Library, Or.14298, f. 18

Folding book containing the *Avalokitesvara Sutra* in Chinese characters, with gilded end piece and silk brocade covers. China, 1705.
British Library, Add. MS. 22690

one of the Buddha's last pieces of advice was that after he was gone the *dharma* would be their guide.

Episodes of the Buddha's life communicate values and concepts; his life, or rather, lives, have established for his devotees a model for the effort and constant resolve needed to overcome the barriers to freedom from the cycle of rebirth.

The focus on Gotama's life story as being instructive for devotees took a more literal turn with the rise of Mahayana Buddhism several centuries after the Buddha's death. Gotama and other Buddhas were seen as representing the body of truth (Pali: *dhammakaya*; Sanskrit: *dharmakaya*), which could only be eternal. Buddhas were also believed to have another form, a 'body of magical manifestation' (Pali: *nimmanakaya*; Sanskrit: *nirmanakaya*) that they could deliberately assume for the purpose of teaching and providing a model. Thus, the enlightenment that Gotama experienced in his lifetime on earth was not real, and neither were his death and *nirvana*, as he is in fact already an enlightened, eternal being; his biography on earth was a disposition of expedient means (Sanskrit: *upaya*) to help sentient beings to liberation. This perspective on the Buddha draws attention to his compassion and has inspired devotees to look after not only their own spiritual progress but also that of others.[9] In Mahayana, all humans are understood to have the innate potential to achieve Buddhahood, which they should aim to do in order to relieve the sufferings of others. Bodhisattvas came to be understood as a class of beings whose purpose is to support the welfare and spiritual advancement of all; for devotees, they became both models to be emulated and important objects of worship. Perhaps the best-known and most popularly worshipped Bodhisattva across Asia has been Avalokitesvara, who has postponed his own Buddhahood until all sentient beings have attained theirs; he is regarded as the very embodiment of compassion.[10]

Lineages of the Buddha

In the *Nidanakatha*, the Buddha Gotama is presented as the latest in a lineage of Buddhas. He is also described as a member of other lineages or lines of descent. Beginning 'four *asankheyyas* and a hundred thousand aeons' ago, Sumedha vowed to become a Buddha, initiating a series of rebirths dedicated to achieving *nirvana*. Upon electing to be born the son of Queen Maya and King Suddhodana, the Bodhisatta joined the powerful Sakya clan. The relative significance of this earthly lineage was made clear in the *Nidanakatha*: when the Buddha returned home to Kapilavatthu after his enlightenment, he walked down the street begging alms. This alarmed his father, who declared that noble Khattiyas descended from Mahasammata did not go around begging. The Buddha replied, 'Your Majesty, this royal lineage is your descent, but mine is this lineage of Buddhas, from Dipamkara, Kondanna and others right down to Kassapa.'[11] The Buddha also initiated the lineage of his own disciples, the community of monks and nuns. His own son, Rahula, was ordained a monk, and the Buddha's wife and stepmother became nuns.

The development of lineages for the Buddha is consistent with the practice of religious teachers of his time in ancient India who supported their claims to expertise by declaring the names of their teachers and their teachers' teachers. However, the Buddha's enlightenment was an achievement rooted in his own efforts, and in fact occurred after he had tried and rejected the methods of two teachers. The Buddha's doctrine was that anyone who followed the path he described could likewise become a Buddha.[12] Following from this, it became plausible that others had also previously been enlightened and discovered this path. The word 'Buddha' is a Sanskrit–Pali term meaning 'awakened'. It signifies a position or state of one who is enlightened and was a term applied to the wise of other Indian traditions. In Buddhism, it came to be used as a status or categorization setting a Buddha in distinc-

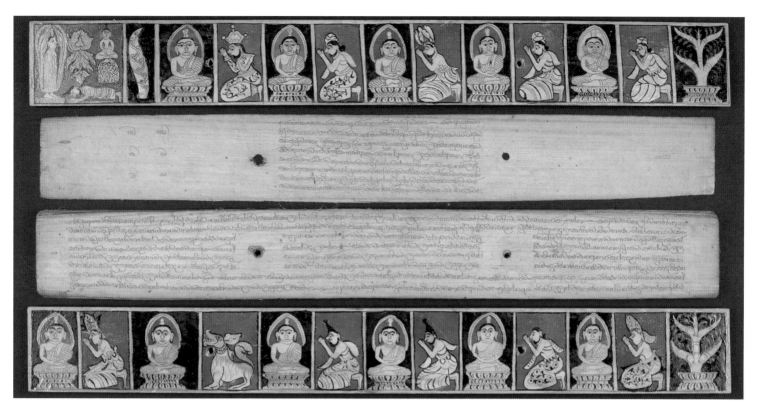

tion from other beings, including humans and gods.[13]

The existence of previous Buddhas is discussed in early Theravada canonical texts such as the *Mahapadana Sutta*, in which the Buddha mentioned six past Buddhas and explained that each Buddha's life story has a similar progression. Emperor Ashoka (r. *c.* 268–232 BCE), who conquered much of the Indian subcontinent and came to be regarded as the model Buddhist monarch, left an inscription referring to doubling the size of a *stupa* for the Buddha Konagamana. Among the carved reliefs at the *stupa* at Bharhut in Madhya Pradesh (second century BCE) is a depiction of seven trees, which an inscription identifies as the trees under which Gotama and six past Buddhas meditated to achieve enlightenment. A relief of seven trees also appears at the temple complex of Sanchi in Madhya Pradesh (first century BCE).[14]

Sinhalese manuscript containing the *Palapandita Sutrasane* for 'two pulpit preaching' with one recitator for Pali and one for Sinhalese, a text intended to be performed during the Suvisi Vivarana Puja ceremony. The cover illustration depicts some of the twenty-four Buddhas of the past who gave the historical Buddha the permissions (Sanskrit/Pali: *vivarana*) of Buddhahood in his previous lives. Sri Lanka, 19th century.
British Library, Or.6600/69

A later Theravada canonical scripture, the *Buddhavamsa* (c. second century BCE) relates the history of twenty-five Buddhas. This provided the basis for the *Nidanakatha*'s account of past Buddhas. For each of the twenty-five Buddhas, including Gotama, the *Buddhavamsa* lists specific aspects of their lives, such as their cities, the names of their parents, wives, sons and chief male and female disciples, bodily height, lifespan, the type of trees under which they attained enlightenment and how their relics were handled after their deaths. The text also mentions but does not describe three Buddhas preceding these twenty-five, so some traditions, as in Myanmar (Burma), honour twenty-eight Buddhas. The *Buddhavamsa* also mentions that the next Buddha to arrive in the world will be Metteyya (Sanskrit: Maitreya). The descriptions of Buddhas' lives as having a particular set of consistent aspects add to the definition of Buddhas as a class of being and suggest how the biography of Gotama was interpreted as reflecting common features of all those who have become Buddhas.[15]

The past Buddhas have been particularly revered as a set in Myanmar (Burma). A long paper manuscript of the nineteenth century unfolds to reveal a vertical series of portraits of the twenty-eight, each presented seated on a throne, their chief disciples kneeling in homage to each side, with deities floating reverently in the skies above. The Buddhas are depicted almost identically while the type of Tree of Awakening of each helps to distinguish them. The Buddhas of the past have also been among the most popular subjects of temple wall painting in Myanmar (Burma) since at least the Bagan period (ninth to thirteenth centuries). In the seventeenth to nineteenth centuries, the twenty-eight Buddhas were often portrayed, appearing virtually identical to each other, in a row at the top of a wall near the ceiling, signalling their high position in a cosmic hierarchy. Below this row of past Buddhas were often scenes of episodes from the Buddha Gotama's lifetime, and below these, taking up the largest amount of wall space, scenes of Gotama's past lives. The art historian Alexandra Green has noted that murals of the seventeenth to nineteenth centuries were part of a holistic design of temples that incorporated paintings, sculpture and architecture to support devotees in their efforts to ensure their security and progress towards *nirvana*.[16] The temple literally enables the devotee to enter and be immersed in a world in which time and space are structured by the Buddha's biography.

The recognition of a lineage of Buddhas also opened a new dimension to the lived worlds of Buddhists: specific places in their communities could be identified as cosmically significant landmarks upon the discovery of links to past Buddhas. For example, in the *Nidanakatha*,

the last event recounted in the life of the Buddha is the donation of the monastery of Jeta's Grove to the Buddha by the rich householder Anathapindika, who paid for the plot of land by blanketing it with gold pieces. The *Nidanakatha* states that in the past the merchant-prince Punabbasumitta had bought that same land by overlaying it with gold bricks and built a monastery for the Buddha Vipassi. Before that, the merchant-prince Sotthiya purchased the land by covering it with elephant feet made of gold and erected a monastery for the Buddha Vessabhu. The land had been gifted in a similar manner for all the other Buddhas as well.[17] This same sense of a place having a deep history by association with previous Buddhas opened up the possibility that places not previously known to be associated with Buddhism could be revealed to be important Buddhist sites visited previously by Buddhas.[18] For instance, in Myanmar (Burma), it seems that sites where local gods had been worshipped were later identified as Buddhist sites and *stupas* built on them. The identification of these spots as those visited by past Buddhas helped to subsume local deity cults to Buddhism, placing the local deities in a hierarchy of worship under the Buddha.[19]

In the Mahayana tradition, as mentioned above, Buddhas were understood as being eternal; this led to a new perspective on the lineage of Buddhas: all Buddhas who have appeared in the past and will appear in the future, being eternal, exist simultaneously. Throughout the cosmos, there are multitudes of Buddhas, each with his own Buddha field or land.[20] The Buddhas make themselves visible to devotees by manifesting their 'enjoyment body' (Sanskrit: *sambhogakaya*). The Buddha Amitabha, for example, is believed to dwell in the pure land of Sukhavati, where beings reside free from suffering amidst trees adorned with gems and precious metals. In China, practices of devotion to Amitabha were known by the fifth century and included voicing the Buddha's name, visualization of Sukhavati and prostration.[21] A Japanese scroll dating to 1636 (see 'The *Lotus Sutra*' in this volume) includes a painting of Amitabha alongside the text of the *Lotus Sutra* (Sanskrit: *Saddharmapundarika Sutra*), perhaps the most famous of Mahayana *sutras*. In the *Lotus Sutra* a scene is described in which Gotama, referred to as Shakyamuni Buddha, is preaching the *Lotus Sutra* when a magnificent jewel-covered *stupa* suddenly rises out of the earth and hovers in the sky. Inside it is the Buddha Prabhuratna. Shakyamuni then sits beside Prabhuratna in the *stupa*, delighting the people assembled below. For several centuries beginning with the fifth, this scene was 'arguably the most popular motif in Chinese Buddhist art' and depicted in murals, reliefs carved on cave walls and metal sculptures, among other forms.[22]

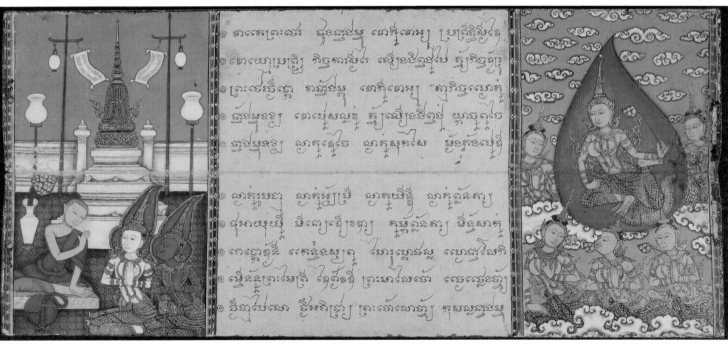

The future Buddha Metteyya (Sanskrit: Maitreya) in Tusita
heaven (top right), and the heavenly *stupa* Culamani Cetiya
with the monk Phra Malai (bottom left) and a female
Bodhisattva (bottom right). Central Thailand, 1849.

Past Lives of the Buddha

As the *Nidanakatha* indicated, the Buddha's life as Gotama is understood as resulting from his previous lives, during which, by undertaking *karma* (Pali: *kamma*) that was wholesome, he developed the virtues and generated the merit that contributed to his ability to achieve enlightenment.

The Buddha gained knowledge of his past lives in the first phase of insights he acquired after his enlightenment under the Tree of Awakening. Later, while teaching others, he narrated *jatakas*, episodes from his past lives, to illustrate his points in different contexts. The *jatakas* present the Bodhisatta in rebirths as humans of different social positions, particularly kings and Brahmins; as deities, including Sakka (also called Indra), king of the gods, and a king of serpent deities (*nagas*); and as animals, including an elephant, a rabbit and a quail. In some *jatakas*, the future Buddha is a saviour or hero; however, in many stories he is not the main character but an observer stating the moral lesson of the stories or giving advice.[23] By the variety of characters, settings and behaviours, not to mention interesting plotlines, these tales help

devotees relate to the experience of progressing towards Buddhahood while furthering their understanding of the workings of *karma* and other Buddhist concepts and values in a variety of situations. The *jatakas* provide parables for devotees at all stages of spiritual development, including monks; some *jatakas* were related by the Buddha in order to instruct proper monastic conduct.[24] Also, each story has an epilogue, in which the Buddha reveals that the characters in the episode were the past existences of specific persons in his vicinity, such as his disciples and family members. These epilogues sketched a *karmic* line between past and present.

For example, the *Silavanaga jataka* was recounted by the Buddha one day at the Bamboo Grove monastery, when the monks were discussing the ingratitude of the Buddha's cousin, the monk Devadatta. The Buddha related that in a past rebirth the Buddha was an elephant king named Silava living in the forest of the Himalayas. One day, Silava heard the cries of a forester from Varanasi who was lost. Silava brought the man to Silava's own home, nourished him with fruits, then carried him to the road to Varanasi. Once the forester returned to the city, he went to ivory craftsmen and

Four of twenty-eight Buddhas of the past, illustrated in a Burmese folding book providing information of their names and places of their enlightenment. Burma, 19th century.
British Library, Or.14823, ff. 23–26

promised to bring them tusks. He re-entered the forest and told Silava of his impoverishment. Out of compassion, the elephant allowed him to saw off the tips of his tusks. The forester returned repeatedly to take more and more of the tusks until he extracted the stumps. As the man walked back to Varanasi, the earth opened, and he was swallowed by the fires of hell. A tree deity nearby recited a verse on the insatiability of ingrates. The Buddha explained that the forester was a past rebirth of Devadatta, the tree deity a past existence of one of his chief disciples, Sariputta, and he himself was Silava.[25]

In the Theravada Canon, *jatakas* may be found grouped in texts such as the *Cariya Pitaka*, which presents Gotama's biography as the result of practice of the perfections or virtues in thirty-five past lives. The largest collection of *jatakas* is the *Jataka atthakatha*, an assemblage of 547 stories compiled in ancient Sri Lanka. The *jatakas* also inspired the creation of 'new' *jatakas*, which imitated their structure and themes, such as the *Pannasa jataka* (*Fifty Jatakas*), stories found in different versions across mainland Southeast Asia and which have also been depicted in temple murals. Some of these *jatakas*

are the source materials for works that are now considered classics of Thai and Lao literature and theatre.[26]

Indeed, for thousands of years and in all the places where Buddhism has spread, the *jatakas* have been popular subjects for artistic and literary production and performance. Whether the *jatakas*, which originally existed in oral form, influenced visual depictions or the other way around is an open question; it may well be that both forms were mutually influential in the development of each story.

Jatakas are illustrated in carvings on some of the earliest surviving Buddhist monuments, such as the hilltop complex of Sanchi, located in present-day north-central India, which by the first century was a flourishing monastic complex. The Great Stupa (Mahastupa) at Sanchi is believed to have been originally built by Emperor Ashoka in the third century BCE and enlarged to its current diameter of 36 metres in the following century. Some time around the early decades of the first century, high stone gateways were installed at each of the cardinal directions around the *stupa*. Carved on to them are reliefs of protective and symbolic figures such as animals, guardians and deities. There are also a number of *jatakas,* presented with figures and landscape arranged within rectangular panels; as the art historian Vidya Dehejia has explained, a sense of narrative action is suggested through various tactics such as the repetition of figures across the space to indicate their progress through time.[27]

Jatakas were also represented artistically in complete sets. In mainland Southeast Asia, these were inspired by the *Jataka atthakatha*'s 547 stories. In Bagan, in present-day upper Myanmar (Burma), there are seven temples or pagodas, all dated to the eleventh to twelfth centuries, each of which is adorned with scenes representing all the *jatakas*. The scenes are depicted on glazed terracotta plaques, which may be either on the interior or exterior of the structures, or frescos on the interior.[28] While visual depictions of particular *jatakas* may have had a didactic function as reminders to devotees of Buddhist ethics and the Buddha's path to enlightenment, many of the plaques are high on terraces or other places that would have been difficult for visitors to see clearly. The art historian Robert L. Brown has suggested that the significance of such sets of *jataka* representations was in their completeness, the ensemble presenting the Buddha through his biography.[29]

A Thai chronicle relates that in the mid-fifteenth century King Borommatrailokkanat of Ayutthaya (in present-day central Thailand) 'cast representations of the 500 lives of the Bodhisatta'. While the whereabouts of these representations are unknown, Forrest McGill has identified three dozen bronze images that may have been part of this set, including several whole statues and a number of heads, which appear stylistically related and may date to the fifteenth century. There are sculptures of crowned figures, Brahmins, a monkey and a dog. No record is available explaining why King Borommatrailokkanat had such sculptures made or where and how they were displayed. McGill observed

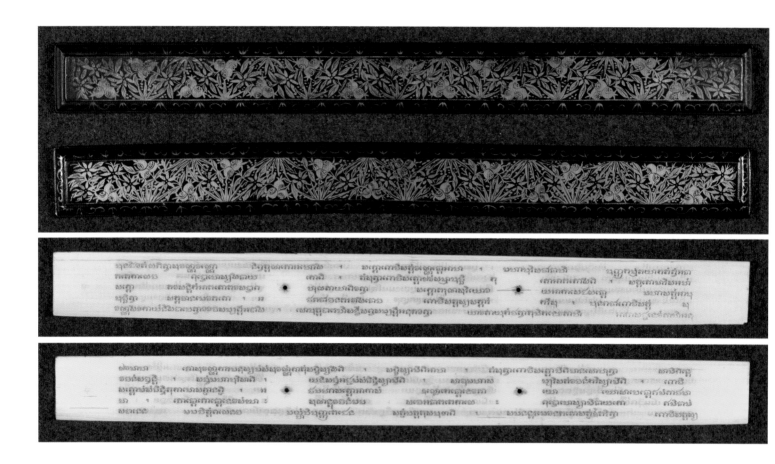

Collection of *Pannasa jatakas*, or extra-Canonical Birth Tales that were created locally in mainland Southeast Asia, in Khmer script. Thailand, 19th century.

British Library, Or.12524, ff. 1v, 2v and covers

that this king had a version in Thai of the *Vessantara jataka*, in which the Bodhisatta was a generous prince, composed and built a temple called Wat Chulamani, ostensibly named for the *stupa* in heaven where the gods enshrined the topknot cut off by the Bodhisatta when he renounced princely life. McGill suggests that through these projects and the creation of the *jataka* set, the king may have been drawing an identification between himself and the Bodhisatta. In the mid-fifteenth century, there may also have been a sense of urgency to support Buddhism as it passed its second millennium since the Buddha's *nirvana*. An ambitious, and perhaps unique, initiative to cast images representing all of the *jatakas*, McGill remarked, 'provided a potent reminder of the round of birth, merit accumulation, death, and rebirth leading towards eventual Buddhahood'.[30]

Particularly in Southeast Asian traditions, the final ten stories of the *Jataka atthakatha* are believed to come from the Bodhisatta's last ten existences before his birth as Gotama and to demonstrate his attainment of absolutely exemplary dedication to the Ten Perfections or virtues. The Last Ten Jatakas are often depicted artistically as a set of wall murals, manuscript illustrations and other forms. In a Thai paper manuscript dating to the eighteenth century (see pages 56–57), each page is divided into three panels, with the two outer panels painted with illustrations from the Last Ten Jatakas and the inner panel inscribed with extracts from various Theravada canonical scriptures. As is common with such manuscripts, the *jataka* representations are unrelated to the textual content, which comes from other canonical scriptures. The texts are the words of the Buddha and the paintings materialize his perfection; each infuses the manuscript with the Buddha's biography and cosmic truth.

Historically, the most popular of the *jatakas* has been the final one, that in which the Bodhisatta was Prince Vessantara (Sanskrit: Vishvantara). It is said that in Southeast Asia this *jataka*'s significance is on a par with that of the *Ramayana* in South Asia.[31] The *Vessantara jataka* has been presented in recitations, written verse, temple murals, dramatic performances and television shows, among other formats. Here follows a summary of the Pali canonical text.

Prince Vessantara was the son of King Sanjaya and Queen Phusati of Sivi. He was constantly inclined to generosity. When Brahmins from a neighbouring kingdom suffering drought came to request his magical rain-causing elephant, he gave it to them. This angered the people of Sivi, and Vessantara's father, the king, banished his son from the kingdom. Before departing, Vessantara spent a day distributing donations in massive amounts. Vessantara's wife, Maddi, insisted that she and their children, Jali and Kanhajina, accompany Vessantara into exile. The four mounted a horse-drawn chariot and set out from the city. On the way, Vessantara gave the chariot and horses away. The prince and his family proceeded on foot and took up residence in a hermitage in the forest, which, unbeknownst to them, had been magically constructed by the gods. Meanwhile, an old Brahmin named Jujaka was living in a village not far away with Amittatapana, his young and beautiful wife. Amittatapana, upset by teasing from the village women about her marriage, demanded that Jujaka obtain Vessantara's children to be her slaves. Jujaka found the family's hermitage and requested the children. Vessantara assented, making the children understand the necessity of the gift for his future spiritual attainment. Jujaka led the children away; they escaped twice, but, although filled with grief, Vessantara sent them back to Jujaka. Maddi had not been present during this time as she had gone into the forest to look for fruits and been detained there by deities, who took the form of wild animals, to prevent her from interfering with Vessantara's giving away of the children. When they did allow her to return, Vessantara did not state what happened, and she searched desperately for the children until she collapsed. Vessantara then related the children's fate. Maddi understood and encouraged him to keep giving. The god Sakka then appeared at the hermitage disguised as a Brahmin and asked Vessantara to give him Maddi. Vessantara agreed, but Sakka returned her to continue to support him. Meanwhile, Jujaka and the children were covertly guided by deities to the court of King Sanjaya, Vessantara's father, who got Jujaka to give up the children in exchange for a huge amount of treasures. The greedy Jujaka stuffed himself with food until he died. The King sent a procession of ministers to seek Vessantara in the forest. Vessantara and Maddi were found, bringing about an emotional family reunion. Vessantara agreed to the ministers' invitation to return to the city.

The suffering of Vessantara and his family endows poignancy and human scale to the Bodhisatta's cosmic journey through numerous lives towards Buddhahood. Naomi Appleton and Sarah Shaw have observed that his path is isolating and lonely, but he was crucially supported by family members and gods. The characters' lives were intertwined at the same time that each had free will to follow his or her own route. Through their dedication to their own advancement and to the wider goal of happiness for all, the other characters protected the Bodhisatta. The sense of larger purpose, Appleton and Shaw note, infuses the action with 'the protective power of a great ritual'.[32]

These aspects of the *Vessantara jataka* are reflected in festive recitations of the *jataka* conducted in villages in present-day northeast Thailand and Laos. During the

three-day annual Bun Pha Wet festival, the *Vessantara jataka* is recited on the last day by monks in narrative with interspersed dialogue, mixing chant with ordinary speech. The villagers enact the invitation of Vessantara and Maddi to return to their kingdom, often dressing up as these and other characters.[33] A distinctive feature of the festival is the *pha yao Pha Wet*, a long cloth scroll illustrating the Vessantara story in painted scenes. The scrolls, found in nearly all the thousands of northeastern Thai temples, are many metres in length; an example studied by Leedom Lefferts and Sandra Cate in Singapore's Asian Civilisations Museum is 31 metres long. The scroll is borne aloft by the villagers when they enact the invitation to Vessantara and Maddi to return from exile. The festival, as Lefferts and Cate remark, shifts the narrative voice from the Buddha, who originally recounted the *jataka*, to monks, artists and festival participants; they become the storytellers, but they also 'become the story', and the scrolls 'help to transform the community of the specific [temple] holding the festival into the subjects of the prince's kingdom'.[34]

The anthropologist Katherine Bowie has observed that the Vessantara story does not exist as a single fixed or 'authentic' text, but as a recital with variations according to the needs of tellers and audiences. In Thailand, through the centuries, the *jataka* has had resonance for past rulers who sought to identify themselves with Vessantara, who is both king and Bodhisatta. But many ordinary villagers in northern Thailand, vulnerable to mistreatment by ruling authorities, historically identified with the figure of the impoverished Jujaka rather than the royal Vessantara; the recounting of the *jataka* thus has provided occasion for political satire.[35]

Photograph of the eastern gateway of the Great Stupa at Sanchi, taken by James Waterhouse in 1861. The Great Stupa of Sanchi is the most important surviving monument of the Shunga era (*c*. 185–75 BCE) and an important pilgrimage destination.
British Library, Photo 1000/12

||◉|| នមោពស្សូរវបនេពារនារពោសមាសអ្មនអក្ស || ||◉||
||◉|| ភុសនានភ្គា អគ្គសនានគ្គា អវ្គ្រុក្ខនានគ្គា ។ នេះ
ភុសគ្គា នមោនភុសគ្គា || ភពវម្មុតគ្គា ភុសរណេនស្ងាំសនេ
នាមានរនុកុសល្បិត្ថ ្ ្ ្ ្ ្ ្ បក្ខ្កភោន សោមនស្សូករអានសិស្ន្
នានរគ្បអុគ្គ ្ ្ ្ ្ ្ ្ បក្ការមនានរ ្ ្ ្ ្ សគ្គរមនានរ ្ ្ ្ ្ នគ្គាភ្ខនានរ ្
រកាភមុនានរ ្ ្ ្ ្ ននន្ត្ខរមុនានរ ្ ្ ្ ្ នមារមុនានរ ្ ្ ្ ្ យ៉ែ៉ំនារ ្
នារច្ចុនិស្សរនេរ ្ ្ ្ ្ នស្ខានោន || ្ ្ ្ ្ វនគោនោន ្ ្ ្ ្ នន
នានានោន ្ ្ ្ ្ ពិនរនោន ្ ្ ្ ្ កុម៉នោន ្ ្ ្ ្ ពិភុក្សូនរនានោន ្
ន ្ ្ ្ ្ នវនានោន ្ ្ ្ ្ សន្ញានោន ្ ្ ្ ្ នវគ្គននោន ្ ្ ្ ្ ពិភុក្សូ ្
ន ្ ្ ្ ្ សន្និ ្

||◉|| សគ្គុនេអាករអសគ្គុនេអា ្ ្ ្ ្ សគ្គុភិនិនរអសគ្គុភិនិ ្ ្ ្ ្ អសគ្គុ
ភិនិនិនសគ្គុភិនិ ្ ្ ្ ្ សគ្គុភិនិ្ស្គុភិនិ្សេន ្ ្ ្ ្ អរសគ្គុភិនិនិនអរ
ច្ខុភិនិ ្ ្ ្ ្ សម្ហ្យ៉ូនពាគ្គា ្ ្ ្ ្ នវ្យ៉ូយេខ្យ៉ូពោ ្ ្ ្ ្ សម្ហ្យ៉ូយខ្ខ្លោន់ខ្ន្យ៉ូ
យុគ្គ ្
យុគ្គ ្

||◉|| នវរគ្គីនខ្គេខ ្ ្ ្ ្ ខគ្ខនរគ្គា ្ ្ ្ ្ អាឧនេខនបគ្គា ្ ្ ្ ្ សាឧន ្

ឣព្ធៃណា ឆ្អឣរឣព្ធៃត សឣ្ថិកឣ្ធៃរឣមឆ្ផៃនាត រាឣឣត្គៃ
ឧឪរាសឣ្ថិកឣ្ធៃរឣមឆ្ផៃ ឧឆាឣសោឣឣព្ធៃណា ឆ្អឣរឣព្ធៃឣាស
ឆ្ថិកឣ្ធៃរឣមឆ្ផៃនាត ឧឆាឣវិតឆ្ញរឣឆាឆាឣិឆិឆ្ញឣ់ឣឆ្ញិឣឣព្ធៃឆា
ឆ្អឣរឣព្ធៃឣាសសឣ្ថិកឣ្ធៃរឣមឆ្ផៃ ៕ ឆាឣឣឣងឆ្ផ្គៃរឆ្ផ្គៃ ឆឆា
សឣ្ថិកឣ្ធៃឣាមឆ្ផៃ ឆគោឆសោឣឣព្ធៃណា ឆ្អឣរឣព្ធៃត សឣ្ថិកឣ្ធៃ
ឣរឣមឆ្ផៃនាត ៕ យៃរឆ្ញឣ់ឣឣវិឣឆ្ផ្គៃឆ្ញៃឣ្ញឣឣព្ធៃណា ឆ្អឣ
ឣរឣព្ធៃត សឣ្ថិកឣ្ធៃឣាមឆ្ផៃ ឆាឆាឆ្ផ្គៃ ឆឆារឣឣិឣឣ្ថៃ :
ឣមឆ្ផៃ ឆគោឆសោឣឣព្ធៃណា ឆ្អឣរឣព្ធៃត សឣ្ថិកឣ្ធៃរឣមឆ្ផៃ
ឆាតឣិឣា ៕ ឆាឆ្ចៃឣឣងឆ្ផ្គៃរឆ្ផ្គៃ ឆឆារសឣ្ថិកឣ្ធៃរឣមឆ្ផៃ ឆ
គោឆសោឣឣព្ធៃណា ឆ្អឣរឣព្ធៃត សឣ្ថិកឣ្ធៃរឣមឆ្ផៃនាត ៕ ៕

ឣាឣឣឣឆ្ធៃឣោ ឣារឆ្ធ្គណាឣឣឆ្ធៃឣោ ឣឣនិឆតឣឆ្ធៃឣោ ឣ
ឣឆ្គៃរឣឆ្ធៃឣោ ឆឣឣឆ្គៃរឣឆ្ធៃឣោ សឣាឣាឣឣឆ្ធៃឣោ ឣឆ្គៃឣ
ឣ្គៃរឣឆ្ធៃឣោ ឣិសឣ្ញឣរឣឆ្ធៃឣោ ឆ្អឣឣិឆ្ញៃឣរឣឆ្ធៃឣោ ឣ
ឆ្នឆាឣរឣឆ្ធៃឣោ ឣឣ្ញាឣាឆរឣឆ្ធៃឣោ ឣាឆសោឆឣឣ្ញឆ្ធៃឣោ :
ឣឣឣឣ្ញ្គៃឣោ ឆ្ទិសឣរឣឆ្ធៃឣោ ឣារឣាឣរឣឆ្ធៃឣោ ឆ្ច្ញៃ
ឣយៃឣ្ធៃឣោ ឣាឣាឆ្ធៃឣោ ឣឣ្គៃឣឣ្ញៃឆ្ធៃឣោ សឣ្ញឣ្ចៃ
ឣ្គៃឣ្ញឆ្ធៃឣោ ឆ្ទិឣ្ញោឣ្ញ្គៃឣឣ្ញៃឣោ រឣ្គៃឣ្ញឆ្ធៃឣោ ឣ្គៃ្ចៃឣ
ឆ្ធៃឣោ ឆ្ទិឣ្ញ្គៃឣ្ញឆ្ធៃឣោ ឣឣ្គៃកឣ្ញឆ្ធៃឣោឣឆឣឆ ៕ ឆ្ធៃ
ឣ្ញឆ្ធៃឣោឣត ឣាឣឣឣាឣសឣ្ញៃឣ្ញ្គៃនាឆ្ថ្គាឆ់ ឣាឆឣ
ឆ្ថ្គាឣឣ្ញឆ្ច្ចៃឣ្ថ្គៃឣ ឆ្អឣឣឆ្ធៃឣោឣឣឆ្ធៃឣោ ឣារឣឣឣាឣឆ្ធៃ

A Thai folding book containing extracts from the Pali Canon
(Pali: *Tipitaka*) in Khmer script, with illustrations of the Last Ten
Jatakas, which symbolize the perfections (Pali: *paramita*) of a
Buddha, or Enlightened One. Central Thailand, 18th century.
British Library, Or.14068, ff. 3, 5, 6, 7, 9

THE LIFE OF THE BUDDHA

Bowie also noted that monastic and lay Buddhists she interviewed about the Bun Pha Wet festival stated that the event was a way to create solidarity among villagers, who must work together to produce the festival.[36] This parallels the theme in the *Vessantara jataka* that journeying towards enlightenment requires the support of others. Vessantara's wife and children were in fact also considered to have been with him in their rebirths down through the millennia.

According to a *sutta* of the *Samyutta Nikaya* cited in both Theravada and Mahayana sources, the Buddha stated that 'it is not easy to find a being who has not formerly been your mother ... your father ... your brother ... your sister ... your son ... [or] your daughter'. The weaving together of interlinked series of rebirths in the *jatakas* depict the Buddha and those with whom he interacts as 'one huge interconnected karmic web transmigrating together across time toward a group fruition of all the good karma combined, realized in salvific participation in the Buddha's own intimate community', as Jonathan S. Walters has described. This sense of *karmic* connection, in which society is seen as composed of transmigrating social units of families, friends and co-workers, is still understood today as shaping Buddhist lives.[37]

I.B. Horner has also pointed out that a Bodhisatta's quest for enlightenment is hardly a solitary endeavour, as shown in the *Buddhavamsa*'s description of how each of the twenty-five Bodhisattas departed home to become a religious seeker. Gotama left on horseback while previous Bodhisattas rode elephants, chariots, palanquins and even flying palaces; one walked. All of the Bodhisattas, Horner observed, left home escorted by others. Gotama, for instance, was accompanied by his groom Channa; the Bodhisatta who went on foot had a whole army as an entourage. It is only when the Bodhisattas were seated under their Trees of Awakening that they were alone.[38] A Buddha's biography is not a tale of heroic individualism but of what may be achieved through the realization of the interconnection of lives.

Scenes from the *Vessantara jataka* representing generosity as a form of compassion of Prince Vessantara in the Last Jataka, or Great Birth Tale. Central Thailand, 19th century. From Henry Ginsburg's collection.
British Library, Or.16552, f. 24

Extensions of the Life of the Buddha: Relics and Images

Though the Buddha died two and a half millennia ago, his life can be said to be ongoing through his *dharma*, which, from his deathbed, he had advised his disciples would lead them. The Buddha's biography also continues as he is seen to exist in his relics and images. After the Buddha's death and cremation, his relics were enshrined in *stupas* in eight kingdoms in northern India. Two centuries later, the great Buddhist Emperor Ashoka is said to have gathered up the relics and redistributed them to 84,000 *stupas* he constructed far and wide. This act demonstrated Ashoka's concern for the welfare of others; as the *Mahaparinibbana Sutta* recounted, the Buddha explained the benefits of worship at a *stupa* enshrining his remains: 'whoever lays wreaths or puts sweet perfumes and colours there with a devout heart, will reap benefit and happiness for a long time'.[39] In Buddhist literature, worshipping the Buddha is overwhelmingly presented not only as an act of good *karma* but also as a means to bring about improvements to a devotee's mental state; devotion was thus regarded as profoundly conducive to one's spiritual progress.[40] By disseminating the Buddha's relics, Ashoka was providing vast numbers of people the opportunity to advance towards enlightenment and happiness.

As John Strong highlighted, Ashoka's act 'centripetalized' the body of the Buddha out of ancient India to territories the Buddha may never have visited himself, extending the Buddha's life to new people and places.[41] The distribution of relics gave rise to new histories, legends and traditions as local history and folklore were entwined with the life of the Buddha. One northern Thai manuscript perhaps dating to the fifteenth century relates that the Great Relic of Hariphunchai was discovered by a king who had built an outhouse for his new palace over the spot where a relic had been interred long ago but forgotten by humans. Upon being informed of the relic's presence by a crow guarding the spot, the king moved his own palace elsewhere and built a palace for the relic. The site is now one of the region's most revered shrines, Wat Phra That Hariphunchai, in Lamphun.[42]

Ashoka is also said to have journeyed to pay respect and erect shrines at thirty-two places previously visited by the Buddha himself.[43] As with the 'centripetalization' of the relics, this act emphasized that places were significant if graced by the Buddha's presence. In the wake of the Ashokan period, Buddhists across Asia began to narrate accounts of how the Buddha himself visited their homelands during his lifetime, personally bringing the *dharma* to their communities, even though Canonical Buddhist texts made no mention of such visits. With these narratives, people and places were integrated into the biography of the Buddha. For example, Sri Lankan tradition dating to at least the fifth century holds that the Buddha visited the island no fewer than three times, during which he subdued ogres (*yakkhas*) and serpent deities (*nagas*), arranged for the protection of the sites where shrines and temples would be built in the future, and stamped his footprint on Samantakuta, today famed as Adam's Peak.[44] Thus, it was the Buddha himself who secured Sri Lanka for the benefit of the religion. The island's importance was reinforced with the later enshrinement there of bodily relics of the Buddha, including the Sacred Tooth, which became an important symbol of legitimacy for local rulers. King Parakkamabahu I (r. 1153–1186) is said to have carried the Tooth on his head in a festival procession after regaining it from rebels who had taken it.[45] A drawing from about 1800 depicts the participation of a wide variety of people in a procession of the Tooth.

Statues of the Buddha, which often have relics embedded in them, have also been instrumental in establishing the Buddha's presence in local communities. In canonical texts, there is no clear authorization given by the Buddha for the making of images. How the Buddha, gone to *nirvana*, may be considered present or accessible in his images is a question that has occupied scholars.[46] Nonetheless, any uncertainty has hardly deterred the enthusiasm of Buddhists for images, and in fact it is probably images and ritual instruments of Buddhism, rather than texts, that have most propelled the spread of Buddhism.

Among the earliest Buddhist artworks that have survived to the present are carved stone reliefs of Buddhist scenes at Sanchi and elsewhere that do not show the figure of the Buddha, but seem to indicate his presence with motifs such as a pair of footprints or an honorific umbrella, surrounded by worshipful devotees. Scholars have suggested that these scenes make reference to the absence of the Buddha, due to his *nirvana*, or are more intended to illustrate rituals of lay piety.[47]

According to the available evidence, images of the Buddha's figure were first produced beginning around the start of the Common Era. Among the early inscribed images found in ancient India, the large majority were sponsored by monks and nuns: the introduction of images in Buddhism was apparently an innovation led by monastics, not the laity.[48] In China, images came to be instrumental in common rituals for monastics. For example, confessing one's faults was often done before a Buddha image. Also, contemplating a Buddha image was a means to train oneself for meditation practices in which one visualized living Buddhas.[49] Through the practice of *anusmrti* (Sanskrit) or 'recollection of the

Buddha', the meditator focuses on the Buddha's qualities and mentally pictures the Buddha, such that the meditator becomes like the Buddha himself.[50]

According to an old tradition known across Asia, the first portrait of the Buddha was made during his lifetime. A version of the story was told by Faxian, a Chinese monk who travelled in India in the fourth century, as follows. When the Buddha was residing in Kosala, in today's Uttar Pradesh, he left for a few months to preach in heaven to his mother, who was living there among the gods. King Pasenadi, ruler of Kosala, missed the Buddha so much that he had a statue of him sculpted from sandalwood and set it on the Buddha's throne. When the Buddha returned, the statue rose to greet him. The Buddha said, 'Return, I pray you, to your seat. After my nirvana you will be the model from which my followers shall carve their images.' The statue then sat down.[51] Faxian remarked, 'This image, as it was the very first made of all the figures of the Buddha, is the one which all subsequent ages have followed as a model.'[52] According to another tradition, the first image of the Buddha was made when a king requested one, and the Buddha cast his shadow onto a piece of cloth, which craftsmen then painted in with various colours.[53]

As noted earlier, the Buddha was considered a being distinct from a human or a god. Becoming a Buddha entailed not only spiritual development but also physical transformation. A canonical Theravada scripture, the *Lakkhana Sutta*, describes the 'thirty-two marks peculiar to a Great Man (*Mahapurisa*)', attributing specific physical features to virtuous actions performed by the Buddha in previous rebirths: for instance, his 'bright complexion, the colour of gold' was due to the donations of clothing he made in former lives; his 'upward-growing body-hairs' and 'ankle high above the foot' were thanks to having taught the *dharma* to others. The Buddha also had 'soft and tender hands and feet'; 'his male organs [were] enclosed in a sheath'; he had 'jaws like a lion's' and 'eyelashes like a cow's', among other characteristics.[54] Mahayana texts describing the Buddha's physical features are even more detailed.[55] As Peter Skilling has observed, 'there is an intimate relation between *jatakas* and the Buddha image. The *jatakas* have, in a sense, culminated in the image.'[56]

There is believed to be a value to seeing a Buddha with one's own eyes. This may stem from the old Indic practice of *darshana* (Sanskrit), the ritual practice of seeing an honoured being. The importance of viewing the Buddha, a being who rarely appears in the world, is indicated in the *Mahaparinibbana Sutta*, which notes that while the Buddha lay dying gods were crowding around to catch a last glimpse of a Buddha, such that 'there is not a space you could touch with the point of a

hair' between them.[57] The Buddha also noted the benefit of seeing when he encouraged the practice of pilgrimage, stating 'the sight' of the places would stir pilgrims' emotions.

Two stories indicate one of the ways in which viewing the Buddha's image could benefit the devotee. A collection of fourth-century Pali tales, the *Sihalavatthuppakarana*, includes the story of Phussadeva, a monk who asked the demon Mara to transform himself into the form of the Buddha. When Mara manifested the Buddha's glorious body, Phussadeva raised his hands in homage, and, with tears in his eyes, recollected the Buddha's qualities. He then described the Buddha's body, first from his feet to the top of his head, and then again in reverse order. After describing each mark of the Great Man, Phussadeva recited that it was 'gone to destruction and not seen'. Phussadeva then achieved enlightenment. Through deconstruction of the image, Phussadeva gained insight into the impermanence of the Buddha's body. A similar message is conveyed in another account of Mara taking on the appearance of the Buddha, this time at the request of the legendary monk Upagupta. Before transforming himself, Mara warned Upagupta that, as he was not the Buddha, Upagupta should not bow down before the image; if Upagupta did so, Mara would burst into flames. Indeed, when Upagupta saw the vision created by Mara, he lamented the 'pitiless impermanence' that destroyed the Buddha's body, but still prostrated before it. Mara ceased generating the image and admonished Upagupta. But the monk replied that he knew the Buddha was gone and that he bowed down before his 'pleasing figure' and not to Mara. As Strong remarked, the two monks understood the image in stages. First, they perceived the magnificence of the Buddha's body. Then, through the recollection of his qualities, they made the Buddha present, before recalling the fact of his absence. The objective of worship of the Buddha's image was to advance towards enlightenment.[58]

Historically, artistic representations of the Buddha have typically been created in a limited range of postures and possess specific physical attributes (including those of the Great Man), which by their combination identify him as the Buddha. The postures and gestures are often linked to episodes in the Buddha's life. One of the most popular postures is of the Buddha seated cross-legged and with his right hand extended over his right knee, with the fingers straightened and pointed towards the ground. This posture is often understood to refer to the meditating Bodhisatta calling the earth to witness his impending enlightenment and the subsequent defeat of Mara; it is known among art historians by the Sanskrit terms *maravijaya*, 'victory over Mara', or *bhumisparsha mudra*, the 'sign of touching the earth'.

Painting of the annual procession of Buddha's Tooth Relic,
Asala Perahera, at Kandy. Sri Lanka, c. 1796–1815.

British Library, Or.11901 (part)

One example is a gilt bronze statue of the Buddha in this posture probably produced in the reign of the Chinese Emperor Yongle (r. 1402–1424). Large for its type, at 37 centimetres high, the figure was probably cast in the imperial workshops, which produced huge amounts of Buddhist images and ritual objects for Yongle, an adherent of Tibetan Buddhism who established religious and diplomatic exchanges with Tibet.[59]

The earliest existing examples of the earth-touching Buddha as a stand-alone sculpture are from sixth-century northeastern India. These depictions of the Buddha appeared at the same time as inscriptions on images and other objects began to appear of a well-known Buddhist formulation: 'All things arise from a cause, the Tathagata [Buddha] has explained the cause. This cause of things has finally been destroyed.

Such is the teaching of the Great Ascetic.' Although the earth-touching Buddha image later became associated with the shrine at Bodh Gaya (also Buddhagaya), where the Buddha attained enlightenment, more images in this gesture were actually produced at Sarnath, the site associated with his first teaching, beginning in the sixth century. Janice Leoshko therefore suggested that these early earth-touching images were not meant to refer to the victory over Mara, as is typically suggested, but to the Buddha's insight into the causal relations stated in the formula. Buddha images may not only have narrative meanings but also signify particular Buddhist concepts.[60]

Buddha statues have been understood to channel the Buddha's biography and doctrine, but they have also been recognized as developing their own individual characters. In China, Buddhist statues were typically

南無華相佛 南無不虛步佛 南無斷疑佛 南無照明佛 南無定意佛 南無寶語佛 南無智勝佛 南無善行意佛 南無德臂佛 南無大名佛 南無龍喜佛 南無龍明佛 南無上師子音佛 南無上尊佛 南無安隱佛 南無遊步佛 南無施額佛 南無法積佛

南無山主王佛 南無覺悟佛 南無善明佛 南無寶相佛 南無無量力佛 南無日明佛 南無無量目佛 南無自莊嚴佛 南無龍手佛 南無天力佛 南無香自在佛 南無華山佛 南無藥藏佛 南無撤高德佛 南無法義別佛 南無衆王佛 南無寶衆佛 南無定義佛

regarded, as John Kieschnick noted, 'as independent, living entities with distinct personalities, rather than as emanations of transcendent Buddhist figures described in Buddhist scriptures'. Images were even said to cause blindness and other injury to those who threatened them. Interestingly, according to Kieschnick, the idea of icons being alive only appeared in China with the arrival of Buddhism. Indeed, Buddhism came to be so closely associated with images that Chinese texts often referred to it as *xiang jiao*, 'the teaching of icons'.[61] Buddha images can develop particular meanings through their integration into the lives of their devotees. As Heidi Tan has observed of home shrines in Myanmar (Burma), images of the Buddha can come to 'embody family memories'.[62]

In northern Thailand, there has been a tradition at least since the fifteenth century of composing biog-raphies of specific Buddha images. The texts narrate how each image was created and then moved across Asia over hundreds of years. For example, the *Tamnan Phra Kaeo Morakot* (*Chronicle of the Emerald Buddha*) explains that the Emerald Buddha image, which is now housed in its own hall at the Grand Palace in Bangkok, was carved in ancient India many centuries ago by the gods from a precious gem at the instigation of a legendarily wise monk, Nagasena, who worshipped the image until he attained his final *nirvana*. Later, due to war, the statue was transported to Sri Lanka, where it was honoured by the island's monarch and people. From there, King Anawrahta (r. 1044–1077), a famous ruler of Bagan, present-day Myanmar (Burma), had it placed on a ship, but the ship was blown off course to Angkor, in present-day Cambodia. After Angkor was flooded by

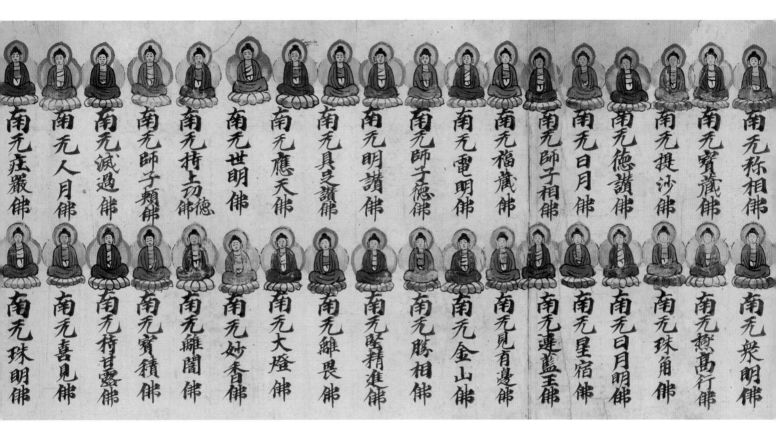

Sutra of the Buddha's names, used for both public and private recitations. Cave 17, Mogao Caves near Dunhuang, China, Gansu Province, *c.* 9th or 10th century.
British Library, Or.8210/S.253

an angry serpent deity, the statue was transported to Thai territories and venerated by Thai kings. The chronicle ends with the enshrinement of the image in northern Thailand.[63]

In this account, a Buddha statue, rather than a founder of a dynasty or sect, provided the focal point for the weaving of networks of persons and places across time. This chronicle connected the northern Thai to a wider landscape and deeper history of Buddhism, positioning them as the heirs to great Buddhist heroes of the past. Through the Buddha image, the community entwined the Buddha with their own histories.[64] The Buddha's biography is in many senses not yet ended, as it continues through his teachings, followers, relics and statues.

Notes

1 In this chapter I use the Pali versions of Indic terms with the exception of terms that have come into common English usage in their Sanskrit versions, such as *dharma* and *nirvana* (instead of Pali *dhamma* and *nibbana*), unless otherwise stated.

2 Kate Crosby, *Theravada Buddhism: Continuity, Diversity, and Identity* (Chichester: Wiley Blackwell, 2014), pp. 72–76.

3 Frank E. Reynolds and Charles Hallisey, 'Buddha' in Lindsay Jones, ed., *Encyclopedia of Religion*, 2nd ed. (Detroit: Macmillan Reference USA, 2005), pp. 1059–1071 (1064). Andrew Skilton, *A Concise History of Buddhism* (New York: Barnes & Noble Books, 1994), p. 20.

4 Crosby, *Theravada Buddhism*, p. 30.

5 The summary of the *Nidanakatha* is based on N.A. Jayawickrama, trans., *The Story of Gotama Buddha: The Nidana-katha of the Jatakatthakatha* (Oxford: Pali Text Society, 1990).

6 The summary of the *Mahaparinibbana Sutta* is based on Maurice Walshe, trans., *The Long Discourses of the Buddha: A Translation of the Digha Nikaya* (Boston: Wisdom, 1987), chapter 16 (pp. 231–278).

7 Ibid., pp. 263–264.

8 Ibid., pp. 264–277.

9 John S. Strong, *The Buddha: A Short Biography* (Oxford: Oneworld, 2001), pp. 13–14.

10 Nandana Chutiwongs, *The Iconography of Avalokitesvara in Mainland South East Asia* (New Delhi: Indira Gandhi National Centre for the Arts and Aryan Books International, 2002), pp. 13–14.

11 Jayawickrama, *The Story of Gotama Buddha*, pp. 121–122.

12 Richard Gombrich, 'The Significance of Former Buddhas in the Theravadin Tradition' in Somaratna Balasooriya et al., eds, *Buddhist Studies in Honour of Walpola Rahula* (London: Gordon Fraser, 1980), pp. 62–72 (64).

13 Crosby, *Theravada Buddhism*, p. 34.

14 Gombrich, 'The Significance of Former Buddhas', pp. 66–67.

15 Crosby, *Theravada Buddhism*, pp. 22–23.

16 Alexandra Green, *Buddhist Visual Cultures, Rhetoric, and Narrative in Late Burmese Wall Paintings* (Hong Kong University Press, 2018), pp. 3, 20, 37.

17 Jayawickrama, *The Story of Gotama Buddha*, pp. 126–127.

18 Strong, *Relics of the Buddha*, p. 41.

19 H.L. Shorto, 'The Dewatau Sotapan: A Mon Prototype of the 37 Nats', *Bulletin of the School of Oriental and African Studies* 30.1 (1967), pp. 127–141 (p. 140).

20 John S. Strong, *Buddhisms: An Introduction* (London: Oneworld, 2015), p. 237.

21 Denise Patry Leidy, *The Art of Buddhism: An Introduction to Its History and Meaning* (Boston: Shambhala, 2008), p. 89.

22 Eugene Y. Wang, *Shaping the Lotus Sutra: Buddhist Visual Culture in Medieval China* (Seattle: University of Washington Press, 2005), pp. 4–5. Strong, *Buddhisms*, p. 237.

23 Naomi K. Appleton, *Jataka Stories in Theravada Buddhism: Narrating the Bodhisatta Path* (Burlington: Ashgate, 2010), pp. 21–28. Jonathan S. Walters, 'The Buddha's Bad Karma: A Problem in the History of Theravada Buddhism', *Numen* 37.1 (June 1990), pp. 70–95.

24 Crosby, *Theravada Buddhism*, pp. 103–105.

25 E.B. Cowell, ed., *The Jataka or Stories of the Buddha's Former Lives*, vol. 1, Robert Chalmers, trans. (Bristol: Pali Text Society, 2013 [1895]), no. 172 (pp. 174–177).

26 San San May and Jana Igunma, *Buddhism Illuminated: Manuscript Art from Southeast Asia* (London: British Library, 2018), p. 155.

27 Vidya Dehejia, 'On Modes of Visual Narration in Early Buddhist Art', *Art Bulletin* 72.3 (Sept. 1990), pp. 374–392.

28 G.H. Luce, 'The 550 Jatakas in Old Burma', *Artibus Asiae* 19 (1956), pp. 291–307.

29 Robert L. Brown, 'Narrative as Icon: The Jataka Stories in Ancient Indian and Southeast Asian Architecture' in Juliane Schober, ed., *Sacred Biography in the Buddhist Traditions of South and Southeast Asia* (Honolulu: University of Hawai'i Press, 1997), pp. 64–109.

30 Forrest McGill, 'Jatakas, Universal Monarchs, and the Year 2000', *Artibus Asiae* 53.3/4 (1993), pp. 412–448 (p. 436).

31 Leedom Lefferts and Sandra Cate, *Buddhist Storytelling in Thailand and Laos: The Vessantara Jataka Scroll at the Asian Civilisations Museum* (Singapore: Asian Civilisations Museum, 2012), p. 1.

32 Naomi Appleton and Sarah Shaw, *The Ten Great Birth Stories of the Buddha: The Mahanipata of the Jatakatthavannana*, vol. 2 (Chiang Mai: Silkworm and Chulalongkorn University Press, 2015), pp. 510, 533–534.

33 Kathryn A. Bowie, *Of Beggars and Buddhas: The Politics of Humor in the Vessantara Jataka in Thailand* (Madison: University of Wisconsin Press, 2017), pp. 83–94.

34 Lefferts and Cate, *Buddhist Storytelling in Thailand and Laos*, pp. 1–4, 42.

35 Bowie, *Of Beggars and Buddhas*, pp. 18–36 and chapter 3 on northern Thailand (pp. 123–166).

36 Ibid., pp. 83–94.

37 Jonathan S. Walters, 'Communal Karma and Karmic Community in Theravada Buddhist History' in John Clifford Holt, Jacob N. Kinnard and Jonathan S. Walters, eds, *Constituting Communities: Theravada Buddhism and the Religious Cultures of South and Southeast Asia* (Albany: State University of New York Press, 2003), pp. 9–39 (pp. 14–16, 22).

38 I.B. Horner, trans., *The Minor Anthologies of the Pali Canon, vol. III: Chronicle of Buddhas (Buddhavamsa) and Basket of Conduct (Cariya Pitaka)* (Bristol: Pali Text Society, 2013 [1975]), pp. xxxv–xxxvi.

39 Walshe, trans., *The Long Discourses of the Buddha*, p. 264.

40 Kate Crosby, 'Devotion to the Buddha in Theravada and its Role in Meditation' in Anna S. King and John Brockington, eds, *The Intimate Other: Love Divine in Indic Religions* (New Delhi: Orient Longman, 2005), pp. 244–277 (pp. 247–248).

41 Strong, *Relics of the Buddha*.

42 Angela S. Chiu, *The Buddha in Lanna: Art, Lineage, Power, and Place in Northern Thailand* (Honolulu: University of Hawai'i Press, 2017), pp. 107–109.

43 John S. Strong, *The Legend of King Asoka: A Study and Translation of the Asokavadana* (Delhi: Motilal Banarsidass, 2016 [1983]), p. 123.

44 Wilhelm Geiger, trans., *The Mahavamsa or The Great Chronicle of Ceylon* (Colombo: Ceylon Government Information Department, 1960), pp. 3–9.

45 Wilhelm Geiger, *Culture of Ceylon in Mediaeval Times*, Heinz Bechert, ed. (Wiesbaden: Harrassowitz, 1960), p. 178.

46 For a discussion of some scholarly views on this topic, see Crosby, 'Devotion to the Buddha'.

Seated figure representing the Buddha Shakyamuni, the historical Buddha, in the earth-touching pose (Sanskrit: *bhumisparsa mudra*).

nn4344.1 ©Horniman Museum and Gardens

View of the pyramidal-stepped *stupa* at the Maha Bodhi temple
complex, Bodhgaya, indicating the place where Buddha is said
to have attained enlightenment. Watercolour painting by
James Crockatt, *c.* 1800.

47 Vidya Dehejia, 'Aniconism and the Multivalence of Emblems', *Ars Orientalis* 21 (1991), pp. 45–66; Susan L. Huntington, 'Aniconism and the Multivalence of Emblems: Another Look', *Ars Orientalis* 22 (1992), pp. 111–156.

48 Gregory Schopen, 'On Monks, Nuns and "Vulgar" Practices: The Introduction of the Image Cult into Indian Buddhism', *Artibus Asiae* 49 (1988/89), pp. 153–168.

49 John Kieschnick, *The Impact of Buddhism on Chinese Material Culture* (Princeton: Princeton University Press, 2003), p. 55.

50 Jacob N. Kinnard, 'Buddhist Iconography' in Lindsay Jones, ed., *Encyclopedia of Religion*, 2nd ed. (Detroit: Macmillan Reference USA, 2005), pp. 4327–4331 (p. 4331).

51 Samuel S. Beal, trans., *Si-Yu-Ki: Buddhist Records of the Western World, Translated from the Chinese of Hiuen Tsiang (A.D. 629)* (London: Kegan Paul, Trench, Trübner, 1906), vol. 1, pp. xliv–xlv.

52 Ibid., vol. 2, p. 4.

53 Charuni Inchoetchai and Khwanchit Loetsiri, *Phra Bot [Buddhist Paintings on Cloth]* (Krung Thep: Samnak Boranakadi lae Phiphitiphan Sathan haeng Chat, 2545 [2002]), p. 11.

54 Walshe, trans., *The Long Discourses of the Buddha*, pp. 441–460 (chapter 30).

55 Strong, *The Buddha*, p. 31.

56 Peter Skilling, ed., *Past Lives of the Buddha: Wat Si Chum – Art, Architecture and Inscriptions* (Bangkok: River Books, 2008), p. 68.

57 Walshe, trans., *The Long Discourses of the Buddha*, p. 263.

58 John S. Strong, 'Buddha Bhakti and the Absence of the Blessed One' in Jacques Ryckmans, ed., *Premier Colloque Etienne Lamotte* (Louvain-la-Neuve: Université Catholique de Louvain, Institut Orientaliste, 1993), pp. 131–140 (pp. 134–139).

59 James C.Y. Watt and Denise Patry Leidy, *Defining Yongle: Imperial Art in Early Fifteenth-Century China* (New York: Metropolitan Museum of Art, 2005), p. 14. Quanyu Wang and Sascha Priewe, 'Scientific Analysis of a Buddha Attributed to the Yongle Period of the Ming Dynasty', *British Museum Technical Research Bulletin* 7 (2013), pp. 61–68.

60 Janice Leoshko, 'About Looking at Buddha Images in Eastern India', *Archives of Asian Art* 52 (2000/2001), pp. 63–82.

61 Kieschnick, *The Impact of Buddhism on Chinese Material Culture*, pp. 53, 68–69.

62 Heidi Tan, 'Art, Power, and Merit: The Veneration of Buddha Images in Myanmar Museums' in Sylvia Fraser-Lu and Donald M. Stadtner, eds, *Buddhist Art of Myanmar* (New York: Asia Society, 2015), pp. 81–87 (p. 84).

63 Saeng Monwithun, trans., *Ratanaphimphawong: Tamnan Phra Kaeo Morakot [Chronicle of the Emerald Buddha Image]* (Bangkok: Krom Sinlapakon, 2510 [1967]).

64 Chiu, *The Buddha in Lanna*, chapter 2 (pp. 19–52).

Knox *Lalitavistara* (IO.SAN.688)

Pasquale Manzo

This Sanskrit manuscript was commissioned by a British resident in Nepal (Captain William Douglas Knox of the East India Company's army) and copied in clear Devanagari writing by the scribe Amritananda in Patan, Nepal, in 1803. It was subsequently owned by H.T. Colebrooke (1765–1837), one of the most important Indologists of his time. A paper with a partial list of the chapters he inserted in the manuscript and some marginal notes are still preserved. The manuscript then came into the possession of B.H. Hodgson, also a British resident in Nepal and pioneer of Buddhist studies, who eventually presented it to the India Office Library. In 1836 Robert Lenz based his analysis of the *Lalita-Vistara-Pourana*, one of the first works ever published in the West about an important Buddhist text, on this manuscript. The yellow-dyed handmade paper leaves are held between two painted wooden boards and the text is illustrated by twenty-seven fine miniatures in opaque watercolour. Captain Knox and Amritananda appear on the inside rear board and in a miniature at the end of the manuscript in which the British official is depicted seated, wearing his uniform and holding a prayer wheel whilst in conversation with the scribe who has the manuscript in his left hand. In the background, a stupa emerges from the trees under the night sky.

The *Lalitavistara Sutra* narrates the extraordinary events in the life of Buddha Shakyamuni (Siddharta Gautama, the so-called historic Buddha) unfolding from his descent from Tushita heaven to the First Sermon (the Setting in Motion of the Wheel of Dharma) in the Deer Park at Sarnath near the holy Indian city of Varanasi. It tells of Buddha's miraculous conception and birth, of the gods and sages saluting him as the Great Bodhisattva who will free all beings from suffering with his wisdom. Here we find the list of the thirty-two special signs (*lakshana*) marking his body and detailed descriptions of his moral attitude and qualities, the tales of his childhood and youth in the Shakya royal palace, and of the four fortuitous encounters through which he sees the reality of impermanence and suffering and decides to find its cause. Further, it details the years of strenuous discipline under various teachers in search of the true path to liberation.

The various episodes narrated in the *Lalitavistara Sutra* have inspired Buddhist art across the Indian subcontinent and beyond: famous examples are found in sculptures from Gandhara, on the reliefs of the great stupas in central and southern India (e.g. Bharut, Sanchi, Amaravati) and at the Borobudur temple complex on the island of Java in Indonesia. The miniatures illustrating the manuscript, whose style shows a Tibetan influence, depict some of the main events described in the text: Buddha's descent from heaven in the form of a white elephant as seen in a dream by his mother Maya; the birth in Lumbini park with the Bodhisattva coming out of Maya's right side as she stands holding a branch of the Shala tree; and the great departure, here represented with a very touching portrait of King Suddhodana, Buddha's father, crying at the sight of his son's horse coming back to the palace. This manuscript is a significant example of British patronage of art and culture in the Indian subcontinent. It ends with the praises of Captain Knox (whose virtues are compared to those of a Buddha) and with a list of his honorific titles.

Lalitavistara Sutra in Sanskrit, Nepal, 1803.
British Library, IO.San.688

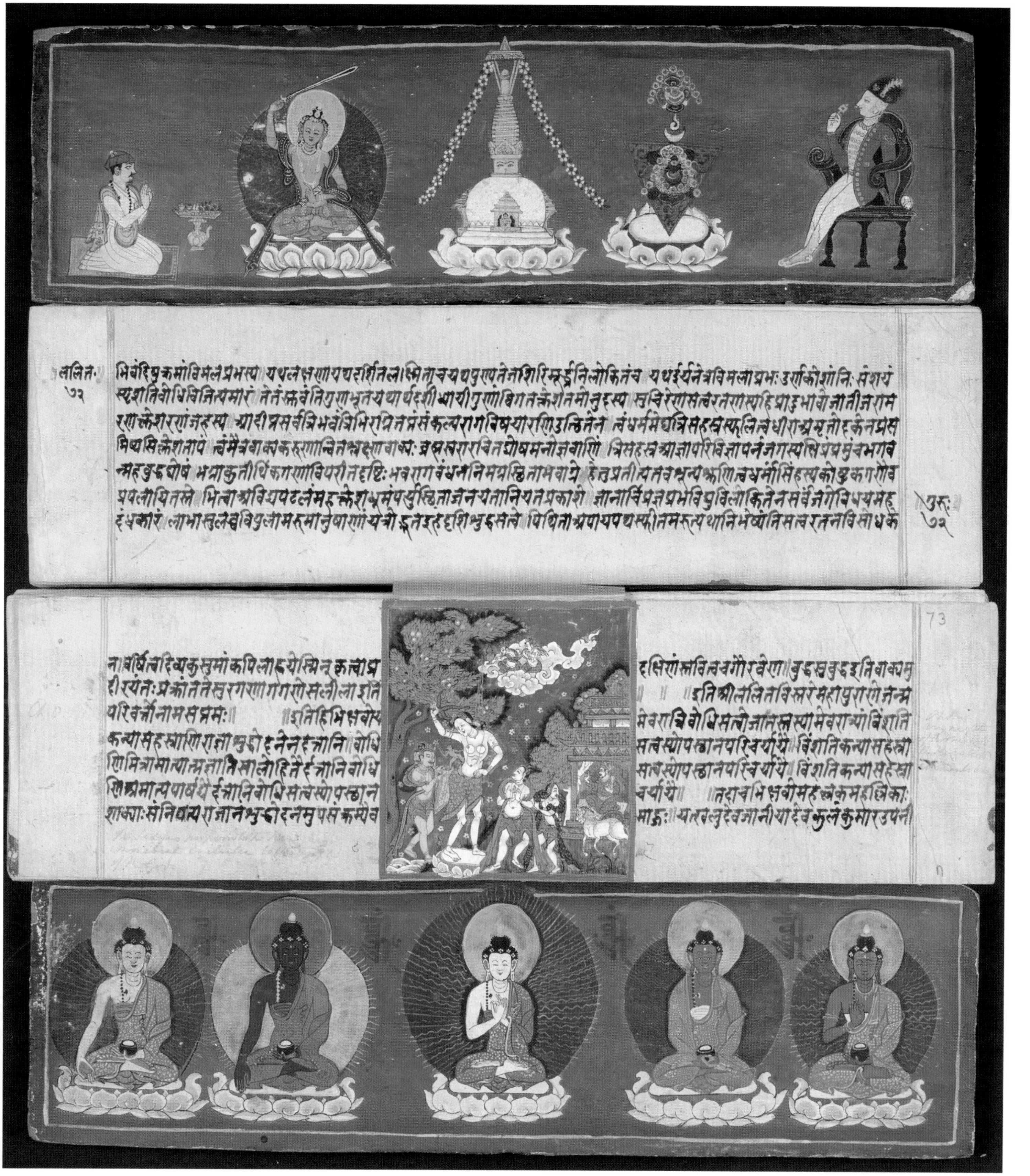

लिलत
२२ भिवंदिद्गुक्मोविमलप्रभस्य यथलक्ष्माएयशशीतलस्मिगूरय्य वपुर्णेनशिरिम्पूईनिलोकितेनं यथर्हयैंनेत्रविमलाप्रभः उर्णीकोशोनि संश्रयं
स्सतिवीषिविनियर्मार नेतंकनंविनिगुणभूतयं यावयदर्णी अरीगुणान्विगतकेशनमोनुस्य चूर्विरेगसत्वगतगाह प्राइभावोज्ञातीज्ञराम
रगक्लेशरांजहस्य आदीप्रसविविभवेविभिरापितप्रसंकल्याणगविश्यारायिलुन्लितेनं लंधर्ममिधिरासहस्रफुल्लिते धीरास्वरसूरीदकेनप्रसा
मिष्यसिक्नोनांदे दंमेवंबबकवक्हरानितिक्ष्णकवाक्षा व्रफूतरारविनीयीवमनोज्ञवाणी विसहस्रस्याप्रोपरिवेशापनंजगस्यसिप्रयमुंभगाव
स्महबुद्धघोषे भवराकूतीर्थिकगणाविरोगितंदृष्टिः भवरागवंधननिगमवूच्छित्तानामवादे हेतुप्रतीद्गनवभूयद्गकुषिग्धर्मसिंहस्यकोष्ठकारीव
प्रवलीयितले भित्वाश्रियपदलेमहकेशो भूमंपदुष्छितांजनयतानियत प्रकाशे ज्ञानार्विप्रतप्रभविप्रविलोकितेनं सर्वजगेरियमहू तुरुः
३२
दंधकारे लाभास्तेविविज्ञोमसमानुवागांयोची इतिहइदृशिभुइसले बिषिनांज्ञाणयप्रयस्थीतमस्त्यां यानिभेव्योनिसतरत्नविलोधके

नार्विचदियकुसुमां कपिलादुयोत्रिनकुचाप्र   दक्षिणांश्रिविरवगौरवेगा बुद्धबुद्दइतिशाक्यमु
रीरयतेः प्रकीतेनेस्तुरगणा गागरोसलीलाशोति   इतिश्रीललितविस्तरेमहापुराणीनेन्द्र
परिवर्त्नीनामसप्तम्म॥ इतिहिमिभवोच   मेवराचिवोचिसतीज्ञानुत्तस्यामेवराब्योविंशति
कन्यासहस्राशिराजा बुद्धेनेनइञ्ज्ञानि बोधि   सत्वस्योपस्थानपरिवर्य्यौ विंशतिकन्यासहस्रा
 णिमित्रामात्यामत्या नैसोलोहितेर्द्गानि बोधि   सत्वस्योपस्थानपरिवर्य्यौ विंशतिकन्यासहस्रा
ष्टिप्रमात्यपार्श्वेय ईर्द्गानि बोधि सर्वस्योपस्थानं   वर्य्यौ तदावमि भवोमहकेलुमहमल्लिका
शाक्याःसनिवयं राजानभुद्गीदनमुपसक्रम्यं   माहुःयतरलुदेवज्ञानीयादेव कुलेकुमारउपनी

73

KNOX *LALITAVISTARA*

71

The *Lotus Sutra*

Hamish Todd

The *Lotus Sutra*, known in Sanskrit as *Saddharma Pundarika Sutra* or *Sutra of the Lotus of the Wonderful Law*, is one of the most influential scriptures of Mahayana Buddhism and is an object of particular veneration in China, Korea and Japan.

Precisely where and when the *sutra* was composed is unknown. The scholarly consensus is that it was written in several stages during the first and second centuries CE. There are said to have been six translations of the *sutra* from Sanskrit into Chinese, of which three have been lost and three are extant. Of these it was the translation by Kumarajiva (343–413 CE), a Buddhist monk from the Central Asian Kingdom of Kucha, completed in 406 and titled *Miao-fa-lian-hua-jing* (in Japanese *Myoho-renge-kyo*), that was most influential in spreading the *sutra's* teachings in East Asia.

The *Lotus Sutra* is seen by many of its adherents as the summation of the teachings of the Buddha. Among its important doctrines are: that there is only one vehicle or path to salvation – the path to Buddhahood; that all sentient beings can attain salvation in their present existence by following its teachings; and that the Buddha is an eternal being, ever-present and concerned for the salvation of all beings. In Japan the *Lotus Sutra* has long been one of the most popular Buddhist texts and is of particular significance for the Tendai and Nichiren schools of Buddhism.

The most popular part of the *sutra* in Japan and China was chapter 25, which concerns the Bodhisattva Avalokitesvara, 'Perceiver of the Sounds of the World', the embodiment of compassion, whose name was rendered into Chinese as Guanyin and into Japanese as Kannon. The *sutra* teaches that Avalokitesvara, who can appear in thirty-three different manifestations, works unceasingly to aid those who call on his name and that invoking the name of the Bodhisattva with true sincerity will bring all manner of assistance and protection to believers.

The manuscript illustrated here belongs to a long Japanese tradition of sumptuously decorated *sutras* known as *soshoku-kyo*. The practice of copying *sutras* by hand (*shakyo*) is believed to accrue Buddhist merit, either for oneself or for one's deceased relations. From the Heian period (794–1185) onwards, members of the imperial family and nobility would commission lavishly embellished copies of the *Lotus Sutra*, generally, as here, with a beautifully illustrated frontispiece, accompanied by the finest calligraphy on richly ornamented paper.

This scroll contains chapter 8 of the *Lotus Sutra* ('The Prophecy of Enlightenment for Five Hundred Disciples'), written in gold on indigo-dyed paper in vertical columns surrounded by double gold lines. The margins above and below the text and the reverse of the scroll are covered in abstract designs in silver and gold. The gilt metalwork on the roller bears the three-leaved hollyhock, the dynastic emblem of the Tokugawa family.

The most striking aspect, however, is the finely drawn frontispiece, depicting two themes from the chapter. In the upper section Buddha grants promises of Buddhahood to his assembled disciples; in the lower are scenes from the parable of a man who leads a life of poverty and hardship, unaware that many years ago a friend had sewn a priceless jewel into his robe, an allusion to the teachings of the Buddha that many forget.

With a provenance reaching back to the Matsudaira family of Shikoku, a branch of the Tokugawa dynasty, this scroll has traditionally been linked to a set of twenty-eight, one for each chapter of the *Lotus Sutra*, commissioned during the Kanbun Era (1661–1672) by the Retired Emperor Go-Mizunoo (1596–1680, r. 1611–1629). These were dedicated to the Toshogu Shrine at Nikko, where the first Tokugawa Shogun, Tokugawa Ieyasu (1543–1616), was enshrined. Ieyasu was the grandfather of the Emperor's consort, Kazuko, known to history as Tofukumon'in (1607–1678), but the relationship between Emperor and Shogun was complicated and often strained, as the former struggled to assert his independence.

Despite the high degree of skill evident in such decorated *sutras*, the identities of the scribes, artists and other craftsmen responsible are rarely known since very few of the scrolls bear any indication of the date when they were created or the names of those involved. However, in the 1990s, repairs to the British Library manuscript revealed a hitherto unsuspected inscription at the very end of the scroll, which had previously been hidden by the roller to which it was attached. This contained the date of the fourth month of the thirteenth year of Kan'ei Era (i.e. 1636) and the signatures of at least ten scribes headed by *daikyoji* (senior scribe) Doi, who held the title of *hogen* ('eye of the Dharma'), the second-highest priestly rank in the Buddhist hierarchy. While the inscription does not tell us what role each of those listed played in the creation of the manuscript, it seems reasonable to assume that Doi would have been responsible for the most important element – the illustrated frontispiece.

The date of 1636 given in the colophon means the scroll was created thirty or so years earlier than previously thought. Significantly, 1636 was the twentieth anniversary of the death of Ieyasu and the year in which the Toshogu was extensively rebuilt on the orders of

the third Shogun Tokugawa Iemitsu. It is known from historical sources that from 1632 onwards the imperial court regularly sent decorated *sutras* to the Nikko Shrine. Comparing the British Library manuscript with examples of these reveals many similarities in terms of calligraphic style and decorative design. So, while there is no categorical proof, there is a strong possibility that this scroll was dedicated as part of the reconstruction of the Toshogu. In any case, it bears testimony both to the importance attached to the *Lotus Sutra* in Japanese culture and to the great skill of monk-scribes like Doi and his fellows.

The *Lotus Sutra* (Japanese: *Myoho-renge-kyo*) in Chinese characters, chapter 8. Japan, 1636.
British Library, Or.13926

WHEEL OF LIFE: PHILOSOPHY AND ETHICS

Khammai Dhammasami

A wheel is found on vehicles of all kinds and is considered to represent a symbol of transport. The Buddha made it clear that his teachings were a means to an end and not the end itself. Seven weeks after his enlightenment at Buddhagaya (Bodhgaya) when he set out for Varanasi to share his newly found way to freedom with a group of five former friends, he met an ascetic who enquired where he was going, and why. The Buddha is said to have answered that he 'was going to turn the wheel of dhamma (*dhammacakkam pavattetum*)'. That turning of the wheel happened at the Deer Park when he gave his first sermon, now known as the 'discourse on the turning of the wheel of *dhamma*'. Before that, the wheel as a symbol had been in use in pre-Buddhist India, where, for example, a righteous ruler was described as a wheel-turning monarch (*cakkavatti/cakravartin*). In the first sermon of the Buddha, the wheel signifies the coming together of various wholesome qualities to solve the problem of suffering. In that first teaching, the wheel means 'the truths' when referring to the Four Noble Truths; 'the way' to realize the truths when discussing the Noble Eightfold Path; or 'enlightenment' when the Four Noble Truths are understood in twelve aspects, as set out later in this chapter. In the same spirit, the Buddha illustrated to the monks, using a wheel with four spokes, that for a person to progress in life there have to be four conditions working together: a suitable location; a good friend; self-dedication; and a good foundation from the past. Later, to explain how life goes on in a cycle of rebirth, or *samsara*, the wheel is used to demonstrate the repetition of suffering and it comes to be known as the wheel of life (*bhavacakka/bhavacakra*). This chapter explains the wheel of life from a cosmological viewpoint, with an emphasis on Buddhist philosophy and ethics.

Some ask a question: given its simple yet profound philosophical outlook based on human experience, does Buddhism need teachings on cosmology? This is the more pertinent if one compares traditional Buddhist cosmology to physics in modern science. Buddhist teachings on cosmology are not a later development, as some would claim, for we know the earliest Buddhist canonical works contain clear references to cosmology. During the moments of his full enlightenment under the Bodhi tree at Buddhagaya, the Buddha is said to have remembered more than a hundred thousand of his past lives (M.1.22).[1] After his enlightenment, the earliest era he is recorded as having recalled is that of ninety-one aeons before that present moment (M.1.483). In Buddhist cosmology, the cosmos also exists in thousand-fold clusters, galactic groupings of these clusters and super-galactic groupings of these galaxies (A.1.227).[2] The *Visuddhimagga* says: 'the physical universe is said to consist of countless world-systems spread out through space, each seen as having a central mountain called Meru surrounded by four continents and smaller islands, which came to be seen as all on a flat disc' (Vsm. 205–206).[3] Another celebrated commentator in Mahayana Buddhism, Vasubandhu, provides a similar account in his *Abhidharmakosa*. For a start, Buddhist cosmology in the fifth century BCE, or for that matter any religious cosmology, was not presented in contemporary scientific terms.

While some scholars, including Tominago Nagamoto (1715–1746) and Donald Lopez Jr (1952–), focus more on the spiritual than on the literal plane of the Buddhist cosmological teachings, others, such as Peter Harvey

(1951–) and Rupert Gethin (1957–), offer an inclusive view and suggest that Buddhist cosmology allows for both symbolic and psychological interpretation alongside a literal reading. A popular example by which to test this theory is the story of the Buddha's own enlightenment. The ascetic Gotama (Sanskrit: Gautama) sat under the Bodhi tree with a vow to not rise again until he had achieved full enlightenment. Mara, the heavenly but demonic figure not unlike Satan, rushed to dissuade him from his efforts, but Gotama refused. Consequently, Mara sent his army to destroy Gotama, but upon approaching him their flying weapons were transformed into flower blossoms. This episode may be read literally if one so wishes, and has indeed translated into a popular belief that on the eve of one achieving anything great, that very imminent success may attract some villainous obstacle that one must then overcome as a final test. Or, on a different plane, one may interpret the raining weapons as a manifestation of anger and fear, until then dormant deep within the mind of the Bodhisattva (Buddha-to-be), which he had to overcome through wisdom and compassion, represented here by the positive presence of flowers.

Further, on being challenged by Mara that he had no right to be on the seat of enlightenment, the Bodhisattva answered that he had earned his right to be there by accumulating merits over countless aeons. This he vouches by extending his right hand and touching the earth, thereby summoning the goddess of the earth (Vasundhara, Sthavara or Dharani, the latter pronounced by Thai and Lao people as 'Thorani') to bear witness to his great virtues. The goddess serves as witness by wringing water out of her hair, leading to the floods that dispel Mara's army. The enormous volume of water from her hair was as much as the amount of libation water poured by the Buddha in his many previous lives while performing generous deeds. Here, the story may be read literally on the one hand, while on the other it may be taken as an illustration of how deeply seated self-doubt can be overcome by revisiting the positive qualities and contributions one has made in the past.

Moreover, after the Buddha's enlightenment, Mara sends his three daughters – Tanha (Craving), Arati (Discontent) and Raga (Delight) – to tempt him. The Buddha remains unmoved and they give up. Here, the Buddha's steadfastness in the face of the daughters of Mara may be seen to stand for the final uprooting of lust and sensual gratification: they may be regarded either as divinity figures or mental manifestations.

Mara may therefore be seen either as a malevolent divinity from without (devaputta-mara/devaputra-mara) or a psychological phenomenon of affliction from within (kilesa-mara). Both interpretations are accepted by Buddhist traditions. Indeed, both the Theravada and Mahayana Buddhist traditions perceive death (maccu) and the aggregates of mind and body (khandha) as Mara. One of the earliest Pali texts, the Parayana-vagga of the Suttanipata, contains a remark by the Buddha to a young man, Bhadravudha: 'Mara is after beings.' Its commentary explains that Mara here is the volition that forms kamma (Sanskrit: karma), for it is this kamma that brings in its wake other forms of Mara such as rebirth, mind and body, and death. Delusion leads to craving and sensual frailty, and consequently one accumulates unwholesome kamma. Therefore, there may be the tendency – within our mind – to be antagonistic towards the idea of liberation from samsara, the cycle of birth and death, which is represented as Mara.

One may well take note of the fact that the three kinds of knowledge (vijja) forming components of enlightenment do not include the defeat of a divine being called Mara. This suggests that it is not necessary to believe and defeat Mara the demonic figure as part of one's spiritual progress towards enlightenment, therefore even Mara as a being is defeated, and that victory would simply be a by-product. It is the deeply rooted affliction (anusaya kilesa) in one's own mind that needs to be overcome. The three kinds of knowledge are: (a) the knowledge of past lives, which confirms how the law of kamma has determined one's existence throughout the cycle of birth and death in different realms (pubbe-nivasanussati/cutupapata); (b) the knowledge of divine sight, which is the realization that all others are also subject to rebirth and death in samsara (dibbacakkhu); and (c) the knowledge of the total extinction of negative emotion (asavakkhaya). These three kinds of knowledge can be interpreted cosmologically in the context of the experiences of many lives – kamma and rebirth in the vast lengths of time in the cosmos – as many have done so traditionally. Or, they may be understood as three psychological aspects of enlightenment in one's life experiences: (a) seeing and accepting the natural law of cause and effect in one's life; (b) confirming this as a universal law, rather than unique to any one individual; and (c) that all beings are governed by their own volitional action, kamma, and there is nothing perpetuating the samsara but the habits of one's own mind.

It is worth noting here that there is a shared heritage among the Indian religious philosophies. Many of the celestial and other living beings found in the Buddhist suttas have been incorporated from previous Indian traditions, just as in pre-Buddhist Brahmanism and Jainism. Figures such as Brahma and Indra (Pali: Sakka); classifications such as Asuras, Gandhabba, Yakkha, Yakkhini, Rakha, Nagas and Garudas; or minor figures such as tree- or forest-dwelling deities all form

Painting of the cosmic ocean with the
mythical Mount Meru surrounded by
seven rivers and mountain ranges, sun
and moon, cosmic pillars, heavenly
palaces and four continents. At the top of
Mount Meru is a heavenly palace housing
the god Indra (Pali: Sakka) and empty
palaces symbolizing realms of
formlessness. Thailand, 19th century.
British Library, Or.16100, ff. 96–100

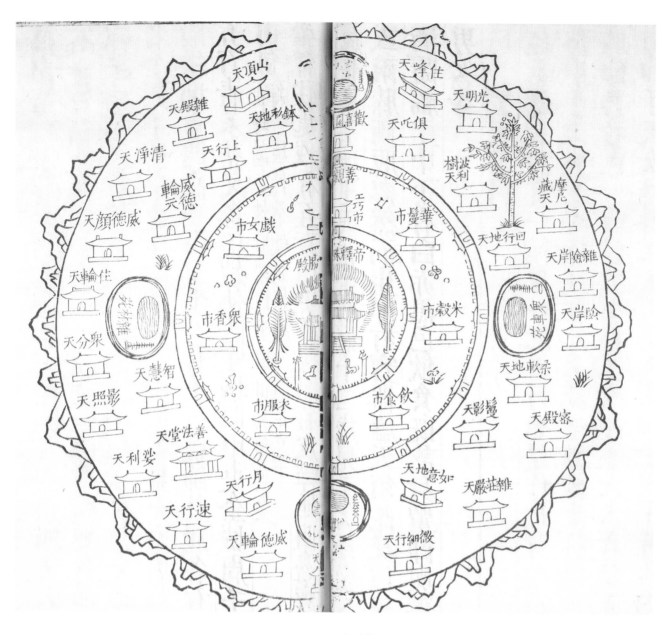

Buddhist cosmological map of one of twenty-eight heavenly realms. Guangzhou, China, c. 1800.

a part of the larger Indian religious folk heritage. As far as Buddhism is concerned, so long as human beings rely on themselves for attaining release from *samsara*, the accommodation of these celestial figures and their realms does not contradict the spirit of early Buddhism. Even outside its homeland of India, Buddhism continues to accommodate local beliefs along this line. Many Buddhists of Burma/Myanmar perform rites connected with *nat,* a deified type of being, while Thai Buddhists worship a similar form of being which they call *phi.* Japanese Buddhists worship *kami* spirits at the Shinto shrines, while Tibetan Buddhists seek the blessings of a whole range of spirits and gods, acknowledging

some as protectors of *dhamma* (Sanskrit: *dharma*). Buddhist monks appeal daily to *devas* to help protect their devotees (*rakkhantu sabba-devata*), and indeed the wholesome qualities of the *devas* are taught by the Buddha as an object of meditation (*devatanussati*). Thus, in early Buddhist texts, deities are said to possess some form of power to help human beings with their daily problems. The *Ratana Sutta* in the *Suttanipata* is one such text that recognizes the power of divine beings or even demi-gods, made evident when Ananda, attendant of the Buddha, appeals to them to be kind to the people of Vesali (Sanskrit: Vaishali). It is what Melford Spiro considers 'apotropaic Buddhism'.[4]

However, if one looks at the pantheon of gods in the Hindu tradition, these gods often take on a different and reduced role when incorporated into the Buddhist scheme. In the table are some examples, with brief descriptions.

Gods	HINDU	BUDDHIST
Brahma	first of the gods and creator of the universe	reigns in Mahabrahma Heaven, being reborn there due to his meditative power
Yama	god of death	king of hell
Indra	storm god of the firmament	king of Tavatimsa Heaven, being reborn there as the result of his previous good kamma
Mara	god of death	tempter

From being worshipped as the creator of the universe and the first among all gods in Brahmanism, Brahma is considered in Buddhism as the king of the Brahma world, consisting of three of the Thirty-One Planes of Existence. A Brahman by the name of Sahampati Brahma is said to have convinced the Buddha – initially sceptical about whether anybody would understand his profound insights – to teach. Sahampati Brahma is believed to have said that the Fully Awakened One *should* teach, for there are people with little dust in their eyes who would be able to understand the *dhamma*. For this intervention through the person of Sahampati Brahma at the inception of the Buddhist dispensation (*sasana*), Brahma is appreciated as a *Dhammapala*, 'Guardian of the Dhamma'. Despite their long life spanning one aeon, and their meditative achievement of the first *jhana*, Brahma and his subjects have to go through the cycle of birth and death like anyone else in the universe.

Yama is considered the king of hell in Buddhist cosmology, not god of death as in pre-Buddhist belief. Although his abode is situated in various realms – heaven (*sagga*), ghosts (*peta*) and hell (*niraya*) – he is a divinity. Birth, decay, illness, punishment of criminals

Burmese painting of the Himavanta region at the foot of Mount Meru, shown here with the lake Anotatta, a place where the Buddha meditated. Burma, 19th century.

Thangka painting of the two-armed Mahakala, a protector deity of the Karma Kagyu School of the Vajrayana tradition. This specific form of Mahakala is called Bernagchen in Tibetan and is dedicated to the protection of the lineage of Karmapas. Tibet, 16th century.

by the government on earth and death are his five messengers reminding people to refrain from evil deeds and be virtuous. According to the *Devaduta Sutta* in the *Majjhima Nikaya*, upon arriving in hell a person is taken by hell-wardens to King Yama, who interrogates the newly arrived as to whether he or she has ever noticed any of the five messengers and performed good deeds of generosity, and restraint in conduct, as a result. King Yama also asks if the person has ever showed respect to parents, elders and the spiritually endowed. If the answer is positive and one is able to recall any previous good deeds, one is then freed from that woeful state. But if all the answers are negative, King Yama decrees that the evil deeds were not done by parents or any others but by oneself. As King Yama falls silent, the evil-doer is taken to various vast torture chambers. Here, as the philosophy of *kamma* in Buddhism relies on natural cause-and-effect to mete out punishment to the evil-doer, King Yama's role is not that of a judge but rather of one who offers the last chance to individuals to remember their good deeds and thereby free themselves from that baleful state. Yama is considered as being among those who register the good deeds performed by human

beings; others in that role include the goddess of the earth (*Vasundhara/Dharani/Sthavara*).

Indra, also known as Sakra/Sakka, who is 'the king of the gods ... [and] who eventually becomes the chief of all divinities in Indian popular religion'[5] is a storm god and a supreme deity in Hinduism, and is seen in Buddhism as the ruler of the gods of the Thirty-Three Realms at the summit of Mount Meru, and also as a guardian of the *dhamma*. As in the Vedic tradition, he is the god most often referred to in Buddhist scriptures. This chief Vedic divinity, Indra, has attained the spiritual purification of a stream-enterer (*sotapanna*) and is thus a protector of the *dhamma*. He has been reborn as Sakra as the result of his previous wholesome *kamma*, and is subject to the nature of *samsara* like any others.

While Buddhism retains much of the cosmological order and beliefs from older Indian religions such as Brahmanism and Jainism, it is clear that Buddhism offers one crucial difference: it presents its cosmology without resorting to a Creator God but putting the responsibility of creation and destruction in the hands of each and every living being. Moreover, unlike contemporary cosmologies that focus exclusively, for instance, on gravity, strong force, weak force and electromagnetic force of the external physical universe in which we live, the principal contemplation in Buddhist cosmology is the inner world – the force of morally intentional actions called *kamma*. The core message from the Buddha is that the key to human happiness and unhappiness lies not in the hands of gods who were believed until the appearance of the Buddha to hold sway over human life, but is determined by our own ethical choices. This applies not just to human beings but also to animals and powerful gods themselves, and not just in this universe but equally in the other 'ten-thousand' universes (*dasa-sahassi lokadhatu*).

Sentient beings – including gods in the heavens, human beings or those in hellish states – are therefore responsible through their own *kamma* for the existence and destruction of the universe. Belief in rebirth, *samsara* and *nirvana* thus becomes an essential part of Buddhist cosmology. Spiritually, it explains how one can take one's course of life into one's own hands, progressing to better lives in the journey of *samsara* – the cycle of life and death – and ultimately achieving liberation from it. *Samsara* is basically seen in Buddhism as a state of dissatisfaction (*dukkha*), and is approached from two angles: cosmological and psychological.[6]

Buddhism does not see any necessity for a creator of the cosmos it postulates, and no beginning to the cosmos or the *samsara* of life.[7] Furthermore, 'if there were a creator he would be regarded as responsible for the suffering which is found throughout the universe'.[8] Indeed, the Buddha himself is reported to have declared that 'the beginning of *samsara* is inconceivable and its starting point cannot be indicated' (SN.ii.178). One is encouraged not to waste time discussing the measurement of the physical universe in time and space, but to focus one's energy on improving oneself ethically and psychologically. This spirit is captured in famous sayings of the Buddha:

> One truly is the protector of oneself; who else
> could the protector be?
> With oneself fully controlled, one gains a mastery
> that is hard to gain.
> (Dh 160, translation by Buddharakkhita)

> Therefore, Ananda, be a light unto yourself,
> be refuges unto yourself,
> seeking no external refuge; let the dharma
> as your island be your refuge,
> seeking no other refuge.
> (*Mahaparinibbana Sutta*, DN 16)

A detailed model of the universe is given in the Thirty-One Planes of Existence, showing the connec-tion between our ethical actions and cosmology in the Buddhist tradition, as preserved in the literary sources, both canonical and commentarial. The Thirty-One Planes are divided into three folds, depending on the spiritual capabilities of the inhabitants of each realm: the sensual sphere (*kama-dhatu*), the form sphere (*rupa-dhatu*) and the formless sphere (*arupa-dhatu*), with the last two determined by the attainment of meditative absorption (*jhana*).

The lowest of the Thirty-One Planes is the realm of hell, which includes many infernal rebirths involving experiences of being tortured. The Buddha himself is said to have told the monks, as recorded in the *Devaduta Sutta* ('The Discourse on Divine Messengers'), in the *Majjhima Nikaya* ('Collection of the Middle Length Sayings'), how evil-doers are tortured. Punishments include a red-hot iron stake being repeatedly driven through one's limbs; limbs being chopped off with axes one by one; being plunged into a red-hot burning copper cauldron; being burnt in four directions in the flames of the Great Hell; being thrown into the Vast Hot Ashes Hell; being put in the Simbali Forest, covered with burning, blazing and glowing thorns, and in the Sword-Leaf Forest, where the leaves are so sharp they cut one's limbs; and being made by the hell-wardens to swallow a burning or molten copper ball when thirsty and asking for water. Furthermore, beings do not die of these tortures and injuries as long as their evil *kamma* is not exhausted. Hell is the comeuppance for an inflicted consciousness, a place where all the experiences of the senses are highly unpleasant and intolerable. While some hells are worse than others, all of the suffering is deemed appropriate for the corrupt deeds evil-doers have committed in their past lives. Though the time in hell is long, it is not eternal, as believed in the Abrahamic traditions. Once the consequences of their evil deeds are over, hellish beings are reborn in the human world. Rupert Gethin gives a clear illustration of the connection of negative states of consciousness in the human world and the actual hell: 'when a human being experiences unpleasant mental states such as aversion, hatred, or depression, then there is a sense in which that being can be said to be experiencing something of what it is like to exist in a hell realm – in other words, he makes a brief visit to the hell realms; when those unpleasant states pass (as they inevitably will), the being will return to the mental state natural to human beings – a mental state which is understood to be essentially wholesome and pleasant.'[9]

Realms that are slightly better but still considered undesirable and lowly include those of the animals and *peta*, or hungry ghosts, with the latter possessing a gross physical body gained through an instant birth, without going through pregnancy. The habitat of the hungry ghosts is on the fringes of the human world because they are extremely attached to earthly experiences. One type of hungry ghost is said to have a huge stomach, insatiable hunger and a tiny mouth and neck, which allow little food to pass.

Together with divine gods and deities (Sanskrit: *deva*), human birth is considered a fortunate birth, the result of having performed generosity and moral practices in a previous life. To develop wisdom and compassion for the attainment of liberation from *samsara*, human birth is seen as ideal because a human being is not so beset by suffering as to be in no position to practise the *dhamma* – as is the case with animals, ghosts and hell beings – and not so intoxicated by pleasure, as are the heavenly beings. Only in the human world could a fully enlightened being like the Buddha appear. Even in the human world, those born in a place and time where a Buddha exists, with capabilities to comprehend his teachings, are considered more fortunate than others. It is therefore not uncommon to see devout Buddhists dedicating the energy of their good deeds towards rebirth at a time and place where they might meet the future Buddha, Arimetteyya (Sanskrit: Maitreya). *Asuras*, or demi-gods, are counted among those of lower rebirth because of their fierce and power-hungry nature.

The twenty-six heavens are once again classified into three. First is the realm of sense-desire (*kama-dhatu*), comprising the six lowest heavens. Together with the human world, these seven are known as the good births or realms of the sense-sphere (*kama-sugati-bhumi*). Beings in these realms perceive the senses through the prism of desirability and undesirability. Above them are the sixteen heavens of pure form (*rupa-dhatu*), progressively refined and calm. The gods of the sixteen realms of pure form perceive objects, but without sense-desire. They are without the senses of smell, taste and touch. They possess the visual faculty and can also listen to the *dhamma*. But they still suffer from attachment and limitation. Last, much more refined and above them all are the four heavens of the formless (*arupa-dhatu*). They occupy a pure mental sphere devoid of any shape or form, however subtle. They possess the characteristics of the consciousness of the Brahmas born there and are known after them, namely 'infinite space', 'infinite consciousness', 'nothingness' and 'neither-perception-nor-non-perception'. Even this highest and most refined form of rebirth, the neither-perception-nor-non-perception realm with a life span of 84,000 aeons is subject to death and rebirth. While still in search of truth, the Buddha-to-be, Gotama, achieved the 'nothingness' state of consciousness under the guidance of Alara Kalama, and the 'neither-perception-nor-non-perception' state under Uddaka Ramaputra. Thus, in the human world, if individuals achieve a highly refined state of concentration

such as these, they thereby orientate their consciousness to the formless experiences and, once internalized, face a rebirth in the formless realms after death.

It is important to note here that a discrete Brahma heavenly realm is assigned to each of the four *jhana* states achieved in deep meditation. For example, the lowest three Brahma realms are for those with the attainment of the first *jhana*. Buddhist cosmology is therefore structured in the form of a moral hierarchy with realms of existence relating to certain kinds of mental states. Apart from the five Pure Abodes where the great Brahmas have attained the state of 'non-returner' and will inevitably attain *nirvana*, the other heavenly beings will continue to wander through *samsara*.

Advanced meditators in the human world are said to be able to visit the various hells and heavenly realms and see for themselves their respective inhabitants. For the rest of us ordinary human beings, only the human and animal realms are visible to us, though heavenly beings may help human beings to perceive the heavenly or hellish states. In one of his previous lives, the Buddha, as King Nemi, was given a tour of the hells and the heavens by Matali, the charioteer of Indra. King Nemi thus witnessed the suffering in various hells and the luxurious lives in various heavens on his way to the Thirty-Three Realms. Inspired by the king's dedication and good work for his people on earth, Indra invited King Nemi to lecture to the gods of the Thirty-Three Realms on the importance of doing good deeds. A later work very popular in Southeast Asia, the *Maleyya Sutta*, details how the monk Maleyya, also known in Thai as Phra Malai, visited various hells, witnessing there those who suffered the consequences of their bad *kamma*; this *sutta* advises individuals to learn, or at least to listen to, the famous *Vessantara jataka*, to be completed in one day, as a form of accumulating sufficient merits for those suffering in hell. The *Vessantara jataka* chronicles the last of the Buddha's 547 previous lives, the life of the extraordinarily generous Prince Vessantara who gives away much, including the white elephant, considered to be crown property, and even his wife and his children. The *Maleyya Sutta* usually forms the introduction to the recitation of the *Vessantara jataka*, encouraging people to be kind, moral and generous, that they might not suffer in hells in the afterlife, and that their relatives in hells may also escape with the hearing of this *jataka*. There is a long tradition of the recitation of this great *jataka*, known as *Thet Maha Chat* in Thailand, *Boun Pha Wet* in Laos, and *Det Tham Wesan* in the eastern part of Shan State, Burma/Myanmar.

In terms of time, *samsara* is measured through aeons (*kappa/kalpa*), 'a vast unit of time used for measuring the coming and going of world-systems'[10], an almost unfathomable age.

Suppose there was a great mountain of rock, seven miles across and seven miles high, a solid mass without any cracks. At the end of every hundred years a man might brush it just once with a fine Varanasi cloth. That great mountain of rock would decay and come to an end sooner than ever the aeon. So long is an aeon. And of aeons of this length not just one has passed, not just a hundred, not just a thousand, not just a hundred thousand.[11]

Indeed, 'more aeons have passed than there are grains of sand on the banks of the river Ganges' (SN.ii.183–84).[12]

A world system, an inhabited universe, in which humans and other living beings exist is called *cakkavala* (also *cakkapada*). It is 'the name of the eight ranges of metallic mountains that are presumed to surround the world system of the sensuous realm (*kamaloka*) and thus sometimes used by metonymy to designate the entire universe or world system'.[13]

Eight concentric mountain ranges are said to surround the central axis of the world system, Mount Meru. The seven innermost ranges are made of gold, and seven seas fill the valleys between these concentric ranges … Located in a vast ocean that exists beyond these seven innermost concentric rings are laid out the four continents, including Jambudvipa (the Rose-Apple Continent) to the south, where human beings dwell; Videha to the east; Aparagoyana (Godaniya) to the west; and Uttarakuru to the north. At the outer perimeter of the world system is a final range of iron mountains, which surrounds and contains the outermost sea. The universe was presumed to be occupied by an essentially infinite number of these *cakkavala* world systems, each similarly structured, and each world system was the domain of a specific Buddha [*Buddha-khetta*], where he achieved enlightenment and worked towards the liberation of all sentient beings.[14]

In other words, the *cakkavala* is structured as a planet sitting on a great circle of wind, which is supported in turn by a great mass of water. The water supports a column of golden earth. On this golden earth are the mountains, the great ocean and the four continents. The great ocean, much greater in size than our earth, is contained by the *cakkavala*, the iron mountain range surrounding the planet. Mount Meru sits at the centre of this planet and situated at the top of Mount Meru are the Thirty-Three realms, where Indra and thirty-two other *devas* live. This is the realm the Buddha is said to have visited seven years after his enlightenment, to deliver a special teaching of the *Abhidhamma Pitaka* to his mother, by then reborn there as a *deva*. James Bogle calculates in his *Buddhist Cosmology* the distance 'from the outermost range of the mountains which encircle Mount Meru to the walls of the iron mountain' as 320,000 *yojana*, or 1,280,000

kilometres/800,000 miles.[15] Bogle also mentions that 'the diameter of the *Cakravala* is around 375 times larger than the Earth's'.[16]

In other words, virtually all living beings in this universe and other inhabited worlds also go through the cycle of rebirth. 'Just as beings go through a series of lives, so do the world-systems: they develop, remain for a period, come to an end and are absent, then followed by another. Each phase takes an "incalculable" eon, and the whole cycle takes a "great" eon.'[17] The cosmos is destroyed progressively by fire, water and wind from bottom up until the lower eight Brahma realms disappear. Only the upper seven Brahma realms and the four formless realms corresponding to the fourth *jhana* are spared from destruction. First, the fire destroys up to the first three Brahma worlds, and beings are reborn in the Realms of Radiance. This indicates that in times of crisis people develop their mind as high as *jhana* states. The Buddha himself discusses this:

> Now after a long period of time there comes a time when this world contracts. As the world contracts, for the most part born beings are in the realm of Radiance. They exist there, made of mind, living on joy, self-luminous, moving through the air, always beautiful; they remain for a very long time. (DN iii, 84–85)

After a long span of time the water destroys three further Brahma realms and people are reborn higher up in the three Brahma Realms of Beauty until those planes themselves disappear, being destroyed by the wind. And, after a long time, due to their *kamma*, the Brahmas are reborn in lower realms, repopulating in the re-evolving physical world.

With regard to the spatial aspect of the physical universe, the Buddha's emphasis on psychological matter could not be more pronounced. One day, the Buddha recounted to a householder by the name of Kevaddha the account of a monk who wished to know where the four elements of earth, water, fire and wind cease completely (DN.i.215–23.) As Gethin says:

> We can understand this as wishing to discover the limits of the physical universe. The monk was a master of meditation (*samadhi*) and so

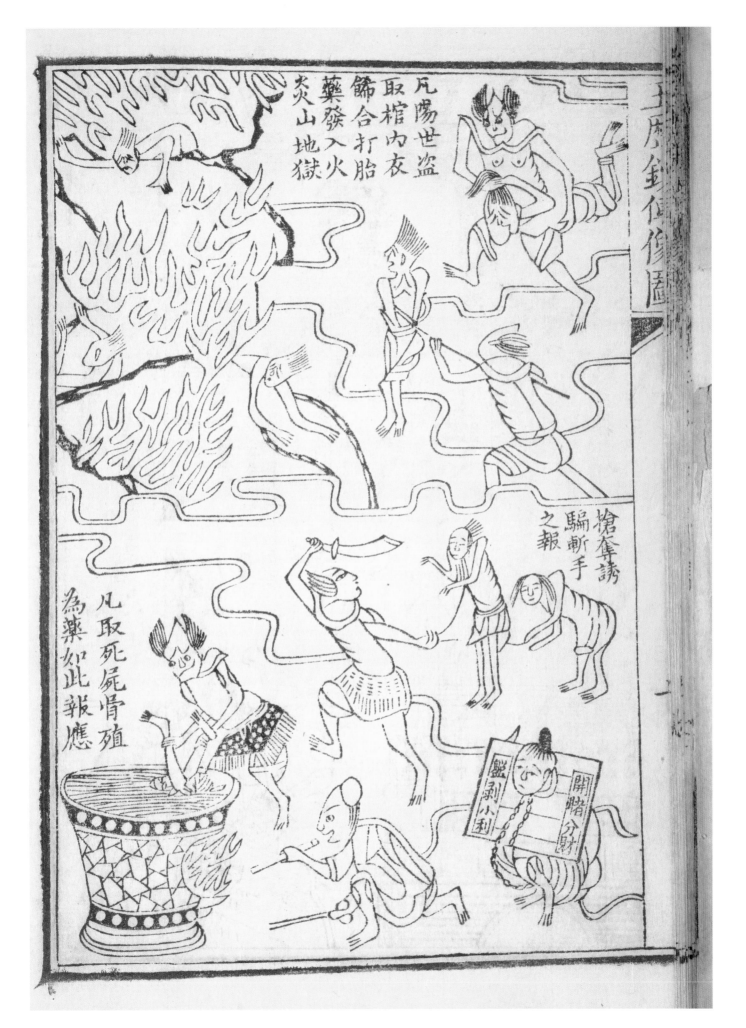

炎山地獄

瓦陽世盜
取棺內衣
篩合打胎
藥發入火

搶奪誘
騙斬手
之報

凡取死屍骨殖
為藥如此報應

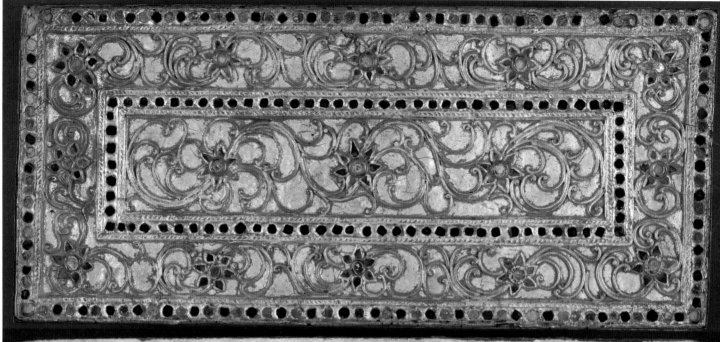

� တရားတော်အမည်ကားအနာဂတ္တဝင် အာဒိမိတ္တယျာဗျူာ

တ� တာ့လဝမှာ ၏ါ၊ ရှိုက်ကြ၊ အ၊ ဂ၊ ဝတ်တဝင်ကာရိမိ တ်ယ ဝတတု တု မြက်ကျ ၏ု ရ ထံသိ င် လ၊ လ၊ တ၊ ယ ၊ ကြ ၊ ၏ါ၊ ရှို ၆ ချ ၊ ေ တ ေ က ၊ မြ ၊ မ ျ ၊ လ ဟ ၊ ခ ၊ ရှ ၆ မ ၊ ဆ င ၊ သ ု ဝ ၄ ၀ ထ ၊ သ ဲ ၊ း ၊ ဗ ှ ၊ ၊ ၊ တ ၊ ၊ ၊ သ ၊ လ ဝ မ ှ ၊ ခ ၊ မ ၊ ဖ ၄ ၆ ၊ ၆ ၊ လ ၊ တ ၊ ၏ ၊ ၊ ကာ ၊ အ ၊ လ ၊ ဖ ၊ ပြ ၊ ရ ၊ ယ ၊ ၏ ၊ ၄ ၄ ၊ ၊ တ ၊ ၊ ၊ မ ၊ အ ေ ၊ လ ၊ ေ တ ၊ ၏ ၊ ၊ ယ ၊ ၊ ၄ ၊ ၊ ၊ ၏ ၊ လ ၊ မ ၊ ဖ ၊ ၊ ၊ လ ၊ မ ၊ ၄ ၊ ၊ အ ၊ ၄ ေ ၊ တ ၊ ၊ ၊ သ ၊ ၆ ေ ၊ ၊ ၊ တ ၊ ၊ ၊ ၊ က ၊ အ ၊ က ၊ က ျ ၊ အ ၊ ရ ၊ ၆ ၊ သ ၊ မ ျ ၊ က ု ၊ လ ၊ ယ ၊ လ ၊ ၊ တ ၊ ၊ ၊ ၊ ၊ ၏ ၊

──────────

နို ၊ အ ၊ တ ၊ သ ၊ ၊ ၊ ၊ ၊ ၊ အ ၊ ရ ၊ ဟ ၊ ၊ ေ ၊ ၊ ၊ ၊ သ မ္မ ၊ သ မ္ဗု ဒ္ဓ သ ၊ ၊ ၊ ၊ မ ိ သ ရ က ၊ း ၊ ၊ အ ဗ ၊ ဝ ဏ္ဏ မ ိ ၊ ၊ ၊ ၊ ၊

သ ဗ္ဗ ဒါ ၊ ၊ ပု သ တ ပ္ဗ သ မ္ဗာ ရ ံ ဗ ၊ က ျ ၊ ၊ ၊ ၊ ၊ ၊ က ္ဗ တ္တ ိ သ ေ ဇ တ္တ ၊ ဟု ၊ ၊ ၊ ၊ ၊ ၊ ၊ ၊ ၊

ထ ၊

was able to visit the realms of various *devas* or gods and put his questions to them. First, he approached the gods of the Four Kings; they were unable to answer his question but directed him to yet higher gods of the Thirty-Three Realms, the Yama gods, the Contented gods, the gods who Delighted in Creation, the Masters of the Creations of Others, the gods of Brahmas. None could answer his question. Finally, he approached Great Brahma himself, who only repeated that he was Great Brahma, 'mighty, unconquerable, all-seeing, master, lord, maker, creator, overseer, controller, father of all who are and will be'. In the face of the monk's persistence, Great Brahma eventually took him aside and confessed that he too did not know where the elements cease, and suggested the monk return to the Buddha and put the question to him. The Buddha's answer, we are told, was that where the four elements cease completely is the consciousness that knows *nirvana* (DN i.215–23).[18]

The Buddha's answer – to help us find all of cosmology – is that we look no further than our own mind.

One may look at a *Buddhapada* – the symbolic footprint of the Buddha – for an idea of Buddhist cosmology. Within the footprint lies the most important symbol of Buddhist cosmology, namely the *Dhammacakka* or the 'Wheel of Law'. This very early symbol encapsulates some of the most profound teachings of the Buddha. In his First Sermon, the Buddha says that he has discovered how the Wheel of Law can be turned (*pavattana*), and then shares that knowledge with his former fellow practitioners, the five ascetics (the *pancavaggiya*). The Wheel of Law with 'four spokes' symbolizes the natural law of the Four Noble Truths: the reality of suffering; the causes of suffering; its cessation; and the way to achieve that cessation. The path to the end of suffering is described by the Buddha himself as the Middle Path, avoiding the two extr§§§§emes of self-indulgence and self-torture. This path consists of eight factors, denoted by the 'eight spokes' in yet another representation of the Wheel of Law. There is a *further* Wheel of Law

OPPOSITE: A lavishly decorated folding book in Shan language containing the *Anagatavamsa*, a text on the coming of the future Buddha Metteyya (Sanskrit: Maitreya). Shan State, Burma, 1893.
British Library, Or.14572

BELOW: Burmese Buddhist cosmology on palm leaves illustrating the Thirty-One Planes of Existence. Shown here is one of the heavens. Burma, 18th or 19th century.
British Library, Or.2770, ff. 10–13

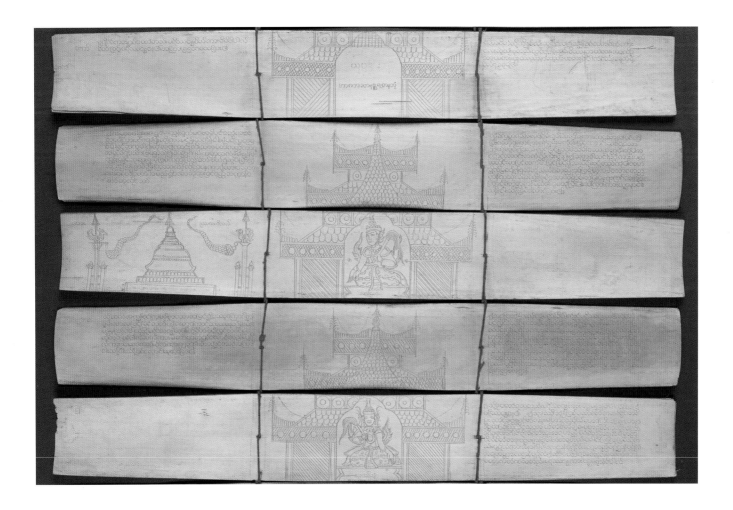

still, with 'twelve spokes', indicating how the realization of the Four Noble Truths actually takes place. In each one of the Four Noble Truths, realization takes place in three dimensions, namely: (a) awakening to what that particular truth is; (b) realizing what to do with it, and; (c) understanding how to evaluate if the task has been accomplished. Thus, the three dimensions multiplied by four equals twelve spokes in the Wheel of Law highlighting aspects of enlightenment. The lessons embodied by the Wheel of Law, with its varying number of spokes, are taught by the Buddha himself in his First Sermon when he provides the criteria for enlightenment.

At the centre of *Thangka* paintings of the Wheel of Life lie the three root poisons of the mind – greed, hatred and delusion – represented by the rooster, the snake and the pig. Moving concentrically outwards, there are the six divisions (the five worlds in the *Mahasihanada Sutta* of the Theravada school, where demi-gods are considered as belonging to the world of gods proper) representing the summary of the Thirty-One Planes into the six classifications of rebirth. These are:

1 Realm of the gods
The most pleasure-filled of the six realms, this realm is subdivided into twenty-six sub-realms. Rebirth in this heavenly realm is believed to be the result of the accumulation of very good *kamma*. A *deva* (god) does not need to work, and is able to enjoy in the heavenly realm all pleasures found on earth. However, the pleasures of this realm lead to attachment (*upadana*) and a lack of spiritual pursuit, thereby making it hard, though not impossible, for one to attain *nirvana*.

2 Realm of the demi-gods
The demi-gods (*Asuras*) occupy the second realm of existence in Buddhism. *Asuras* are notable for their anger and certain supernormal powers. They fight with the *devas* (gods proper), or trouble human beings through illnesses and natural disasters. They accumulate *kamma*, and are reborn.

3 Realm of human beings
Buddhism asserts that beings are reborn in this realm with vastly varying physical endowments and moral natures that result from each being's past *kamma*. A rebirth in this realm is considered fortunate because it offers a greater opportunity to attain *nirvana* and thereby end the cycle of *samsara*.

4 Realm of animals
This is the state of existence of a being as an animal. This realm is traditionally thought to be similar to a hellish realm, because animals are believed in Buddhist texts to be driven by impulse and instinct, and to prey on each other and suffer.

5 Realm of the hungry ghosts
Hungry ghosts and other restless spirits (*peta*) are rebirths caused by *kamma* of excessive craving and attachments. They are invisible to human beings and constitute only the 'subtle matter' of a being. Buddhist texts describe them as beings who suffer from being extremely thirsty and hungry, in possession of very small mouths and very large stomachs. Buddhist traditions in Asia attempt to care for them on ritual days, every year, by leaving food and drinks out in the open, to feed any hungry ghosts nearby. When their bad *kamma* runs out, these beings are reborn in another realm.

6 Realm of hell
Beings in hell (Pali: *naraka*; Sanskrit: *niraya*) enter this realm for evil *kamma* such as theft, lying and adultery. Texts vary in their details, but typically describe numerous hellish regions, each with different forms of intense suffering, such as eight extremely hot hellish realms and eight extremely cold, as well as realms in which beings are partially eaten alive, beaten or subjected to various other forms of torture – all this in proportion to the evil *kamma* accumulated. After their evil *kamma* has run its course, the beings in this realm will die and get another chance in the human world. The realm of hell is not similar to the hell in the afterlife in Christianity or other Abrahamic traditions because in Buddhism there is no realm of final damnation and existence; this realm of hell, too, is a temporary state.

Moving outwards, the next annulus divided into twelve sections is a graphical depiction of the twelve links of Dependent Origination (*paticcasamuppada*). This ring depicts a blind man or woman (representing ignorance), potters (formation), a monkey (consciousness), two men in a boat (mind and body), a house with six windows (the senses), an embracing couple (contact), an eye pierced by an arrow (sensation), a person drinking (thirst), a man gathering fruit (grasping), a couple making love (becoming), a woman giving birth (birth) and a man carrying a corpse (death). The creature holding the Wheel of Life in his hooves is Yama, the lord of the hell realm.

Drawing of Buddha's footprint with 108 auspicious symbols (Pali: *Buddhapadamangala*). The Buddha footprint was one of the early symbols representing the Buddha. Burma, 19th century. British Library, MS. Burmese 203, f. 11

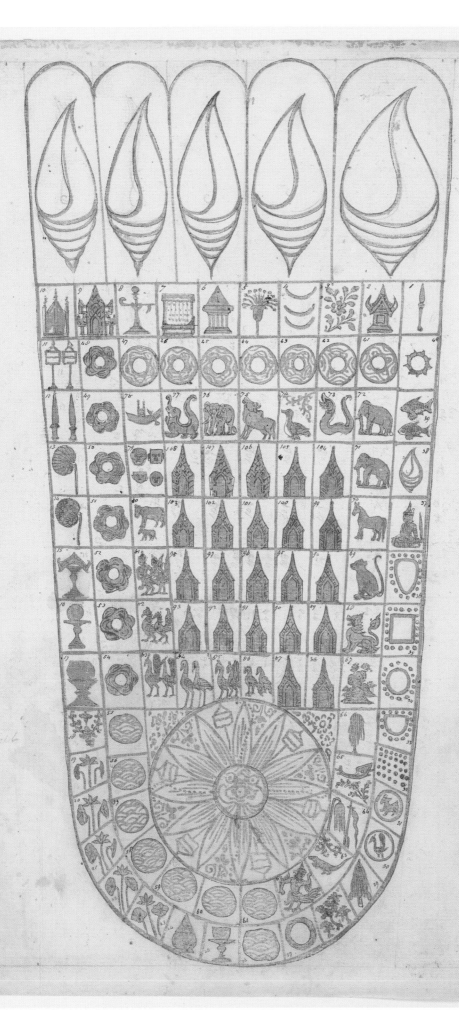

Impression of the Sole of Gautama's Foot - 108 marks

 လက်လာ မင့်

Kamma and Rebirth

Wandering around *samsara* or the psychological aspect of the *cakkavala* is governed not by the will of a Creator God but by the natural law of *kamma*: action causes reaction, good or bad, like the laws of physics. In pre-Buddhist Brahmanism, *kamma* was a significant ritual intended to improve the quality of human life, and involved the recitation of the sacred texts, the Vedas, by priests who could only be drawn from the Brahmin caste. The *kamma* ritual, in other words, was the exclusive domain of the Brahmins, and members of no other caste could perform it, for the Brahmins alone 'knew' – supposedly – the wishes of God and how to please Him to grant a favour to a devotee. For the Buddha, however, *kamma* has nothing to do with ritual; rather, it is the intention of individuals, related to the choice of their ethical conduct.

In the Buddhist understanding of *kamma*, each intentional action has a real consequence and each and every individual, regardless of gender or social status, is responsible for his or her own actions. One cannot blame the gods for his/her misfortune, nor seek their favour. There is no one such as a Creator God to punish or reward; it is one's own volitional acts that lead to affliction or to positive results. Living beings owe the outcome of their actions to their own actions. Intention is the psychological impulse behind all our actions. The Buddha's own statement on this is 'it is intention, O monks, that I call *kamma*; having willed, one acts through body, speech or mind' (A. iii. 415).

It is human beings who have to be, and who have the *capacity* to be, mindful of the nature of their actions, be they individual or collective, because their actions alone – and not the will of any creator – change this physical universe we live in. Even powerful gods, including those in the realms of *nimmanarati* and the various planes of Brahmas, are subject to the law of *kamma*. 'A person's action moulds their consciousness, making them into a certain kind of person, so that when they die their outer form tends to correspond to the type of nature that has been developed.'[19] So, a more meditative person with an achievement of *jhana* plus loving-kindness is reborn in the Brahma world. One who has accumulated much greedy consciousness may be reborn as a hungry ghost, never feeling contented with anything. People with a strong nature of anger and hatred have a similar experience as that in the hellish realms, and the last consciousness in a given life may direct them to one of the woeful rebirths. So, *kamma* and rebirth are closely related. Moreover, the accumulated effect of *kamma* is such that stinginess leads to poverty, harming people to sickness, and anger to being ugly. Of course, efficiently strong *kammic* action will lead to rebirth while other weaker *kamma* may bear results only after one is reborn (through subsequent *kamma*).

But these connections between certain *kammic* actions and their results are not to be taken as fixed. The Buddha criticized determinism as one of the extreme forms of philosophy. In other words, the law of *kamma* is not deterministic; whether it is good or bad *kamma* from the past, our present *kamma* can still alter its result. *Kamma* is not a single cause but a very important component of a network of conditions working together to bring about a result. Other conditions such as the natural laws of the physical world (*utu-niyama*), the natural laws of the biotic world (*bija-niyama*), the natural laws of the mind (*citta-niyama*) and the natural laws of spiritual attainment (*dhamma-niyama*) play their role in determining one's experiences in life. How long one lives is partly due to *kamma*, but is also due to one's psychological health, and whether the conditions of one's social and ecological environment are conducive to wellbeing, including access to healthcare and food. The Buddha talks about the proportionate effect of *kamma* as salt in water, with the degree of volume of each diminishing the impact of the other (AN i.99). For one who has accumulated a lot of good *kamma*, certain unwholesome actions – so long as they are not the weighty ones – may not have a transformative result. The bad *kamma* accrued

Contemporary *Thangka* painting by Master Buddha Lama depicting the Wheel of Life (Sanskrit: *bhavachakra*) which illustrates the cycle of birth, death and rebirth (Sanskrit: *samsara*). The wheel is gripped by Yama, the lord of hell. These popular paintings are used both as meditation and teaching tools in the Vajrayana tradition. Bhaktapur, Nepal, 2019

by Angulimala – the robber who had killed nearly a thousand people, whose fingers he collected – did not lead to a rebirth in hell, because he had transformed his mind through meditation, uprooting all conditions for ripening of *kamma*, including the wholesome ones. His most powerful wholesome act – the eradication of greed, hatred and delusion – cancelled out all his past bad *kamma*. This is the nature of the mind overruling the nature of *kamma*. Angulimala's mind was substantially transformed, cancelling out the potential of his bad *kamma*. Similarly, King Ajatasattu, who committed patricide, was not able to attain any spiritual achievement despite his great efforts late in life because the weighty unwholesome *kamma* of killing his father prevented the potential of his realization of the *dhamma* from coming to fruition.

Effort made to ensure we have more of wholesome intention than its opposite, and subsequent *kamma* in both modes of speech and action, is at the heart of Buddhist practice. The Buddha said, 'Mind is forerunner. Mind is chief. The world is mind-made. Speak or act with an impure mind, and suffering follows one as the cart follows the ox … Speak or act with a pure mind, and happiness follows one as one's own shadow' (Dh 1–2). The result of an action may come in this very life or in one of the rebirths after this life.

The concept of rebirth is common to many religious traditions. The Abrahamic traditions believe in one rebirth, often to take place on the Day of Judgement in a permanent heaven or hell, and according to the will of the creator. Indian religions, including Buddhism, believe in more than one rebirth. Beings wander through the cycle of life, *samsara*. While the various Indian religious philosophies present the path to liberation from *samsara* differently from one another, they all require cosmology to explain *samsara* and *moksha* (freedom from ignorance).

Unlike the Abrahamic religions, Buddhism does not believe in anything permanent, which also applies to the states of heaven and hell. Even when one is reborn in one of the heavenly realms, all of which have an unimaginably long life-cycle as compared to life-cycles in the human world, it is still temporary. One's good *kamma* is comparable to an investment in a grand stately home that is available only on a leasehold because it belongs to the public. Once the lease is over, one has to move on. Every inch of the universe belongs to all beings who 'choose' to stay where they do through their own moral or immoral actions. The opportunity for residency is equally open to all for every part of the universe. Thus, even when one has secured a place in one of those many heavens, except in the *Suddhavasa*, one is still subject to losing one's place. The *Suddhavasa* Brahmas will attain *nirvana* – cessation of *samsara* – there without having to move on to another realm. It is said that Indra often comes to the human world to perform generous deeds, a way of topping up his credits, so as to renew his position in the plane of the Thirty-Three Gods. Such an opportunity for renewal does not occur often in the heavenly worlds, because all are either spoiled and cosseted in sensual pleasures in *kamadhatu*, or are in a state of constant meditative absorption in the Form and Formless States.

The Middle Path

In Buddhism, the way to increase one's wholesome *kamma* and decrease one's bad *kamma*, ultimately liberating oneself from *samsara*, is the Middle Path, also called the Middle Way or Noble Eightfold Path. This Middle Path is at the core of Buddhist philosophy alongside the Four Noble Truths. The Four Noble Truths teach that life in *samsara* has some unavoidable problems such as sickness, old age and death, regardless of our station in this universe. Not knowing how to manage these natural sufferings effectively leaves living beings subconsciously piling upon themselves troubles they can do without. Recognizing the fact that there are inherent pains associated with birth, and that they are experienced universally, is the essential basis for the development of right view. Also considered as right view is the acknowledgement that happiness and unhappiness are caused mainly by one's own intentional actions. Meditators sit in silence to observe the physical and emotional pains within themselves, in order to discern which pain is inherent and which is brought on by ourselves. For example, by observing the physical discomfort experienced during a session of sitting meditation, we come to discover how much of that pain is inescapable and how much of the pain is due entirely to our own mental habits. Thus, a substantial change in our worldview, in our mental state and in our moral conduct will have significant transformative potential.

Sutra of the Ten Kings, describing ten stages during the transitory phase following death and illustrating the six forms of rebirth, here represented as hell; hungry ghosts; snakes; animals; humans; and Buddhas. Cave 17, Mogao Caves near Dunhuang, China, Gansu Province, 10th century.
British Library, Or.8210.s.3961

The Four Noble Truths are:

1 Suffering exists, and it is universal
Anger, for example, is considered suffering. Whoever experiences anger suffers, no matter what their social status or belief. But anger is an option, and we can choose to not be angry if we train our minds thus.

2 The cause of suffering
Personalization and clinging lie at the root of suffering, arising from not viewing suffering as a universal truth. For example, when one is unfairly criticized one does not usually remember that everyone else has been criticized at some point or another, that no one is unique in being criticized. This forgetting leads to personalization and judgemental feelings, leading one to feel threatened and insecure within, hence anger as a reaction. This personalization becomes a habit, and one subconsciously repeats it whenever one is criticized. Thus, if anger is a symptom of suffering, this habit of personalization is the cause of that suffering.

3 An end to suffering
Observing suffering and its causes can help us bring an end to suffering. The truth of the end of suffering is therefore the Third Noble Truth. If the First Noble Truth starts with the recognition, observation and acceptance of suffering as a reality, the Third Noble Truth offers hope that suffering can be overcome.

4 The way to bring an end to suffering
The Fourth Noble Truth is to do with how one brings suffering to an end. The way to do so is called the Middle Path or the Noble Eightfold Path. By developing the factors of this path, such as mindfulness, one is in a position to observe and examine suffering. Through mindful observation, one discovers the causes of suffering and removes them.

Thus, for each of the Four Truths there is a task to achieve, and one achieves them simultaneously, namely: (a) the understanding e.g. anger as suffering with its universal dimension, (b) the removal of the causes of suffering e.g. personalization and clinging, (c) the attainment e.g. the internalization of a non-angry state or a totally calm and clear state of mind, or *nirvana*, and (d) the cultivation e.g. the development of the eightfold factors of the Middle Path. Here, as the original order of the Four Noble Truths goes, the attainment (c) is placed before the cultivation (d) of the path. This has confused many. The reason that the path comes after its supposed result is to highlight the point that once the causes of a problem are understood, there arises a belief that the problem can be solved. It is similar to a doctor reassuring his patient after a thorough diagnosis that an illness can be cured, even before the patient is given any treatment.

The eight factors forming the Middle Path are:

1 Right view
This is about the observation and acceptance of suffering (*dukkha*) as a universal or an impersonal phenomenon (*anatta*), and that everything including suffering is impermanent (*anicca*). In other words, it is to see life in the context of the Four Noble Truths.

2 Right emotion/right intention
This is about using right view to train and transform one's emotions from clinging on to letting go, from ill-will to unconditional love, and from hatred to compassion. Once our intention is based on letting go (*nekkhamma*), unconditional love (*abyapada*), and compassion or non-violence (*avihimsa*), our intention is pure and benevolent towards all beings. This second factor of the path overwhelmingly emphasizes the role of compassion in positive emotional development as a component of the path. In other words, compassion is considered as part of wisdom: a wise person is compassionate.

Right view and right intention form the Buddhist worldview and are considered to consist of wisdom training. Both are based on the understanding that sentient and non-sentient beings are all interdependent; their actions affect one another. Peaceful co-existence is the only way for all to survive and the Buddhist Five Precepts (no killing, no stealing, no sexual misconduct, no telling lies and no intoxication) demonstrate the pragmatic importance of living peacefully together. These precepts have human beings' welfare and wellbeing at their heart.

3 Right speech
Refraining from verbal misdeeds such as lies, divisive speech and slander, harsh and abusive language, frivolous speech and gossip, and instead promoting truthful and compassionate speech that brings harmony.

4 Right action
Refraining from physical misdeeds such as harming living beings, stealing and sexual misconduct, and instead practising compassion, generosity and faithfulness.

5 Right livelihood
Abstaining from any livelihood that is directly or indirectly harmful to others such as trading in weapons, alcohol, animals for slaughter, poison or human trafficking; practising a livelihood that is not harmful to others, and leading a life balanced between income and expenses.

The Tibetan book *Bar do thos grol,* a text in the Vajrayana tradition associated with Padmasambhava (8th century) and Karma Lingpa (14th century). It is intended as a guide through the stages of death and the intermediate state between death and rebirth. Tibet, 18th century.
British Library Or.15190, f. 1

Right speech, right action and right livelihood form ethical training in Buddhism. They are the same as the Five Precepts.

6 Right effort

This is the endeavour to abandon unwholesome states of mind that have already arisen, prevent unwholesome states of mind that have not yet arisen, sustain wholesome states of mind that have already arisen, and develop wholesome states of mind that have not yet arisen. In brief, it is an intelligent effort to identify one's weaknesses and strengths and accordingly apply appropriate effort to overcome one's shortcomings and consolidate one's positive qualities.

7 Right mindfulness

This is about being aware of the four foundations of mindfulness: the nature of one's physical body, of one's physical sensations, of one's thoughts/emotions and of the *dhamma*. It is the foundation of all the other seven factors of the path. Through the contemplation of the four aims mentioned here, a person should focus on two mental habits: aversion towards craving for pleasant experience (*abhijjha*) and unpleasant experience (*domanassam*) – the two emotional behaviours of the mind. Knowing and transforming these two major emotional patterns is the main task of this mindfulness-led Eightfold Path.

三世諸佛光明寶燈

A royal manual of esoteric Buddhism with paintings of altars for all Buddhas and Bodhisattvas, including Bodhisattva Mahamayuri (Great Peacock Wisdom King) on the left. On the right a Bodhisattva is seen in a stylized wheel with eight spokes, in between which the names of 'Three Buddhas' are spelled: Shakyamuni Buddha, Amitabha Buddha and Bhaisajyaguru Buddha (or Medicine Buddha). China, 18th century.

British Library, Or.6627, f. 2

孔雀明王明光佛寶燈

Extracts from the *Sutta Pitaka* (Sankrit: *Sutra Pitaka*), which is
one part of the *Tripitaka*, the scriptures containing the teachings
of the Buddha, or *dharma*. Written in Pali in Khmer script.
Central Thailand, 19th century.

British Library, Or.16009, f. 5

Manuscript of the Tibetan translation of the *Perfection of Wisdom Sutra in Eight Thousand Verses* (Sanskrit: *Astasahasrikaprajnaparamita Sutra*). Written in gold ink on dark indigo-coloured paper. South-central Tibet, 18th century.

British Library, Tib.I.232, front cover and ff. 1–2

Text belonging to the class of *Perfection of Wisdom Sutras* (Sanskrit: *Prajnaparamita Sutra*) of the Tibetan Canon, a very popular text in the Mahayana tradition that highlights the insight into the empty nature of all phenomena. Tibet, 18th century.

British Library, Or.16445, f. 1 and front cover

8 Right concentration

This is the ability of the mind to focus on one single object without being disturbed by the Five Hindrances (desire for sensual pleasure, aversion, sloth and torpor, restlessness and regret, and doubt) and the state where all eight factors come together and unite for one purpose, which is to transform suffering into wisdom and compassion.

Right effort, right mindfulness and right concentration ensure we have the habit of stabilizing our mind, important for anger management and the development of compassion.

The Middle Path is about developing these eight factors and integrating them so that they work in harmony in bringing an end to the causes of suffering. Here, suffering is likened to a disease, personalization and craving to the causes of the disease, and the end of suffering to the cure and the path to treatment. So, it is the realization of the Four Noble Truths that is called enlightenment in Buddhism, that state of attainment in which one has uprooted completely from one's mind the distractions of greed, hatred and delusion – the three root causes of all the problems in the world.

As we have seen, personalization and craving, or the three root causes, are what make beings wander endlessly from life to life in the *cakkavala,* and they are the summary of what is sometimes called the Ten Fetters (*samyojana*) that bind the mind to the cycle of rebirth. They are: wrong belief in a permanent self (*sakkaya-ditthi*), sceptical doubt (*vicikiccha*), clinging to mere rules and rituals (*silabbata-paramasa*), sensuous craving (*kama-raga*), ill will (*byapada*), craving for existence in the realm of fine material (*rupa-raga*), craving for existence in the realm of the non-material (*arupa-raga*), conceit (*mana*), restlessness (*uddhacca*) and ignorance/delusion (*avijja*). Through the practice of the Middle Path, when one has eradicated the first three of the Ten Fetters, one is considered to have attained the first of the four spiritual stages of the noble, called stream-enterer. In the next stage, of the once-returner, one has further overcome sensuous desire and ill-will in their gross form, while their subtle form is uprooted at the third level of spiritual achievement, that of the non-returner. At the last and final stage, that of the *arahant*, one is freed from all Ten Fetters. Upon that complete purification of the mind, one is endowed with wisdom and compassion. One no longer behaves in a way that causes suffering to oneself or to others.

One can thus see that the practice of the Middle Path relies entirely on one's own effort. The only aim is to reduce and ultimately eradicate suffering by transforming our own mental habits. The eight factors of the Middle Path are often summed up as three right and transformative trainings (*ti-sikkha*) comprising wisdom (right view and right emotion), ethics (not harming oneself or others through wrong speech, wrong action or wrong livelihood), and meditation (right effort, right mindfulness and right concentration). Gotama Buddha achieved the end of suffering, or *nirvana*, at the age of thirty-five, and for the remaining forty-five years of his life he taught others how to achieve it, too. Often, he summed up his teaching as consisting of only two things: suffering and the end of suffering. He concerned himself only with helping others to understand suffering and attain release from it in the present.

Though it appears rather a simple list of practices, the Middle Path is not that easy because the practice itself goes against our usual emotional tendencies: the path teaches (a) generosity and contentment as opposed to the accumulation of wealth, (b) restraint of anger and hatred, and the cultivation of compassion as opposed to force and violence, and (c) acceptance of suffering as it is rather than fighting it or ignoring it. Furthermore, the Buddha formulates this path into a simpler set of observances, the Five Precepts.

For lay people, the Five Precepts – also known as the Five Mindfulness Trainings – are the minimum restraints recommended to ensure they accumulate good *kamma* and keep away from bad *kamma*. Refraining from harmful behaviour towards others, from stealing and from adultery are three manifestations of *kamma* in physical action; refraining from untruthful speech is a verbal deed. The last of the five, avoiding intoxicants, is considered as action to prevent transgressions of both body and speech. Simply put, in order to own – metaphorically – a good or even a grand place, such as exists in the heavens of this universe, individuals need not go on bended knees to a divine being but need only seriously and mindfully take charge of their thoughts, speech and action so they are non-violent and kind towards others.

At the heart of the Five Precepts, or indeed of any other Buddhist moral code, is the realization that all living beings are interdependent, for good or ill, and that all fear death. For both survival and happiness, we are intertwined and our actions affect one another. This wisdom of the law of interdependence gives rise to a sense of connection with many, if not all, and helps sustain compassionate behaviour towards others.

While the Five Precepts take care specifically of our physical and verbal actions, they do not directly purify the mind, though they lay a good foundation for it. For, while one may not harm others physically, that does not necessarily translate into loving them or even empathizing with their pain. So, one who wishes to purify his or her mind has to train oneself in wisdom and meditation too. As discussed, wisdom here denotes the realization that suf-

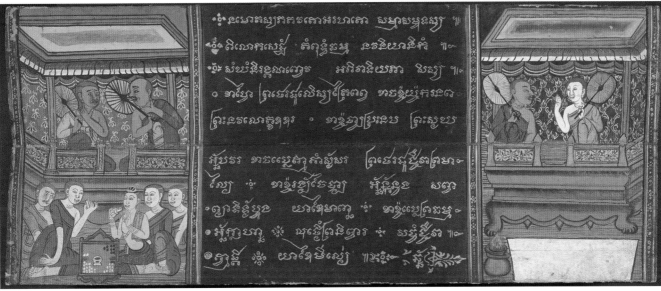

fering is universal and that there is a potential for humans and many celestial beings to find a way out of it. Wisdom also includes the shedding of negative habits of destructive emotions such as ill-will, violence and craving, and the nurturing of positive emotions. Meditation includes training the mind to develop a faculty strong in sensible effort, mindfulness and concentration. Together wisdom and meditation directly purify the mind and ensure the ethical codes of the precepts are strengthened.

Thai funeral book with extracts from the *Vinaya Pitaka* and the seven books of the *Abhidhamma Pitaka* (Thai: *Aphitham chet khamphi*), together with the legend of the monk Phra Malai. Illustrations highlight right and wrong behaviours of Buddhist monks as prescribed in the *Patimokkha* of the *Vinaya Pitaka*. Central Thailand, 19th century.
British Library, Or.14664, ff. 3, 6

Modern copy of the *Heart Sutra of the Perfection of Wisdom*
(Sanskrit: *Prajnaparamitahrdaya*, Japanese: *Maka hannya
haramitta shingyo*) on a silk-backed scroll. Calligraphy in regular
(*kaisho*) style by Miyamoto Chikkei (1926–2002). Calligraphy
and copying of Buddhist scriptures are sometimes practised as
forms of meditation and right concentration. Japan, 1995.

Meditation and Mindfulness

The emphasis in the threefold training (wisdom, ethics, meditation) or the Noble Eightfold Path is on the self-training of the mind, which is undertaken directly in various meditation practices. Traditionally, Buddhist meditation is divided into two major categories: Cultivation of Tranquillity (*samatha-bhavana* or 'calm meditation'), which stresses the crucial component of concentration as the leading factor in transforming the mind, and Cultivation of Insight (*vipassana-bhavana* or 'insight meditation'), which highlights more the role of seeing things as they are. Although early Buddhism appears to have integrated both of these categories, there have been over many centuries separate practices for them in the actual process of meditation. The Cultivation of Tranquillity lists about forty types of practices, including certain reflective techniques (*anussati*) as well as the observation of colours (*kasina*). Even the compassion exercise is considered part of the Cultivation of Tranquillity. For the Cultivation of Insight, the main criterion is to develop insight into three characteristics (*ti-lakkhana*) that form the Buddhist worldview: impermanence, unsatisfactoriness and non-self. There are many discourses that the Buddha has given to different practitioners, tailored to the listeners' temperaments.

But since the early twentieth century, a meditation movement in Burma/Myanmar has concentrated its focus on one of the many *suttas* on meditation, the *Satipatthana Sutta*. This discourse, now translated as *The Foundations of Mindfulness*, has thus become better known than the others for the purposes of meditation instruction. Nyanaponika Thera, a German-born Buddhist monk who practised *satipatthana*-based insight meditation in Burma/Myanmar, records the practice in his book, *The Heart of Buddhist Meditation*, as taught in the Mahasi meditation tradition, with sufficient information on both the text and the practice. It is this work that scientists in the West have taken as a manual in their research in the field that has come to be known as the 'secular mindfulness movement'. *The Heart of Buddhist Meditation* itself is a faithful compilation of the practice as preserved in the Buddhist traditions. Nyanaponika's description of the function of mindfulness as bare attention without pre-conceived notion has been the source of what is now widely known as non-judgemental mindfulness. It is the awareness of information coming through the senses and our reaction to them, without judging them to be good or bad, but simply recognizing the experience as it is and letting it pass.

Jon Kabat-Zinn (1944–), a physician from the University of Massachusetts Medical School who founded Mindfulness-Based Stress Reduction (MBSR) in the 1970s, defines mindfulness as 'paying attention in a particular way: on purpose, in the present moment, and nonjudgmentally'.[20] This is to direct one's attention to a chosen object such as one's breath, pain, thought or emotion as these arise in the present moment, without being judgemental about them. If the breath is short, one should simply observe it as a short breath and not judge it as any better or worse. The same with restlessness, physical discomfort or an angry thought: one should merely register these as they are, and then release them. Learning to register or accept the experience and to release it are the main exercises at the beginning. One usually uses breathing as the primary object to which one keeps returning if distracted, for instance, by sound, pain or automatic thoughts. Constant practice will help the practitioner see a certain pattern in his or her mental behaviour and enable him or her to direct the mind to a chosen object, without endlessly wandering. Dr Kabat-Zinn initially experimented with this practice with chronic patients at the University of Massachusetts Medical School; people who were reliant on painkillers found this meditation technique helpful in managing their pain.

A few years later, using MBSR as the basis, Kabat-Zinn and his colleagues from Toronto, Bangor, Cambridge and Oxford, developed Mindfulness-Based Cognitive Therapy (MBCT):

> to help people who suffer repeated bouts of depression and chronic unhappiness. It combines the ideas of cognitive therapy with meditative practices and attitudes based on the cultivation of mindfulness. The heart of this work lies in becoming acquainted with the modes of mind that often characterize mood disorders while simultaneously learning to develop a new relationship to them.[21]

Since then, a whole range of new interventions based on mindfulness has come into existence, from mindfulness for CEOs and sportspeople, to women and recipients of healthcare. The UK Parliament has formed its own all-parties mindfulness committee and in October 2015 released its report: *Mindful Nation UK 2015*. It recommends the introduction of mindfulness in four areas – education, health, prisons and the civil services – to boost the wellbeing of individuals. Prior to the report, mindfulness training in schools had become popular. While in 1982 there were only two scientific papers on mindfulness, by 2007 more than seventy scientific papers had been published on the subject; ten years later, in 2017, there were more than 690 papers published in English by the scientific community worldwide.

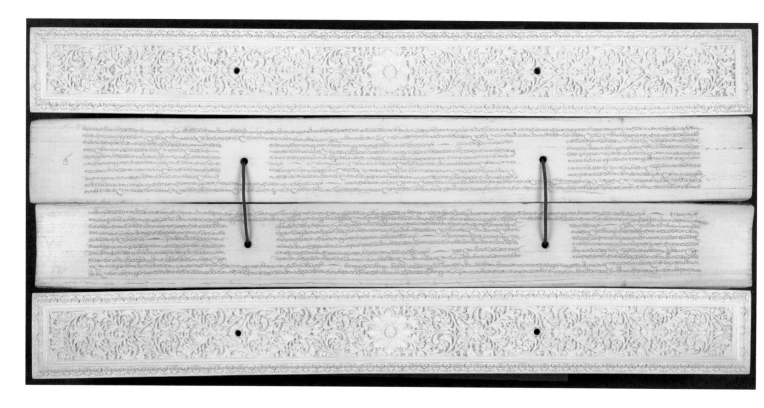

Sinhalese palm leaf manuscript with ivory covers containing the *Visuddhimagga*, a commentary in Pali condensing the teachings of the Buddha and emphasizing the practice of *kasina*-meditation by Buddhaghosa, a 5th-century scholar whose writings were of defining importance in the development of Theravada Buddhism and its meditation practices.
Sri Lanka, 19th century.
British Library, Add. MS 11658

This mindfulness movement is considered secular because it does not require one to subscribe to any Buddhist beliefs such as *kamma*, rebirth, cosmology or *nirvana*. It is accessible, and has proven beneficial, to both believers and non-believers. Professor Mark Williams, the founder of the Oxford Mindfulness Centre and one of the principal researchers of MBCT, is an ordained priest of the Church of England and there is no tension for him in running the eight-week course of mindfulness. Indeed, in many instances, the leading practitioners of secular mindfulness barely mention Buddhism at all. Others merely refer to mindfulness coming from an Eastern tradition. By and large, Buddhist followers themselves have no objection to this secular movement of mindfulness, although some point out its limitation when ethics is taken out from mindfulness practice.

Mindfulness practice has been growing, particularly among psychologists and neurologists. Several new initiatives based on mindfulness have been introduced. Professor Paul Gilbert (1951–) of Derby University, for example, founded Compassion-Based Therapy (CFT), using mindfulness as the stepping stone. Professor Jeffrey M. Schwartz of the UCLA School of Medicine and columnist Sharon Begley's *The Mind and the Brain: Neuroplasticity and the Power of Mental Force* challenges traditional behaviour therapy for Obsessive Compulsive Disorder, arguing for the use of mindfulness instead. The collaborative work between Professor Richard J. Davidson (1951–) at Wisconsin University and several Buddhist meditation teachers through the initiative of the Mind and Life Institute have taken the subject much further in connecting various meditative qualities with different areas of the brain. Mathieu Ricard (1946–), a biologist turned Buddhist monk, was both a collaborator and a meditator on that research project and his books *Happiness* and *Altruism* offer some details of the findings, as does Davidson's *The Emotional Life of Your Brain*. Work on mindfulness and the brain, including Norman Doidge's *New York Times* bestsellers *The Brain that Changes Itself* and *The Brain's Way of*

Healing, has gained increased attention, while Davidson and his former colleague at Harvard, Daniel Goleman, author of *Emotional Intelligence*, have declared meditation a science because this spiritual practice is now backed by hard evidence. Harvard Business Review Press has published summaries of selected research findings on mindfulness as part of its *Emotional Intelligence* series. Mindfulness research is now expanded to include other positive qualities such as resilience and empathy. Many medical schools – for example Harvard and UCLA in the US – introduce mindfulness into their courses. Mindfulness has fully entered the mainstream, becoming a component in clinics, universities, schools, hospitals, politics and management.

Internationally, there have been mindfulness conferences of clinicians and academics who – in Europe – first gathered in Italy at Sapienza University in 2013, with the fifth conference, which aimed to look at the clinical effectiveness of mindfulness as critically as possible, having taken place in the World Trade Centre, Zaragoza, Spain in June 2018. In August 2018, ELTE University in Budapest hosted the first mindfulness conference to be organized in Hungary, titled *Mindfulness and Science*, looking at ethics and compassion. Around two hundred Hungarian psychologists, as well as scholars from other parts of the world, attended the three-day event. Professor Kabat-Zinn, who said he has been meditating for more than fifty years, urged all psychologists in his keynote address to meditate more because, he said, simply knowing psychology is not enough: one actually needs to strengthen one's meditation practice.

Increasingly, there are both charitable and commercial organizations offering mindfulness to enhance wellbeing. One of them is Edward's Trust, whose webpage says:

Mindfulness is a well-respected and comprehensively researched technique which has been clinically proven to help reduce depression, anxiety and stress. The technique involves simple meditation practices which, over time, can bring about changes in mood and increase a sense of wellbeing. In our support of bereaved parents, many have found that Mindfulness has reduced levels of insomnia and anxiety and generally helped them to manage daily activities more easily. Mindfulness is a beautifully simple strategy which has been endorsed by the NHS and forms part of their NICE guidelines for improved mental health.[22]

Another is the Mindfulness in Schools Project (MiSP), '[e]stablished by teachers from amongst the country's most successful schools' and aimed at improving 'the lives of children by making a genuine, positive difference to their mental health and wellbeing'. Many of MiSP's programmes can be viewed on YouTube.

While there is no reason to object to the use of mindfulness in the secular domain if it helps reduce stress and suffering, the Buddhist position has always been that mindfulness comes in a package as part of the Noble Eightfold Path and is more effective if presented in that natural context, particularly taking into consideration its ethical components and the Buddhist worldview. Indeed, a handful of clinical psychologists, including one of the MBCT pioneers, John D. Teasdale of Cambridge University, have been using the key Buddhist philosophy of the Four Noble Truths in their mindfulness research and teaching.

Laywomen practising sitting meditation on an Uposatha day (day of observance) at the Buddhapadipa temple in Wimbledon, London, in April 2019. Meditation techniques aim to develop equanimity, mindfulness, concentration, tranquillity and insight. Meditation sessions and retreats are offered by many Buddhist centres across the world and are open to both Buddhists and non-Buddhists.

Notes

1   References to Pali scriptures are indicated by an abbreviation and numbers used in the Pali Text Society editions of the Pali Tipitaka.

DN = *Digha Nikaya*
M = *Majjhima Nikaya*
A = *Anguttara Nikaya*
SN = *Samyutta Nikaya*
Dh = *Dhammapada*
Vsm = *Visuddhimagga*

2   Peter Harvey, 'Buddhas, Past and Future' in Damien Keown and Charles S. Prebish, eds, *Encyclopedia of Buddhism* (London: Routledge, 2007), 161a–165a.

3   Ibid.

4   Melford E. Spiro, *Buddhism and Society: A Great Tradition and its Burmese Vicissitudes* (London: George Allen and Unwin, 1971), pp. 144-7.

5   Robert E. Buswell Jr and Donald S. Lopez Jr, *The Princeton Dictionary of Buddhism* (Princeton and Oxford: Princeton University Press, 2014), p. 372.

6   Rupert Gethin, *The Foundations of Buddhism* (Oxford: Oxford University Press, 1998), p. 112.

7   Nyanaponika Thera, *The Heart of Buddhist Meditation: The Buddha's Way of Mindfulness* (San Francisco: Weiser, 2014).

8   Peter Harvey, *Introduction to Buddhism: Teachings, History and Practices* (Cambridge: Cambridge University Press, 2013, 2nd ed.), p. 36.

9   Gethin, *The Foundations of Buddhism*, pp. 122–223.

10 Harvey, 'Buddhas, Past and Future', 161a–165a.

11 Gethin, *The Foundations of Buddhism*, p. 113.

12 Harvey, *Introduction to Buddhism*, pp. 32–33.

13 Buswell Jr and Lopez Jr, *The Princeton Dictionary of Buddhism*, p. 163.

14 Ibid.

15 James Emanuel Bogle, *Buddhist Cosmology: The Study of a Burmese Manuscript* (Chiang Mai: Silkworm, 2016), p. 30.

16 Ibid., p. 29.

17 Harvey, 'Buddhas, Past and Future', 161a–165a.

18 Gethin, *The Foundations of Buddhism*, pp. 113–114.

19 Harvey, *Introduction to Buddhism*, p. 39.

20 Jon Kabat-Zinn, *Wherever You Go, There You Are: Mindfulness Meditation in Everyday Life* (New York: Hyperion, 2004), p. 4.

21 See www.mbct.com.

22 https://edwardstrust.org.uk/mindfulness.

သဿန္တသိုင်

ကဏ္ဍလသိုင်

Tengu no dairi

Yasuyo Ohtsuka

Tengu no dairi ('The Palace of the Tengu') is a tale describing the childhood visit of Minamoto no Yoshitsune (1159–1198), one of the most popular samurai warriors in Japanese history, to the Palace of the Tengu or Long-Nosed Goblins, and how he was taken on a miraculous journey by their king.

Yoshitsune was the ninth son of Minamoto no Yoshitomo (1123–1160), head of the Minamoto clan when they were defeated by the rival Taira clan. He later joined his elder brother Minamoto no Yoritomo (1147–1199) to fight against the Taira. However, Yoshitsune's glorious days as a young samurai warrior did not last for long. There were numerous misunderstandings between the brothers and eventually Yoshitsune was killed by his elder brother's army. Yoshitsune's dramatic but tragic life became so popular that these panegyrics came to constitute a literary genre of their own, known as *Hoganmono* (literally 'Tales of the Magistrate') after one of his official titles. However, Yoshitsune's early life is not well recorded in Japanese historical resources, which gave rise to numerous narratives recounting the legends of his childhood.

The story format of *Tengu no dairi* is a Japanese folktale, more specifically the type of story known as *Otogizoshi*, in *Nara ehon* manuscript style. *Otogizoshi* is an umbrella term used to identify a miscellaneous body of Japanese short narratives, covering a wide range of subjects from fairy tales to war epics, Shinto myths to Buddhist legends. These texts started to appear from about the late Kamakura period (1185–1333) until the Muromachi period (1333–1568), but their popularity continued well into the Edo period (1603–1868). Between the late Muromachi and mid-Edo periods they were often reproduced as fine *Nara ehon* manuscripts, which were ornamented with colourful hand-painted illustrations elegantly illuminated with gold and silver foil.

At the start of the story Yoshitsune is fifteen years old and is already renowned for his devotion to the study of Buddhism at Kurama temple. He also harbours the secret desire to one day avenge his father and reinstate the samurai honour of the Minamoto clan. While Yoshitsune is at the temple, he becomes curious about rumours surrounding the Palace of the Tengu on Mount Kurama. The Tengu are mythical beings dwelling deep in the mountain forests with red faces and extraordinary protruding noses. In most cases, Tengu are described as the enemies of Buddha who wilfully break his precepts. Consequently, they belong neither to heaven nor hell and are able to fly unhindered between the two realms.

The Buddhist deity Vaisravana of Kurama temple appears to Yoshitsune and shows him the way to the Palace of the Tengu, hidden deep in the mountains, where Yoshitsune is told his late father was reincarnated in Amitabha's Pure Land. The Tengu king whom Yoshitsune meets in his palace is generous enough to agree to fly him through numerous hells to the Pure Land to see his father. While travelling with the Tengu king, Yoshitsune sees departed souls who are trapped in the various hells. When they visit the Hell of Hungry Ghosts, he sees one ghost who is greatly relieved to know he will be rescued from damnation because his descendant has become a monk to pray for his ancestor's soul. Amid a scene of carnage, Yoshitsune comes across samurai warriors fighting endlessly. One man catches his eye and Yoshitsune believes this man is committing ritual suicide as his punishment for a lack of filial piety in not defending his father's honour.

Yoshitsune now comes face to face with a dilemma: should he become a monk and keep praying for the peaceful repose of his lost father and the Minamoto clan according to the precepts of Buddha, or should he avenge the name of his father and reinstate the clan's samurai honour by taking to the battlefield against the Taira?

Finally, the Tengu king takes Yoshitsune to Amitabha's Pure Land, where he is reunited with his late father, who has been reincarnated as Vairocana. Although his father has already been transformed into a higher spiritual being, he confesses that he is still concerned that his rivals the Taira remain in power and he would prefer his sons to take revenge on the Taira to restore the honour of the Minamoto clan rather than to offer *sutras* for him. Yoshitsune decides firmly that his fate is to take up arms for the sake of his father and the Minamoto.

The closing of the tale leaves us ultimately in doubt whether or not the Tengu king really took Yoshitsune to Amitabha's Pure Land. It might strike us as rather contradictory for Vairocana, who must have reached personal enlightenment, still to be suffering from his own desires and to prefer his sons to take revenge on and kill his rivals, rather than live a life of prayer and contemplation. Surely Yoshitsune had not forgotten the images of the various hells and especially the hungry ghost telling him that prayers of his descendant would rescue the departed souls trapped in hell?

When Yoshitsune's curiosity towards the Palace of Tengu deepens, despite the Tengu's questionable attitude to the precepts of the Buddha, it is Vaisravana of Kurama temple who shows him the way, as though he is on a dangerous quest. It is Yoshitsune himself who believes the words of the Tengu king when he tells him his father has been reincarnated in Amitabha's Pure Land and so makes the decision to abandon his life of

devotion at the temple. This fateful choice to follow the samurai code of honour leads to his tragic end, hinting to us that the moral of the tale centres on the eternal plight of humanity's *karma*; freeing oneself from the vicious circle of human revenge is hard and following the precepts of Buddha is a still long way off. It was a dilemma often faced by the samurai warriors – whether to live by the sword or the *sutra*, or to balance precariously between both.

The Japanese tale in a *Nara ehon* manuscript scroll. Japan, 16th century.
British Library, Or.13839, vol. 1

The *Patimokkha* of the *Bhikkhu* and *Bhikkhuni*

San San May

Bhikkhu Patimokkha and *Bhikkhuni Patimokkha* are two sets of rules for monks (*bhikkhu*) and nuns (*bhikkhuni*) contained in a manuscript from Burma. It is written in the Pali language in Burmese square script and dates to the nineteenth century. The *Patimokkha* constitutes the nucleus of the *Vinaya Pitaka*. It is recited during the fortnightly assemblies (*uposatha*) of the *sangha* (the Buddhist monastic order) by monks and nuns who gather inside a purified *sima* boundary.

This Pali text, inscribed on fifty-two palm leaves, lists the monastic rules of discipline that fully ordained Buddhist monks and nuns have vowed to follow. The edges of the leaves are gilt and the volume is elegantly inscribed in black ink. A note on the margin of the first leaf records that the manuscript was commissioned as an act of merit by King Mindon (r. 1853–1878), founder of Mandalay and patron of Man Aung Yadana Pagoda, and his chief queen. The leaves are enclosed in gilt boards with red ornaments. There are also ornaments on the margins of the leaves.

The First Buddhist Council was held at Rajagaha, shortly after the Buddha's death, in around 400 BCE. Five hundred of the most senior Buddhist monks convened to recite and verify all the sermons they had heard during the Buddha's forty-five years of teaching. They systematically arranged and compiled Buddha's teachings into three main divisions now known as the Pali Canon or *Tipitaka* (literally meaning 'three baskets'). It consists of three parts: monastic discipline (*Vinaya Pitaka*), discourses (*Sutta Pitaka*) and higher teachings (*Abhidhamma Pitaka*). The three elements are distinct. The *Vinaya Pitaka* contains texts concerning the rules of conduct that govern the daily affairs within the *sangha*. There are three major divisions: *Suttavibhanga*, *Khandhaka* and *Parivara*. The *Suttavibhanga* includes the *Patimokkha* sets of rules for monks and nuns with explanations and commentaries, the *Mahavibhanga* or *Bhikkhuvibhanga* concerns the rules for monks and the *Bhikkhunivibhanga* contains the rules for nuns.

A *bhikkhu* is a fully ordained Buddhist monk who observes 227 precepts, which include rules entailing expulsion from the monastic order, rules requiring a meeting, rules entailing confession, rules on training, rules on settlement and so on. A *bhikkhuni* is a fully ordained Buddhist nun who observes 311 precepts, 181 of which are shared with the *Bhikkhu Patimokkha*. Most of the additional precepts for nuns are designed to regulate the interaction between nuns and to protect them from inappropriate or exploitative behaviours. For example, a rule that prohibits nuns from serving monks prevents the inequality and stereotype of women serving men.

Important monks and nuns have been recognized since the earliest times. The *Apadana*, the thirteenth book of the *Khuddaka Nikaya* of the Pali *Suttanpitaka*, includes hagiographies of 547 senior *bhikkhus* and 40 *bhikkhunis* who lived during the lifetime of the Buddha. *Theragatha* or the *Verses of the Elder Monks* and *Therigatha* or the *Verses of the Elder Nuns* are poetic texts attributed to early Buddhist monks and nuns. The lives of a number of the noble monks and nuns are described in these texts.

There are at least ten *bhikkhunis* who have been praised by the Buddha for their specialities in various aspects. The first *bhikkhuni* is Gotami, also known as Mahapajapati, foster mother and the aunt of the Buddha who became the first Buddhist woman to be ordained as a *bhikkhuni*. Following the death of King Suddhodana, the Buddha's father, the widowed queen Mahapajapati Gotami went to the Buddha and asked him to allow women to be fully ordained. The Buddha refused her request, believing that the reality of life as a nun posed serious hardship for the women who wished to undertake it. After Ananda pleaded, the Buddha granted Gotami's request subject to her promise to accept eight conditions for ordination. These included respecting *bhikkhus* and male novices, not travelling further than six hours from the monastery of permanent residence and consulting *bhikkhus* on observance days. She played the most important role in the admission of the *Bhikkhuni Sangha*. After her ordination, and that of her 500 followers, increasing numbers of women left domestic lives to become nuns during the Buddha's lifetime. The other nine *bhikkhunis* were: Dhammadinna Theri, foremost in wisdom and who had a great ability to preach; Patacara, foremost in the Vinaya, the rules of the discipline; Bhadda Kapilana, foremost in remembering past lives; Bhadda Kundalakesa, foremost in swift intuition; Sukula, foremost in the celestial eye; Sona, foremost in strenuous will; Khema and Uppalavanna, foremost as models among the *bhikkhunis*; and Kisa Gotami, foremost in wearing rough cloth.

There are a number of *Patimokkha* codes that are still followed in the main Buddhist traditions today: the *Theravada Patimokkha* in Sri Lankan and Southeast Asian Buddhism; the *Dharmaguptaka Pratimoksa* followed mainly in Chinese, Korean, Japanese and Vietnamese Buddhism; and the *Mulasarvastivada Pratimoksa* followed in Tibetan Buddhism. The ordination of *bhikkhuni* was initially introduced in Sri Lanka by the daughter of Emperor Ashoka, Sanghamitta, in the third century BCE. It was lost temporarily in the Theravada tradition

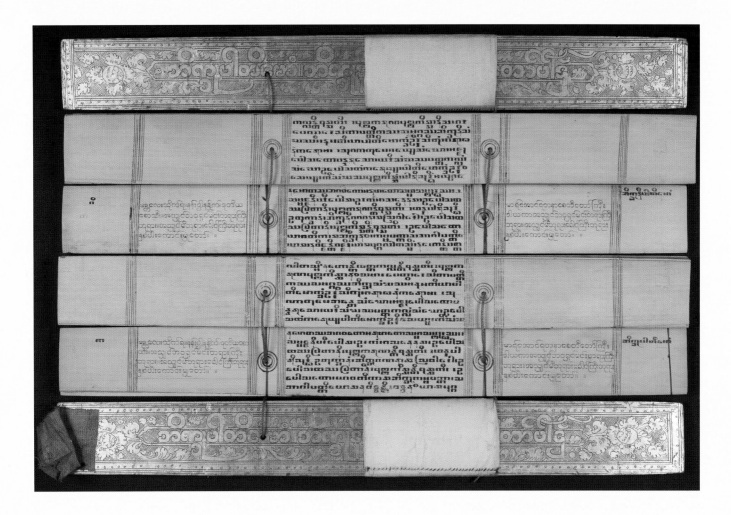

for approximately one millennium but was revived in the 1990s in Sri Lanka through nuns in East Asia belonging to a lineage that could trace its origins back to the Theravada school. *Bhikkhuni* lineages have existed without interruption in the Mahayana tradition.

Patimokkha of the *Bhikkhu* and *Bhikkhuni* written in the Pali language in Burmese square script on palm leaves. Burma, 19th century.

An *Abhidhamma* Commentary in Shan Language

Chaichuen Khamdaengyodtai

A folding book with the title *Sankhara bhajani*, written in Shan poetic language, contains a meritorious commentary on the *Abhidhamma*, or 'life and soul commentary', commissioned by Phrah-takah Sarngjah and his wife Phrah-takah Nang Lah. The scribe's name was Raharn Hsipaw and it was completed in 2460 BE (1917 CE) at Mueang Lakorn, Pah Kham village in northern Thailand. It has 278 folios and two lavishly decorated covers.

The Shan people, an ethnic group that live in Burma/ Myanmar, South China and Thailand, have an old saying: '*Toh lu tsue yah haue haai* [the body perishes; do not let the name disappear], *toh taai laai yah haue nau* [the body dies; do not let the knowledge and skills disappear]'. The Shan way of life still follows the wisdom prescribed in this proverb as much as possible.

For Shan Buddhists, the act of making merit is of great importance. When a house-warming ceremony is carried out, a novice monk ordained into the Buddhist *sangha*, a newly sculpted Buddha image blessed, or a monastery or a pagoda built, Shan families commission a book of offering in commemoration of that particular event. Also, when a family member has passed away, such a book of offering would be made in commemoration of the deceased person and in order to transfer merit to the deceased to enable a fortunate rebirth. These books of offering are kept either in a place of worship in their family homes or at Buddhist monasteries. As a result, each Shan family would own at least one or a small number of such books, whereas a larger collection of books of offering could be found in the house of a *mo-lik* (learned scholar or writer), and entire libraries would be kept in monasteries, which are present in every Shan village. Although printing has largely replaced the tradition of making books of offering by hand, some people still specialize in this art and young people are trained to take it up as a profession.

Two forms of paper books are known in the Shan manuscript tradition: *pap top* (folding book) and *pap ken* (curled or scrolled book). In the West, *pap top* is also often called a *leporello* or accordion book. Before the scribe can start work, the bookmaker must make the paper – usually from the bark of mulberry trees – and shape the appearance of the book. Sheets of paper have to be glued together and folded carefully to make a folding book, or bound together by way of a stitched binding to make a curled book. The neat and spotless appearance of the book even before the text is written reflects the great value attached to its production and its role in Buddhist ritual. The text is usually written in *Lik Tai* (Shan) script with black ink, and the scribe has to make great efforts to write in a neat hand or with elements of calligraphy.

Once the text is finished, the bookmaker may use *nam men* or *nam men lohng* (natural oils) to apply a thin layer on the manuscript which prevents insects from attacking the paper. Then red lacquer is applied on all sides of the folded book and gold leaf is applied in an even manner before the lacquer has fully dried up. The finished book of offering looks like a solid block of gold.

Commemorative *pap top* can be decorated in a special way to add more meritorious value. This special technique of decorating the book involves several steps: when the bookmaker has covered the manuscript in red lacquer, he mixes a thin paste from plant materials (*sah law*) before the lacquer has fully dried out. Then he lays out a pattern with a fine thread of the paste on the front and back covers of the book. Flower designs are usually made by applying some *sah law* in the appropriate places and pressing coloured pieces of mirror-glass, precious stones and pearls into the paste. Finally, just before this elaborate decoration has fully dried out, the bookmaker will carefully rub gold leaf on all surfaces. He then lays a cloth cover on the surface and gently rubs the cloth, causing the gold to stick on all surfaces that are not glass, precious stones and pearls.

The *Sankhara bhajani* consists of thirteen chapters. The subject of this text is the *Sankhara*, which is a concept in Buddhist philosophy that generally refers to conditioned phenomena (which arise due to causes other than themselves) and specifically to *karma* that leads to conditioned arising and dependent origination. This means that all phenomena are interconnected and dependent on one another. Everything is subject to impermanence: birth, growth, decline, decay, rebirth and so on. The mind, *citta*, perceives impermanence as suffering. *Samsara* (the cycle of transmigration) or *samsara dukkha* (the ill of transmigration, suffering caused by perceptual repetition of birth and death or compounded things which are impermanent) is perceived as a continuous cycle of sufferings. Buddha's teachings prescribe the way to escape from *samsara*, which includes the practice of generosity (*dana/pariccaga*), keeping the Buddhist precepts (*sila*) and meditation (*bhavana*).

To practice generosity, offerings (*dana*) or donations (*pariccaga*) should be made out of compassion and respect. Offerings must not be made with the expectation of receiving something in return. True generosity is thought to be one of the many factors leading to *nibbana*. Observing religious precepts (*sila*) means to be mindful of others and not to harm, distress, disturb and

Commentary on the *Abhidhamma* in the Shan language.
Mueang Lakorn, Thailand, 1917.
British Library, Or.16079

encroach on others. Lay followers can decide to observe five, eight or ten precepts, but Buddhist monks observe 227 precepts and nuns observe 311 precepts.

There are two types of meditation (*bhavana*), namely cultivation of concentration (*samadhi-bhavana*) and deep meditation or insight meditation (*vipassana-bhavana*) on three common characteristics, which are impermanence (*anicca*), suffering (*dukkha*) and non-self (*anatta*). *Vipassana* meditation uses the power of concentration (*samadhi*) on sensations within the body and so is concerned with the universe within as it is in their essentiality beyond the realm of concept. It purifies the mind to enable it to gain insight (*vipassana nyana*) leading to imagination of the way (*magga*). It is the main branch of mental development (*bhavana*) to attain *nirvana*.

THE BOOK:
MANIFESTATIONS OF KNOWLEDGE AND CULTURAL EXCHANGE

Beth McKillop

The spread of Buddha's teachings from their homeland to many countries of Asia and beyond has taken myriad physical and intellectual forms, creating a rich and complex story of transmission, translation, adoption and reverence. After the death of the Buddha, his words were remembered by disciples who passed them by word of mouth from teacher to student, from monk to monk, over generations. The practice of committing teachings to memory and reciting them was deeply rooted in Indian and Nepali tradition. Convenient mater-ials for writing texts were not widely available in the early centuries after the Buddha's death. It was only around 250 BCE that the Pali Buddhist scriptures were written down, in Pataliputra (Patna) at the Third Buddhist Council held under the patronage of Emperor Ashoka. The materials for writing were local. In much of India and Southeast Asia, the *talipat* or writing palm *Corypha umbraculifera* was widely used, with reed pens or metal styluses to indent the leaf.

After scoring, ink or a mixture of soot and plant oils was smeared into the grooves. Palm leaves could also have incised illustrations or illustrated covers, and sometimes the text was written with ink on the leaves (not incised) and colour paintings added. Birch bark was also used as a carrier of texts in the Himalayan region. The British Library holds a group of early texts in Kharosthi, from Gandhara, that date to the first century CE and which were preserved in scroll format, in poor condition, in a jar. These texts on birch bark are a remarkable survival and are believed to have been ritually buried in antiquity.

During the centuries that followed the death of the Buddha, while Buddhism as a formal philosophical doctrine was evolving, a number of meetings of monks took place to recite and agree the teachings of the Buddha. The literature, known as a basket or collection of writings – *pitaka* – was organized into categories. Initially, there were two: *Vinaya Pitaka* (basket of monastic discipline) and *Sutra Pitaka* (basket of discourses). Later, around the second century BCE, a third basket, the additional teachings, *Abhidharma Pitaka*, was added. These three groups of texts have evolved into a rather stable Canon of Buddhist teaching and have been continuously studied, explained, recorded, published and circulated around the world, in a number of different versions, from ancient times until today. Although they were committed to written versions long after the Buddha's lifetime, their importance was widely recognized and their content was debated and discussed by the itinerant monks and disciples who spread the Buddha's message as they travelled. In modern times, there are various standard versions of the Buddhist Canon, reflecting the development of different doctrinal schools in the areas where Buddhist communities live and practise. Together, the three parts of the Canon of Buddhist texts form the Three Baskets, the *Tripitaka*.

The earliest surviving version of the *Tripitaka* is in Pali, an early Indian language that survives in written form in various scripts, like Sinhalese, Burmese, Khmer, Thai, northern Thai and Lao, although its precise origins are debated. This is the only version of several

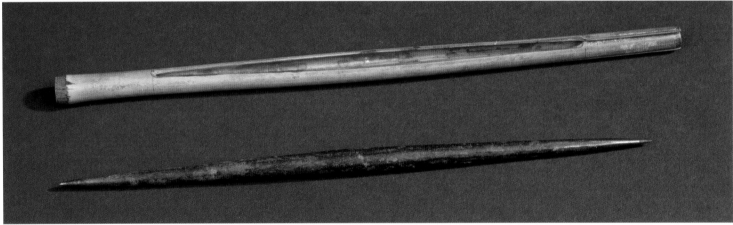

TOP: A Sinhalese palm leaf manuscript with the title *Akhyanapadang likhisang*, containing a textbook for learners of Pali grammar, compiled by scribe Tapassi on the request of a novice named Yasasi. Sri Lanka, 19th century.

British Library, Or.6608/43

ABOVE: Stylus for incising text on palm leaves, which is afterwards rubbed with a mixture of soot and plant oils to make the text more visible. Burma, 19th or early 20th century.

British Library, Or.15951

RIGHT: Fragments from a collection of birch bark scrolls containing various texts from the *Tripitaka* in the Gandhari language and Kharosthi script. These are among the earliest surviving manuscripts containing Buddhist scriptures. Gandhara, North West Frontier Province of Pakistan or Afghanistan, 1st century CE.

British Library, Or.14915

BELOW: Clay water pot with an offering inscription in Kharosthi script which reads 'This water pot [is a gift] to the universal community in the possession of the Sarvastivadin teachers in the Purnaga grove'. It contained texts from the *Tripitaka* in Kharosthi script on birch bark. Gandhara, North West Frontier Province of Pakistan or Afghanistan, 1st century CE.

British Library, Or.14915/B

ABOVE: Printed palm leaves containing short extracts from the *Tipitaka* in northern Thai (Lanna) Dhamma script for chanting for the monastic and lay communities. Wat Doi Saket, Chiang Mai, Thailand, 1960s. From Søren Egerod's collection.

British Library, Or.16994/A

OPPOSITE: Title page of the first volume of the *Taisho Tripitaka* (Taisho 13). Tokyo, Japan, 1924–1934.

British Library, 15102.c.1, vol. 1

in early Indian languages to survive and is regarded as the canonical record of teachings for the Theravada school in Sri Lanka, Myanmar (Burma), Thailand, Laos and Cambodia. Theravada, deriving from the Pali term meaning 'elder', is associated with monastic Buddhism and close adherence to the Vinaya, the rules for monks and nuns. Modern printed versions of the Pali *Tripitaka* exist, along with translations into different languages, including English. There are ongoing projects to publish the sacred texts online such as Pali Canon Online, the Vipassana Research Institute, Sutta Central and the Sinhala *Tripitaka* (this last an initiative of the Sri Lankan government). These published sets of the Pali Canon typically number between forty and sixty volumes. By contrast, the modern Sino-Japanese Canon is the largest *Tripitaka* in length. It reflects many centuries of translations of texts from the earliest times onwards and is associated with Mahayana schools. Mahayana,

the 'Greater Way', emphasizes altruism and generosity. Its teachings stress the benevolence of those who try to alleviate the suffering of all sentient beings. Today, the standard version of the Sino-Japanese Canon is the *Taisho Tripitaka*, in 100 volumes. It comprises of 3,360 works, totalling 11,970 chapters.

Turning to the content of the *Tripitaka*, it is striking that the oldest and shortest part is the Vinaya, the Monastic Rules. Buddhist communities of monks and nuns lived apart from secular society and followed the rules of behaviour taught by the Buddha. At first, the simple message of the Buddha's teaching was sufficient to guide the members of the *sangha*, as the Buddhist order of monastics is called. Over time, as instances of actions and behaviours that contravened the spirit of the Buddha's guidance occurred, the community codified types of crime and misdemeanour and applied appropriate punishments to the offender. These monastic

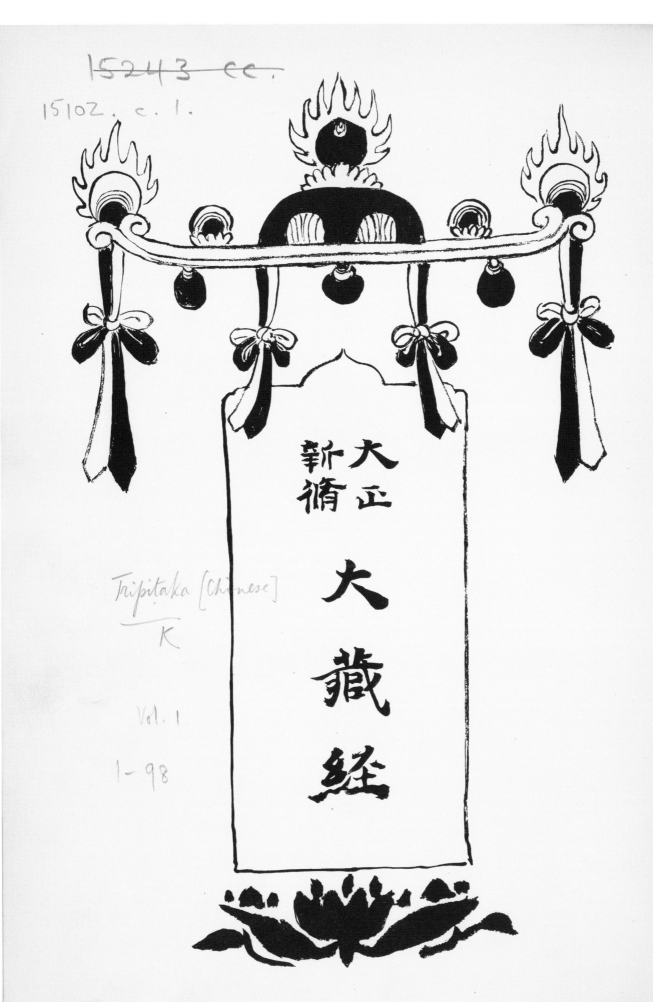

大正新脩 大藏経

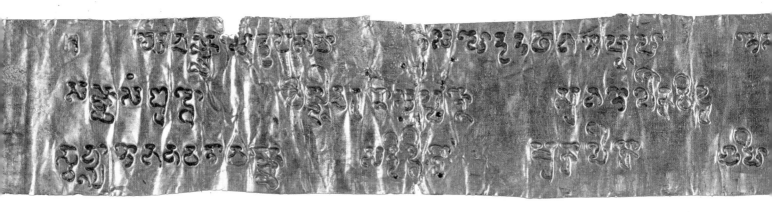

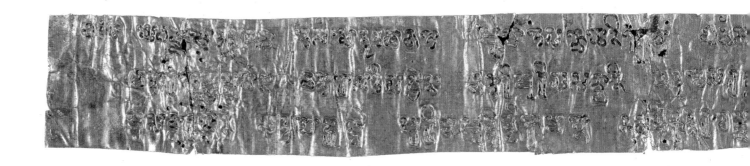

rules are known as *Vinaya Pitaka*, the 'basket of monastic discipline', and have been actively studied and used for nearly 2,600 years. The monastic rules that survive into modern times are in different versions and are associated with different sects. The Pali version contains 227 rules for monks and 311 rules for nuns. The rules are divided into sections. After a confession of faith, monks and nuns would learn the details of the rules of behaviour. Some formed a kind of liturgy, a reminder of the unifying force of the discipline. Reciting or chanting rules on particular days would cement the community together, as well as offering an occasion for confession and a way of identifying those who had violated the code. A separate section of the monastic rules consists of a more detailed exposition, including explanation of the human circumstances that might offer a context for each rule, commentary on its meaning, and discussion of exceptions and punishments. There are also regulations discussing broad issues relating to disharmony in the community, alongside more practical questions about

clothing, the use of leather and dispute procedures. As the monastic community grew in size and wealth, and as its rules evolved over time, the *Vinaya Pitaka* came to include extra texts of later date.

The second section of the Buddhist Canon is the *Sutra Pitaka*, the 'basket of discourses'. The word *sutra* derives from a Sanskrit term 'to sew' and carries the idea of a thread of argument. First transmitted orally, the sermons were recorded in writing some centuries after the death of the Buddha. The Pali Canon, still actively studied and followed in Sri Lanka and most of mainland Southeast Asia today, is believed to have been recorded in writing by monks in the first century BCE because economic hardship and conflict at the time had resulted in a shortage of reciters able to speak the words of the *sutras*. In the lands where Theravada Buddhism is practised, the warm and humid climate is hostile to preserving written texts for posterity, although much effort has been made to keep manuscripts safe from damage by storing them in custom-made lacquered wooden

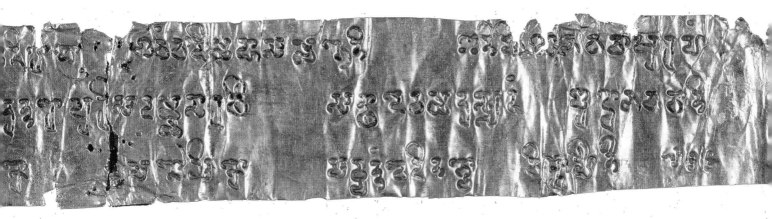

chests and cabinets. They were placed in temple libraries that were constructed in a way that supported air
circulation, thus reducing humidity. These libraries were
in fact often built on stilts above water to protect the
written texts from destruction by fires and rodents. The
text in a damp or mouldy manuscript could be copied,
but a text destroyed by fire was lost forever.

Another region where the Buddha's teachings spread
to new communities was Central Asia. Here, the climate
and topography fortuitously preserved many ancient texts.
The dry desert conditions of the Central Asian lands led to
the survival of numerous objects and documents dating
from ancient times. In the early centuries of the Common
Era, the Kusana Empire united the Indian heartlands with
Central Asia, and Buddhist teachings travelled north
towards China.

Later, travellers in the opposite direction played a
part in transmitting the Buddha's teachings outside of
their homeland. Stories of the Chinese and Central Asian
monks who overcame terrifying hardships while travelling

Fragmented extracts of the *Vinaya Mahavagga* in Pali, written in
Pyu script on gold sheets, which mimic the palm leaf format,
excavated at Maunggan, Burma in 1897. Pyu kingdoms, 5th
century.

British Library, Or.5340/A–B

to India in search of sacred texts began to circulate. The scriptures they brought back with them were translated into many languages by monks, some of whose names are known to us because they were recorded on the manuscripts. The languages of these early translations include Khotanese, a language spoken in part of what is now the Xinjiang region of western China; Tocharian, a language of the Tarim Basin, also in Xinjiang; Uyghur; and Sogdian. The *sutras* were translated both into local languages and into Chinese. Over the centuries, as population centres were abandoned for political or economic reasons, doc-uments including Buddhist texts were preserved in the stable climate conditions of the region, which experiences very low humidity in its atmosphere. The availability of paper in China and the adjacent lands facilitated the production and circulation of written documents. The Chinese habit of recording written texts on hard surfaces – bone, stone, bronze – has ancient origins, and led to the production there of simple printed prayer sheets and images of the Buddha. The much longer sacred texts themselves were also carved onto blocks of wood and printed, a tradition that continued into the twentieth century.

OPPOSITE: Carved and gilded wooden manuscript chest for the storage of Buddhist texts, made in the artistic style of the Rattanakosin era depicting scenes in the Himavanta forest. Central Thailand, 19th century. From Doris Duke's Southeast Asian Art Collection.
British Library, Foster 1058

ABOVE: A wood-carved Tibetan printing block for the production of a Buddhist scripture. Tibet, 20th century.
British Library, Or.14729

Certain *sutras* were translated in multiple versions and the Chinese versions of the *Tripitaka* include variant texts for certain *sutras*. In contrast to the Theravada tradition, where *sutras* are limited to the texts in the *Sutra Pitaka*, in Mahayana Buddhism *sutras* include a large number of texts composed between the first century BCE and the seventh century CE. The oldest extant versions of these *sutras* are in Chinese, although many of them may be translations from older Sanskrit texts.

The *Flower Ornament Sutra* or *Avatamsaka Sutra*, for example, exists in numerous translations into Chinese, including a thirty-four-chapter version translated by Buddhabhadra (359–429) and a forty-chapter version translated by Shikshananda (652–710).[1] The *sutras* themselves follow a conventional form, starting with 'Thus have I heard', reflecting the oral tradition of the Indian lands where the Buddha had preached. In the *Sutra Pitaka*, texts are organized by length, and include 'long sayings', 'middle-length sayings' and minor works.

The third basket is the *Abhidharma Pitaka*, a later addition. Here, explanations of the theoretical terms contained in the *sutras* are expounded. The *Abhidharma* lists and systematizes the terms and concepts studied by Buddhist philosophers. In its philosophical enquiry and its quest for unifying themes derived from the more prosaic teachings of the *sutras*, the *Abhidharma* attempts to approach the nature of truth and existence, to aid the perception of the true nature of the world, and thus to eliminate harmful emotions.

The *Tripitaka* is thus the monumental achievement of Buddhist teaching and thinking in written form and is universally recognized as one of the world's great bodies of sacred texts. In addition to the *Tripitaka* and its associated commentaries, which exist in numerous versions and languages, Buddhist books from the earliest times also include other types of literature. For example, beautifully illustrated sets of stories about the life of the Buddha were produced in Nepal, China, Korea and Myanmar (Burma) at various times. New *sutras* or teachings were composed over the centuries, sometimes purporting to belong to the agreed canonical corpus of texts. Scholars, teachers, monks and nuns composed devotional and meditative works, and still do. Because Buddha taught about incarnation and *karma*, and because it is understood that his teachings were pre-existing doctrines revealed rather than created by him, Buddhist texts are not intrinsically divine; instead, they record a number of eternal truths that predate the human being who became the Buddha.

The Buddhist pantheon abounds with figures whose stories are familiar to believers. Many have local and historical associations. Manifestations of the Buddha-nature take myriad forms. Aspects of the Buddha's

Manuscript volume belonging to the Tibetan *Kangyur* (collected teachings of the Buddha) in 108 volumes produced in 1712 at Shelkar monastery, southern Tibet.

British Library, Or.6724, dalba (1)

power and wisdom are taught and worshipped across the Asian continent. A particularly powerful and distinctive school of teaching is the esoteric or Tantric school, whose adherents used rituals and meditative techniques as they sought to gain enlightenment.

In the context of the Bodhisattva ideal, where the Buddhist believer aspires to Buddhahood for the bene-fit of all sentient beings, Tantric schools teach that enlightenment can be reached, with the guidance of a teacher, in one lifetime. From origins in India, developing during the latter centuries of the first millennium of the Common Era in the Bihar and Bengal regions of the subcontinent, Tantric Buddhism gained adherents across the Buddhist world. After the collapse of northern Indian Buddhism around the time of the Muslim invasions of the thirteenth century, Tantric Buddhism was embraced by the Tibetans. The Tibetan version of the Buddhist Canon includes Tantric texts. It consists of the *Kangyur*, or *Translated Words*, supposed to have been said by the Buddha himself, and the *Tengyur*, or *Translated Treatises*, a collection of commentaries, treatises and *Abhidharma* works. The *Kangyur* is normally in 108 volumes and the *Tengyur* in 225.

One of the most important ritual implements of Tantric Buddhism is the thunderbolt, *Vajra*, which gives its name to the Vajrayana or Thunderbolt Vehicle school. The thunderbolt represents the powerful nature of wisdom. Vajrayana teaches that enlightenment can be attained through the guidance of a guru, who can interpret the many symbols and magic formulae that lead the student to enlightenment. Tantric teaching and ceremony represent aspects of the Buddha-nature through images such as the male in union with the female, compassion joined with insight, conveying the ideal of the Bodhisattva. Other images and gestures associated with protection, or with meditative or spiritual states, also populate the Tantric world. In the context of monastic celibacy, the Tantric belief in psycho-sexual energy exchange continues to surprise believers and non-believers alike. The figure of Samvara, a conquering Buddha, is an example.

Ceremonial union (in Tibetan *yab yum*) between the male and female in the service of Buddhist teaching was practised literally in some Tantric traditions and viewed as a symbolic ritual in others. Chanting special syllables, *dharani* and *mantra*, is another practice reflecting esoteric Buddhism's belief in supernatural powers. Groups of words were recited in an atmosphere of reverence and concentration in the belief that an entire doctrine could be conveyed in one word.

In written or printed form, a powerful *dharani* (magical invocation) could protect a building or a community. In eighth-century Korea, a tiny paper scroll with such a text was rolled up and interred inside part of a royal Buddhist temple. The building's founders hoped that the protective force of the text would safeguard the Buddha Land Temple, Pulguksa, from harm. It was discovered in 1966 when the historic building underwent repairs.

Chinese esoteric meditation mandala in the shape of an opened pomegranate, with the central figure of Yi-dam representing the enlightened mind in embrace with his *prajna* (wisdom) counterpart, together with twenty other divinities in Vajrayana Buddhism. China, 17th or 18th century.
British Museum, 1939, 0118.1

The life of Prince Siddhartha, the historical Buddha, was a rich source of stories and legends. Long before his last life, the Buddha had taken a vow to achieve Buddhahood. In a succession of lives, he performed virtuous deeds as he prepared for his final life as the son of King Suddhodana and Queen Maya. Stories about these preparatory lives were popular and were replete with tales of the previous lives of the Buddha in the form of various humans and animals. An example is a work in the British Library Burmese collection depicting an ox named Saramba who resists the harsh words of his Brahmin owner. Only when the Brahmin realizes his mistake and uses gentler language does the ox perform the feat of pulling 100 loaded carts.

Guides to Buddhist sites were printed for the convenience of pilgrims and visitors. Records of festivals and religious rites were produced, as were stories of exceptional Buddhist believers and monks, such as the legend of Phra Malai, which is particularly popular in Thailand and Laos. This is the story of a monk who visited the Buddhist hells and heavens, where he met the future Buddha Maitreya. Upon his return to the human world he told his fellow humans about the horrors awaiting condemned souls and the blissful delights enjoyed by those who, as a result of accumulated merit, will be reborn at the time of the future Buddha. The legend of Phra Malai is based on Bodhisattva Ksitigarbha.

Vasudharanamadharani, a hymn to Bodhisattva Vasudhara, in Sanskrit language in Siddhamatrika script. It is written in gold and silver ink on blue-black paper, with coloured illustrations. Nepal, 1184.
British Library, Or.13971/A, f. 1v, 2r

Extracts from the *Abhidhamma Pitaka* with the legend of Phra
Malai in a Thai folding book with illustrations of monks in the
style of the Rattanakosin era. Central Thailand, 19th century.

British Library, Or.15257, f. 4

THE BOOK

131

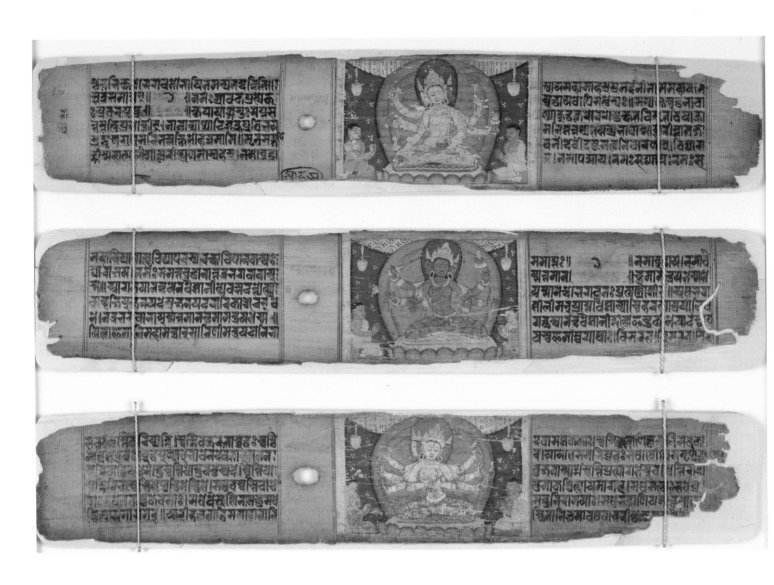

ABOVE: A rare early illustrated palm leaf manuscript containing
the *Pancaraksa*, ritual texts on the Five Protections, in the
Sanskrit language in the Nagari script. Nepal, c. 1130–1150.
British Library, Or.14000

OPPOSITE, BELOW: Carved wooden covers for a paper
manuscript containing the Tibetan version of the *Perfection
of Wisdom Sutra in Eight Thousand Verses* (Sanskrit:
Astasahasrikaprajnaparamita Sutra). Tibet, 14th century.
British Library, Tib.CC.135

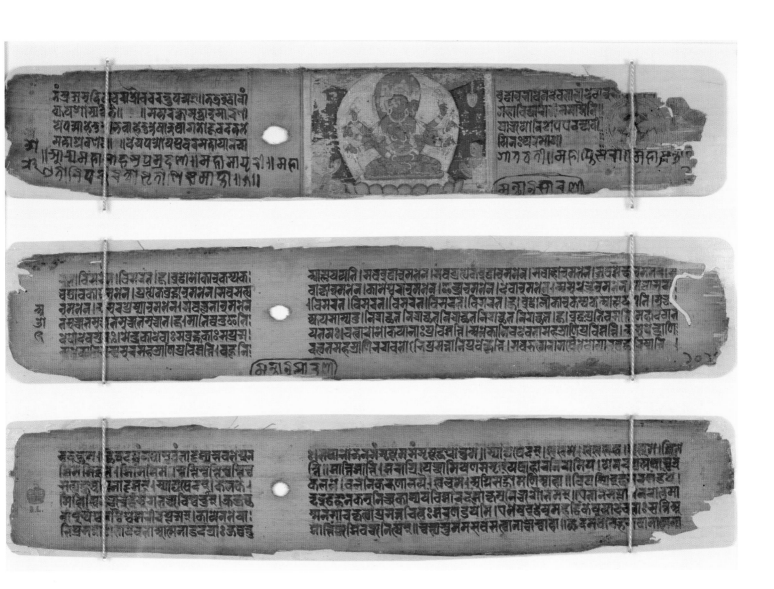

The Word of Buddha in Written Form: Sacred Scriptures in India, Nepal and Tibet

In Nepal and in eastern India, illuminated manuscripts survive from about 1000 CE. An exquisite standard of painting and calligraphy was achieved throughout the eleventh and twelfth centuries. After the Mongol conquest of northern India, refugees arrived in Nepal, bringing manuscripts and later the practice of copying texts on paper rather than on palm leaf.

In Tibet, manuscript and printed text production was practised on a large scale, with temples and private dwellings requiring copies of holy texts as part of the fabric of daily life. From beginnings in the seventh century, through the doctrinal shifts of later centuries, Buddhist books and libraries were an enduring feature of Tibetan life. As well as books, single sheets to aid the chanting of spells and formulae were produced, such as the nineteenth-century Spell of the Victorious Goddess Aparajita Sitatapatra.

The Book, Carrier of Faith and Knowledge in Central Asia

Books and texts played a leading role in the unfolding drama of bringing the Buddha's teachings through the Central Asian lands to China, Korea and Japan. The treacherous deserts and high mountain ranges separating Central Asia from the subcontinent were a formidable barrier against all forms of contact and trade, but intrepid monks braved the elements to seek out teachings in the form of *sutras* and other writings associated with the Buddha. Faxian (*c.* 337–422), who was born in Wuyang, Shanxi Province, embarked upon a pilgrimage to India in 399 CE. He travelled west to Dunhuang and continued across the desert to reach Khotan, where he stayed for three months. Over the next six years he visited Gandhara and many of the Buddhist sacred sites and monasteries in India. He returned to China by sea via Sri Lanka, in order to collect further important Buddhist texts there. After returning to China, Faxian translated many of the Buddhist texts he had collected. His reminiscences formed the *Record of the Buddhistic Kingdoms*, an important source of information on Buddhism and the Silk Road. Another well-known monk pilgrim who travelled from China to India is Xuanzang (602–664 CE), who carried hundreds of important texts overland to China and translated many.

Because of the decline of Buddhism in its Indian birthplace, and the destruction of the monasteries there in the twelfth century, most early versions of the *Tripitaka* were lost. It was an exciting revelation when, in the early twentieth century, sites in Central Asia were excavated and yielded a vast collection of early Buddhist texts in Sanskrit, Chinese and other languages. At that time, archaeologists and explorers vied to reach and collect ancient artefacts and manuscripts from once-vibrant settlements in places such as Dunhuang (Gansu Province), Khotan (Xinjiang Province), Niya (Xinjiang Province) and many others. These thriving settlements had grown up along the Silk Roads that linked East Asia with the Middle East and Europe. Depopulated after many centuries, they were open-air museums for the evidence of early religious life in an area of economic, religious and cultural exchange between West and East. Buddhists were by no means the only religious people to live and work along the ancient Silk Road. Nestorians, Manicheans, Zoroastrians, Jews and Muslims also peopled these trading communities and created sacred and secular texts as required in practising their faith. In the twenty-first century, excavations continue to reveal more evidence of the varied and impressive scriptures used by the inhabitants of Central Asia in its heyday. Exhibitions such as those at Shanghai Museum in 2014 and Hong Kong History Museum in 2018[2] have presented highlights of the finds to an eager public. The Chinese government has permitted international cooperation in certain archaeological excavations and this has allowed Japanese and French historians to contribute to China's energetic efforts to research and document these early West–East contacts. The early Silk Road scholar-monks of Central Asia laid the foundations for centuries of later religious scholarship and devotion.

Painting of a travelling monk with a fly-whisk and a back-carrier of Buddhist scrolls found at the cave complex at Mogao near Dunhuang, China, Gansu Province, 9th century.
British Museum, 1919, 0101, 0.168

Unlike the Indian experience of oral transmission of important lessons and stories, the Chinese preferred to record important events and ideas – whether of religious, administrative or archival nature – in writing. In part, this habit may have its origins in China's early use of writing. Inscriptions on ritual bronzes and on animal bones used during divination ceremonies go back to *c.* 1300 BCE. Paper was made in China from about 200 BCE onwards, although by tradition its introduction is credited to a court official, Cai Lun, who mentioned it in 105 CE. Being lightweight and easily carried, as well as flexible and easy to produce in a variety of sizes and qualities, paper undoubtedly pushed the Buddha's message north and east. Since the monks who travelled to India in search of *sutras* had to pass through western China and Central Asia, these continental lands became a kind of translation crucible where the *Tripitaka*, and other written texts of varying lengths, were studied and translated. In many cases, the names of the monk-translators have survived. For example, translations into Chinese of the *Flower Ornament Sutra – Avatamsaka* in Sanskrit, *Huayan* in Chinese – include that of an Indian monk, Buddhabhadra (359–429) and a later version by Shiksananda (625–710), a monk from Khotan. The second version was based on a more complete text than the first and was done at the request of a Tang dynasty empress. Khotan, a Buddhist kingdom on the Silk Road, was famous as an important centre for transmission of Buddhist teaching into China. Another important text that was translated multiple times is the *Diamond Sutra*. The earlier version, from around 401, was followed by several seventh-century translations and one of 703 by Yijing. The famous printed *Diamond Sutra* of 868 CE (see pages 22–23) is the 401 translation. Kumarajiva, the translator, lived from 344 to 413 and was born in Kucha, another Buddhist kingdom on the northern Silk Road.

In addition to acting as intermediaries who passed on Buddhist teachings as they travelled eastwards and northwards towards China and its neighbours, local Buddhist believers required their own translations. Numerous *sutras* and monastic rules were translated from Sanskrit into the languages spoken and written in the ethnically diverse communities of the Silk

Scroll containing the *Incantation to the Blue-Throated Avalokitesvara of Nilakanthadharani* in Sanskrit. Alternate lines of late Gupta (Siddham) and Sogdian scripts in ink on paper. A *dharani* in honour of Bodhisattva Avalokitesvara as Nilakantha. Dunhuang, China, Gansu Province, 7th or 8th century.
British Library, Or.8212/175

Aurel Stein's photograph of the interior of an empty Cave 16 at the Mogao Caves near Dunhuang where ancient Buddhist manuscripts were found in Cave 17. Dunhuang, China, Gansu Province, *c.* 1906–1908.

British Library, Photo 392/59

Road region. These languages included Khotanese, Sogdian and Tocharian (the language of the kingdom of Kucha). As a result of early twentieth-century expeditions in Central Asia led by Sir Aurel Stein (1862–1943), the British Library holds rare and precious Buddhist *sutras* and administrative documents that reflect the multilingual culture of the Silk Road, such as the eighth-century Sanskrit and Chinese *Perfection of Wisdom Sutra* in folding book format, and the seventh-century Sogdian and Sanskrit incantation in honour of blue-throated Avalokitesvara (see opposite).

Dunhuang, first established as a garrison town of Han dynasty China (206 BCE–220 CE), lies at the junction between the northern and southern Silk Roads. At a cliff near the town, a community of Buddhist believers created caves, the walls and ceilings of which were painted and carved with Buddha images. Soldiers, monks and merchant travellers passed through Dunhuang for over a thousand years, leaving rich documentary evidence of

�᭄ᬓᬾᬦ᭄ᬢᬾᬭᬾᬦ᭄ᬤᬾᬭᬾᬦ᭄ᬤᬾᬭᬾᬦ᭄ᬤᬾᬭᬾᬦ᭄ᬢᬾᬭ

ᬦ᭄ᬤᬾᬭᬾᬦ᭄ᬤᬾᬭᬾᬦ᭄ᬤᬾᬭᬾᬦ᭄ᬤᬾᬭᬾ

ᬤᬾᬦ᭄ᬤᬾᬭᬾᬦ᭄ᬤᬾᬭᬾᬦ᭄ᬤᬾᬭᬾᬦ᭄ᬤᬾᬭᬾᬦ᭄

ᬓᬾᬦ᭄ᬤᬾᬭᬾᬦ᭄ᬤᬾᬭᬾᬦ᭄ᬤᬾᬭᬾ

ᬤᬾᬦ᭄ᬤᬾᬭᬾᬦ᭄ᬤᬾᬭᬾᬦ᭄ᬤᬾᬭ

Buddhist devotion in the form of thousands of scrolls. In 1907, Stein discovered a walled-up cave at the cliff temple complex, where thousands of Buddhist and secular texts had been hidden away. He persuaded the guardian of the caves to allow him to take a selection of the material and these manuscripts and paintings, now in the British Museum, British Library and National Museum of India, have constituted a seminal historical source for twentieth-century historians of China and Central Asia. The great majority of the Dunhuang manuscripts are Buddhist. The Buddha had taught that 'the pen and ink being aids to supreme knowledge are to be venerated, preferably with the hundred-syllable mantra so as to make them highly potent'.[3] The careful preservation of thousands of sacred texts in the Dunhuang cave library is evidence that for Buddhist believers, the imperative to preserve and honour the powerful sacred images and writings that aided meditation and virtuous behaviour remained a powerful force.

It was at Dunhuang that the *Diamond Sutra* of 868 CE (see pages 22–23), the world's earliest dated printed book, was concealed among a huge cache of sacred images and texts to protect it from harm.

The product of a mature printing industry, the *Diamond Sutra* is one of countless copies of holy texts commissioned by believers. In earlier times, Buddhist communities had listened together to recitations of the Buddha's teachings. As the *sutras* were carried to foreign lands, they acquired almost supernatural powers. Believers would commission a *sutra* to be copied by hand or printed, in order to accumulate merit and benefit for themselves or their family members. In a similar way, paintings of the Buddha or Bodhisattvas were sponsored with the intention of benefitting the soul of a loved one. This is the case with the *Diamond Sutra*: it was produced so that the parents of Wang Jie could accumulate merit. Like many East Asian standardized copies of the holy texts, the *Diamond Sutra* of 868 takes the form of columns of text, read from right to left and from top to bottom, preceded by a pictorial scene of the Buddha preaching. In this way the origins of its contents – as the holy words of the Enlightened One – were connected to the reader of the physical object.

OPPOSITE: Scroll containing six Buddhist texts in Sanskrit and Khotanese. Cave 17, Mogao Caves near Dunhuang, China, Gansu Province, 943 CE.
British Library, IOL.Khot.S.46

RIGHT: Photograph of Islam Akhun (see page 140) taken by Aurel Stein after his interview of the forger at Khotan in 1901.
Library of the Hungarian Academy of Sciences, Stein Photo 3/6(19)

The diverse communities and writing traditions of the Central Asian centres meant that in addition to Chinese-language scriptures many documents were written in local languages. Canonical texts, stories about the Buddha's life and monastic regulations were transcribed in formats that mimicked the Indian *pothi* manuscript. The Uyghur kingdoms of the late first millennium CE ruled over parts of western China. They too required Buddhist texts, examples of which survive in the British Library.

Among the rich heritage of translating, copying, printing and distributing texts across Central Asia, the remarkable stories of forgers and swindlers should not be overlooked. Among the best known is Islam Akhun, who duped the Oxford scholar Rudolf Hoernle (1841–1918) and others into believing that his homemade booklets were evidence of a lost ancient language. Eventually debunked by the archaeologist Aurel Stein, Islam Akhun is a sobering example of the widespread phenomenon of production to meet demand: where there is a market for cultural artefacts, there will be unscrupulous tricksters ready to satisfy it.

Buddhist Books and Texts in China

Buddhist ideas and concepts travelled into China by the later Han dynasty (25–220 CE) but the dissemination of *sutras* and other holy texts was a lengthy process requiring translation of texts and their circulation throughout the country. During the third to sixth centuries CE, China was in a period of weakened central control. The Confucian state had fallen, and powerful western neighbours were in contact with India and its religious ideas. Almost all the translators of the *sutras* of all schools were Central Asian. During the Tang dynasty (618–907), Buddhism enjoyed imperial patronage and different schools developed, with an apparently relaxed attitude to scholastic differences. Pure Land Buddhism became a pervasive element in Chinese society, emphasizing devotion to Amitabha and the promise of a Western Paradise for the virtuous. Chan, meditative schools, also developed, tracing their origins to Bodhidharma (c. 470–520 CE), an Indian monk supposed to have travelled to China, where he taught the importance of direct transmission of the Buddha's teaching.

The Buddhist Canon was recorded numerous times in China, evidence of tireless devotion to the faith and of an enduring belief in the *karmic* efficacy of reproducing sacred texts in a variety of media. An early version is the *Fangshan Stone Sutras*, numbering 14,278, still today stored in caves near Yunzhu temple, south of Beijing. Printing texts on paper as a large-scale enterprise had

its origins in the southwest of the country, in Sichuan Province. The entire *Tripitaka* was carved onto blocks of wood there and printed between 971 and 983. This first Chinese *Tripitaka* is known as the *Kaibao Tripitaka*. The printing blocks, 130,000 in number, were then sent north to the capital, Kaifeng, where the work was formally presented to the emperor.

In the eleventh century, a new version of the *Tripitaka*, the *Chongning Tripitaka*, was printed in Fuzhou, Fujian Province. Fujian, a coastal region, emerged during the Song dynasty as an important centre for printing. More editions of the *Tripitaka*, all of a massive scale, were printed during the Song, reflecting a tenacious and widespread belief in gaining merit through reproducing and reciting sacred texts. These are the *Pilu Tripitaka*, 1112–1272, in Fujian; the *Yuanjue Tripitaka*, 1132, in Zhejiang; the *Cifu Tripitaka* of 1175, again in Zhejiang; and the *Qisha Tripitaka*, in Jiangsu, begun in 1232 under the Southern Song but completed only after the Mongol conquest of 1269. During the period of division, when northern parts of China were successively under the rule of the Khitan and Jurchen (the Liao and Jin dynasties), yet more *Tripitakas* were produced. The *Liao Tripitaka* does not survive, but the *Jin Tripitaka*, printed in Shanxi Province, is partially extant. The Tangut, a Manchurian kingdom whose language lacked a writing system before the Tangut script was invented in 1036, also required Buddhist texts and a *Tripitaka* in Tangut printed in Hangzhou in 1302 survives.

With the advent of Mongol rule in 1269, the production of large-scale woodblock-printed versions of the *Tripitaka* did not cease. The *Hongfa Tripitaka* of 1277–1294 and the *Puning Tripitaka* of 1278–1294 complemented the *Qisha Tripitaka*, which was finally completed at Suzhou in 1363 towards the end of the Mongol period. The *Qisha Tripitaka* has been widely reproduced outside China and there is a large holding in the Gest Oriental Library at Princeton University. Its frontispiece illustrations are notable for depictions of the preaching Buddha amidst assembled worshippers, and for scenes showing dialogues between Tibetan and Indian monks.

With the expulsion of the Mongols and return to Han Chinese rule under the Ming dynasty in 1368, production of large-scale sets of Buddhist texts continued. In 1372, a *Tripitaka* of 1,610 works in 6,331 chapters was imperially commissioned and produced in Nanjing; it is known as *Nanzang* or *Southern Tripitaka*. Between 1410 and 1440 another version, numbering 1,615 works in 6,361 chapters, was made to imperial command at the new capital, Beijing, and is known as *Beizang* or *Northern Tripitaka*.

The *Jiaxing Tripitaka* was first printed in China during the early Qing dynasty. The woodblock carving had begun in 1579. Interrupted during the Ming–Qing transition, the work was completed nearly a hundred years later, in 1677. It was compiled and printed as a private monastic effort. The project began in Shanxi Province on Mount Wutai, the realm of Manjusri, but it was later moved to a temple in Jiaxing, near the eastern coast. It includes a number of Chan (meditation) school works, which have not otherwise survived. The Qianlong Emperor, who reigned from 1735 to 1796, was a devout Buddhist; he initiated a project to print Buddhist texts, and this was completed in 1738. This *Tripitaka* was the last Chinese Buddhist Canon printed in China in the classical style. The *Qianlong Tripitaka* is also commonly called the *Longzang* – the *Dragon Store*. Dragons, as well as *nagas* (serpents), were believed to hold immense, incomparable libraries of scriptures.

The widely used *Taisho Shinshu Daizokyo* (*Taisho Tripitaka*) is a modern standardized typeset edition originally published in Tokyo between 1924 and 1934 in 100 volumes. It contains over 3,500 titles. For Chinese editions of the *Tripitaka*, most scholars use the *Great Chinese Tripitaka/Zhonghua Dazangjing*, published in 1984–1987 by Zhonghua Shuju in 106 volumes, reproducing the texts from original woodblock editions.

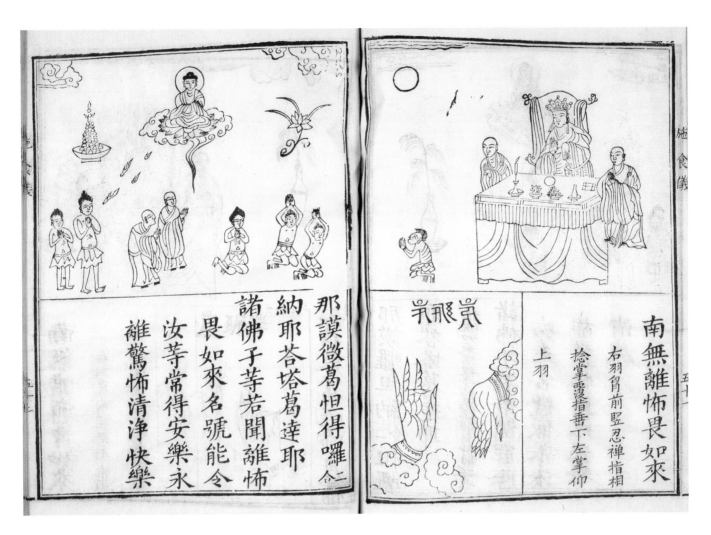

An example of a printed and bound book containing a Buddhist text on the essentials of the cultivation of compassion and almsgiving. Printing made it possible to mass-produce extracts from the *Tripitaka* and to distribute them for educational purposes. China, 1737.

Korea

The great Buddhist temples of the Korean peninsula before the Koryo dynasty (918–1392) have been lost, but the written and material evidence for Buddhism as a courtly and a popular religion is substantial and impressive. Cultural and political links to China were close, and texts were copied by hand onto paper from an early date. A fine eighth-century scroll of the *Avatamsaka Sutra* survives, copied at the behest of a priest at Hwangnyong Temple in Kyongju, a huge wooden temple that was destroyed during the Mongol invasions of the thirteenth century. The colophon following the text records that eleven scribes, four painters, two overseers, one paper maker and one 'painter of the sixth grade, leader of the group' took part in making the *sutra*, which consists of forty-three sheets of white paper rolled around a wooden spindle with crystal knobs at both ends. Like the great majority of Buddhist texts produced in Korea in premodern times, it is written in Chinese, the international language of Buddhism in East Asia.

As mentioned earlier, the city of Kyongju was also the location of a tiny scroll printed with *dharani*. The scroll is only 6.5 centimetres high and was enclosed inside a *stupa* at Pulguk Temple, an important foundation of the mid-eighth century. The *dharani* scroll was printed before the temple's consecration in 751 and is therefore one of the world's earliest datable printed texts.

RIGHT AND OVERLEAF: The Korean version of the *Flower Garland Sutra* (Korean: *Taebang kwangbul Hwaomgyong*, Sanskrit: *Avatamsaka Sutra*), an influential text of the Mahayana tradition on various topics such as the Bodhisattva path, the powers of meditation and the equality of all things in karma. Korea, *c.* 1400.
British Library, Or.7377

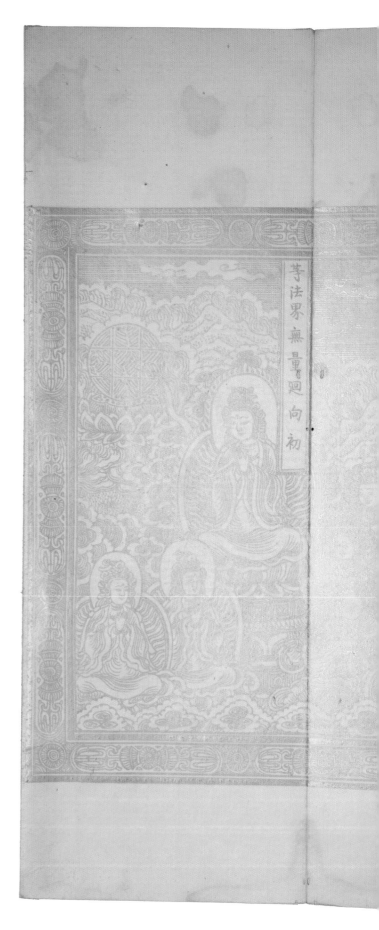

大方廣佛華嚴經卷第三十二周

Korea is also known for magnificent hand-copied Buddhist *sutras* of the Koryo dynasty done in gold pigment upon paper dyed with indigo to a deep blue-black colour. These sumptuous manuscripts were carefully copied under supervision at temples where monk-scribes, papermakers, editors and artists trained to paint the conventional frontispiece scenes, which were set before each text, gathered to copy out the holy texts.

Between the eleventh and fourteenth centuries, the Korean peninsula was invaded a number of times from the north, not to mention the persistent raids mounted by pirates all around the coast. Both at a personal level and for the Korean nation, the Buddha's protection was regarded as a real and necessary support in pursuit of a safe and virtuous life. The great monasteries of the land performed rituals designed to protect the country from danger; Buddhist believers commissioned *sutras* and holy images that would accrue benefit for the souls of parents and other relatives. Sacred texts were so precious that travellers would set out on the dangerous journey to China and beyond to locate and acquire the parts of the *Tripitaka* that were lacking. The monk Uich'on (1055–1101), fourth son of King Munjong, travelled to China to collect Buddhist books and compiled a supplement to the *Tripitaka*, *Sok Changgyong*.

As in China, woodblock printing was the preferred way of making multiple copies of Buddhist texts. The Song Chinese *Tripitaka* of 971 was the model for the first Korean *Tripitaka*, made between 1011 and 1087. When the woodblocks that were used to print it were destroyed during Mongol invasions of the early thirteenth century, a second set was produced between 1236 and 1251. The blocks of that second cutting, currently numbering about 81,000, have given this *Tripitaka* its traditional Korean name, *P'alman Taejanggyong*, the *Tripitaka of Eighty Thousand*. Today, they are still carefully stored at Haein Temple in a mountainous area of South Korea in a remarkable fifteenth-century building, which has preserved the blocks successfully for over 500 years. The *Tripitaka Koreana* in its secluded storehouse has been designated a site of world heritage by UNESCO.

As well as large-scale collections of the scriptures, individual books of sermons, philosophical teachings of monks, stories of Buddhist saints, prayers and incantations were also published. One of the outstanding Koryo Buddhist texts is the apparently modest volume of *Essentials of Buddha's Teachings Recorded by the Monk Paegun*, a collection of hymns and poems printed using metal movable type at a temple in the city of Cheongju in 1377. This date, verified from the colophon, which also names the printers and the sponsor, means that the *Essentials* comprise the world's earliest book printed using metal movable type. Korea's outstanding catalogue of printing accomplishments in medieval times was stimulated and driven by the pious impulse to circulate and duplicate holy texts.

After the Koryo dynasty, Korea went through a period when Buddhism no longer occupied its former role as the nation-protecting religion. With the shift of the Choson kings to a more universal practice of Confucian morality throughout the country, Buddhist monasteries and scriptoria continued to influence people at every level of society, but lost wealth and influence in comparison to their earlier pre-eminent position. During the fifteenth century, a writing system for the Korean language was devised and introduced. Known today as 'Hangul' ('Korean writing'), the new syllabary was put to use in various compositions of the time, including a small number of Buddhist texts. 'Song of the Moon on a Thousand Rivers'/'Worin Cheongang Chigok' was written by King Sejong (r. 1418–1450) in 1447 to praise the Buddha and pray for the happiness of his late queen.

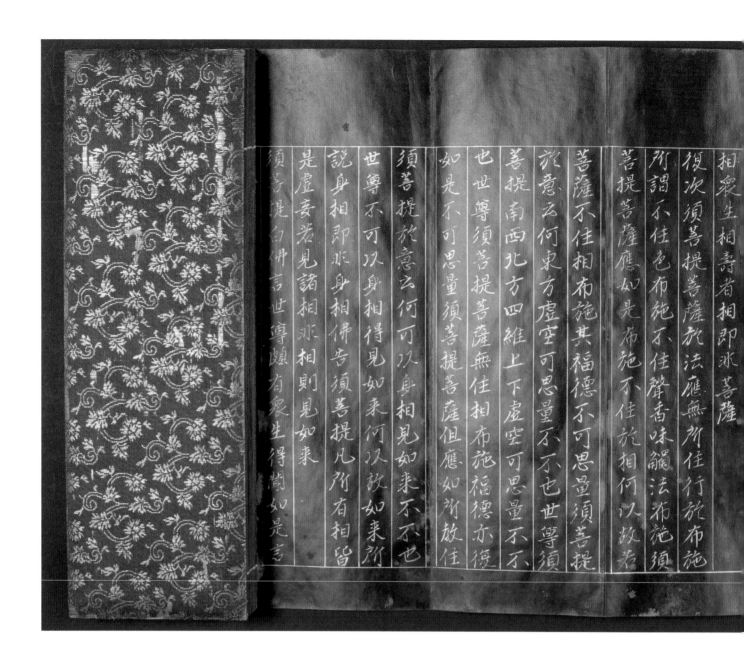

相眾生相壽者相即非菩薩

復次須菩提菩薩於法應無所住行於布施

所謂不住色布施不住聲香味觸法布施須

菩提菩薩應如是布施不住於相何以故若

菩薩不住相布施其福德不可思量須菩提

於意云何東方虛空可思量不不也世尊須

菩提南西北方四維上下虛空可思量不不

也世尊須菩提菩薩無住相布施福德亦復

如是不可思量須菩提菩薩俱應如所教住

須菩提於意云何可以身相見如來不不也

世尊不可以身相得見如來何以故如來所

說身相即非身相佛告須菩提凡所有相皆

是虛妄若見諸相非相則見如來

說言世尊頗有眾生得聞如是言

須菩提是白佛言

Korean version of the *Diamond Sutra of the Perfection of Wisdom* (Sanskrit: *Vajracchedika Prajnaparamita Sutra*), a key Mahayana text emphasizing the practices of non-attachment and non-abiding. Korea, 18th century.

British Library, Or.15263

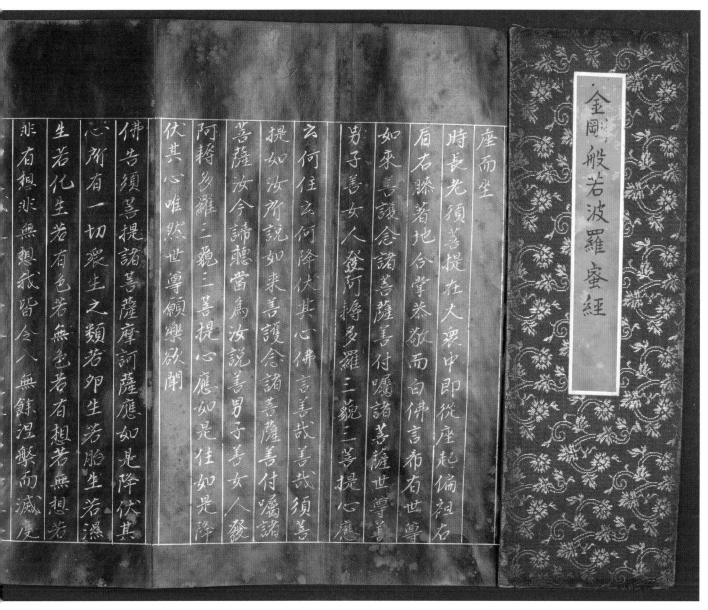

非有想非無想我皆令入無餘涅槃而滅度

生若化生若有色若無色若有想若無想若

心所有一切眾生之類若卵生若胎生若濕

佛告須菩提諸菩薩摩訶薩應如是降伏其

伏其心唯然世尊願樂欲聞

阿耨多羅三藐三菩提心應如是住如是降

菩薩汝今諦聽當為汝說善男子善女人發

提如汝所說如來善護念諸菩薩善付囑諸

云何住云何降伏其心佛言善哉善哉須菩

男子善女人發阿耨多羅三藐三菩提心應

如來善護念諸菩薩善付囑諸菩薩世尊善

肩右膝著地合掌恭敬而白佛言希有世尊

時長老須菩提在大眾中即從座起偏袒右

座而坐

RIGHT: Wooden printing blocks for the Korean *Tripitaka* at Haein temple, a UNESCO World Heritage Site.

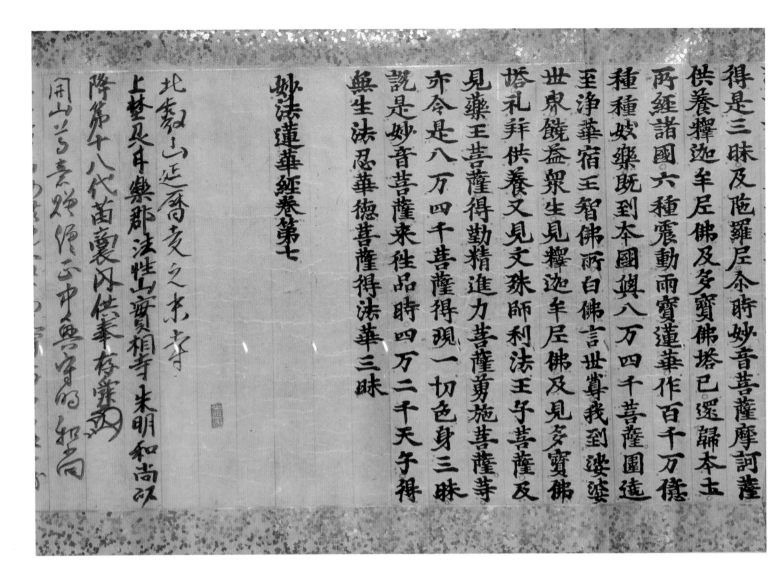

Myoho rengekyo, the Japanese version of the *Lotus Sutra* (Sanskrit: *Saddharmapundarika Sutra*), copied on a paper scroll with gold decorations. Japan, *c.* 1240–1480.
British Library, Or.64.b.35

Japan

The extraordinary effect of Buddha's teaching in early Japan can scarcely be measured unless one imagines a country with an externally derived culture of writing and books. Japan's early literature and book production derives entirely from China. From the earliest times until the coming of internationalism in the nineteenth century, Japanese Buddhist texts and scholarship were founded upon the Chinese language and Chinese traditions. The Buddha's teachings having travelled by land and sea into China by about the third century CE, the practice of copying *sutras* took root and spread across China, Korea and Japan. The earliest surviving manuscript in Japan is a *Lotus Sutra* from the early seventh century, thought by some scholars to be composed by Prince Shotoku (573–621). Like other Buddhist texts from Japan, it is in the Chinese language, the lingua franca of Buddhism in East Asia.

The earliest printed Buddhist documents in Japan are the remarkable *Hyakumanto darani/One Million Pagoda Dharani* (opposite). Four small-format texts were printed on hemp paper, about 5 centimetres wide and of varying length, between 764 and 770, from *Vimalanirbhasa Sutra*, in various forms and placed inside miniature wooden pagodas for distribution to monasteries in western Japan. In ordering the printing of the charms and their distribution to the temples, Empress Shotoku (718–

770) gave thanks for the defeat of a rebellion against her court in 764. It was believed that reproducing a *dharani* was an effective means of accumulating religious merit. Often known as the *Million Charms* (historical records state that one million were produced), the Empress Shotoku's *dharani* and their pagodas have survived in large numbers, indicating that a very large number, even if not one million, were distributed.

In the Heian period, 794–1185, Buddhist *sutras* and other doctrinal texts were printed from woodblocks at the capital, Nara, and later the practice of printing Buddhist texts spread to other regions. In 983, the Emperor of China, Taizong, presented a copy of the *Kaibao Tripitaka* to a Japanese monk, Chonen. Texts of the esoteric and meditation (Zen) schools were also printed at the temples maintained by these sects. Because all these works were in Chinese – and had been translated from Sanskrit – a high level of education was necessary for readers. In the history of printing and book production in Japan, it is Buddhist works that predominate. Such was the pre-eminence of Buddhist temples in the history of printing in Japan that secular works were printed as well as Buddhist texts in the major temples of the Kamakura period, 1185–1333. The domination of Buddhist temples as printing centres endured well into the Tokugawa or Edo period (1603–1867) and persisted after the remarkable short-lived introduction of movable-type printing technology of 1600–1650. This innovation in book production is associated both with the Hideyoshi invasions of the 1590s, when the warlord Hideyoshi Toyotomi brought back printing equipment after his unsuccessful military exploits on the Korean peninsula, and with the Jesuit missionaries who brought a printing press to Japan around 1590. The Jesuit press issued thirty complete works before a strict anti-Christian policy closed down its working.

A feature of Buddhist books in Japan is the ongoing practice of producing finely illustrated manuscript copies of the holy texts. In part, this can be attributed to the believer's pursuit of virtue and merit, and in part to a thirst for holy texts, in some cases based on copies collected by itinerant monks who travelled to China for the purpose.

Notable Buddhist printing enterprises of the Edo period include a movable-type *Tripitaka* printed between 1637 and 1648 at Kan'ei Temple by the Monk Tenkai and a woodblock-printed *Tripitaka* of 1669–1681 by the monk Tetsugen of Kyoto. In the twentieth century, the *Taisho Tripitaka*, compiled and published in Tokyo between 1924 and 1934, became the de facto standard used by scholars of East Asian Buddhism to standardize references to texts and versions. The vast enterprise of transferring the sacred texts of Buddhism into Chinese was already a staggering achievement, and the additional project of typesetting, printing and distributing (and later digitizing) all these texts is recognized as a monumental achievement in the global history of transferring knowledge and wisdom.[4]

The *One Million Pagoda Dharani* (Japanese: *Hyakumanto darani*) are one of the oldest examples of printing in Japan, commissioned between 764 and 770 by the Empress Shotoku as an act of atonement and reconciliation following the suppression of the Emi Rebellion led by Fujiwara no Nakamaro in 764. They contain the Japanese versions of four short texts from the *Vimalanirbhasa Sutra*.

British Library, Or.81.c.31 (pagoda) and Or.78.a.11 (scroll)

けいへんらたし
にもかい
てらま事を
かいりしみく
をよ
ふみを
なひ

そのかなりの
うちを
ほうてに
あくせくとて
まいる
いとし
これを
みせたまへ

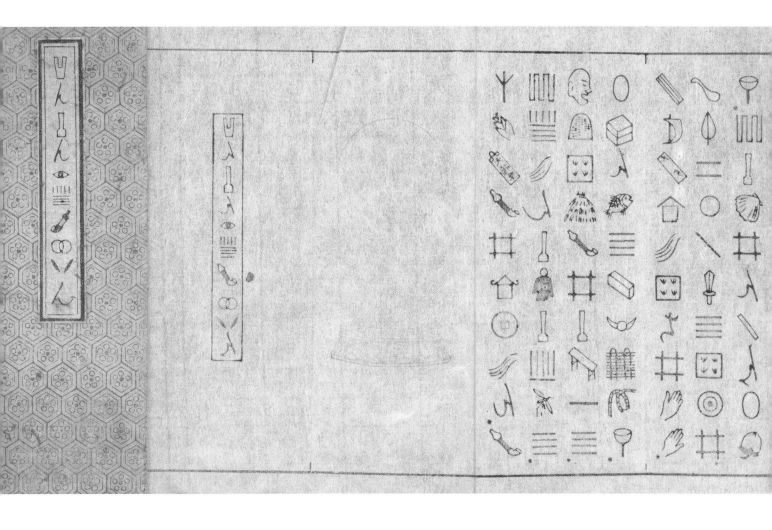

The Global Era

In the modern era of mass communication, the Buddha's teachings have travelled beyond Asia, reaching every corner of the globe. Starting with *The Sacred Books of the East*, a fifty-volume set of English translations of Asian religious writings, edited by Max Müller and published by Oxford University Press between 1879 and 1910, holy texts from Asia began to enter the libraries of scholars and theologists in an increasingly systematic manner. A ground-breaking organization in the study of Buddhist scriptures was the Pali Text Society, founded in 1881 by T.W. Rhys Davids 'to foster and promote the study of Pali texts'. It continues to publish Pali texts in roman characters, translations into English and books for students of Pali. Most of the classical texts and commentaries have now been edited and many works translated into English. The Fragile Palm Leaves Project, supported by

the Society, supports the conservation and identification of Southeast Asian manuscripts. In 2019, the Society's website listed five projects, encompassing translation, dictionary publication and archival papers, supported by the Pali Text Society. Japan has also been an important centre for Buddhist studies of different schools, including translation programmes, research resources and of course the *Taisho Tripitaka*, the widely used standard version of the Sino-Japanese Buddhist Canon.

Outside the academic and scholarly realm, Buddhists across the globe are active in meetings, in inter-faith dialogue, and in a range of charitable foundations broadly aiming to further the values and beliefs of their faith. Since the subtle and complex differences of approach that have developed in different schools of Buddhism can appear daunting to the interested person seeking a teacher to guide a journey of exploration of the ideas and values of Buddhism, publishers

Mekurakyo, a chanting book for illiterate people using pictures
and symbols for the pronunciation of a Sanskrit chanting text.
Japan, 20th century.

of books and digital resources play an important part in opening up the Buddha's insights and sermons to new readers, in Asia and beyond. Pan-Buddhist societies have been founded, which aim to teach the Buddha's truths in a mutually respectful atmosphere. The Network of Buddhist Organisations of the United Kingdom, for example, seeks 'to advance Buddhism in the UK for the benefit of the public through the holding of meetings, lectures, producing and/or disseminating literature and news on Buddhism, to inform and enlighten others about Buddhism' and lists fifteen institutions, geographically spread over the country and affiliated to different Buddhist schools, as members. Similar groups and networks exist around the world, all requiring texts and digital resources to enable their teachers and students to advance in the practice of Buddhism.

Book publishers of Buddhist works in the Western world have taken forward the project of making the voluminous literature of the Theravada, Vajrayana, Mahayana and Meditation schools available, using all the commercial, scholarly and distribution models and tools familiar to publishers, booksellers and readers in the twenty-first century. As well as large-scale, active centres including

Shambhala Publishing, working out of Denver, Colorado, university presses in the United States and United Kingdom have made important contributions to the ongoing project of translating Buddhist texts. These include Columbia, the publisher of many of Burton Watson's translations; University of Hawai'i Press's Classics of East Asian Buddhism series; and the Clay Sanskrit Library, which works with New York University Press and issues parallel text translations of Sanskrit works.

Perhaps most important in assessing the contribution of books to the exchange of Buddhist ideas is the way serious believers read and study. Monks, nuns and lay people alike read the texts repeatedly. They chant or receive the holy words, sometimes in very long passages. Parts of *sutras* are memorized. After a text has been 'mastered' by a student, he or she may return to it at a later stage for further exploration. These study habits are typical of the immersive manner of reading and studying that can bring strong foundations of knowledge and practice to Buddhist believers. The immense corpus of Buddhist literature fulfils its principal purpose as an aid for those who set out on the path to enlightenment, in modern times as throughout its history.

Notes

1   Thomas Cleary, trans., *The Flower Ornament Scripture: A Translation of the Avatamsaka Sutra* (Boston and London: Shambhala, 1993).

2   Online at http://www.shanghaimuseum.net/en/special/special_readmore.jsp?id=229; https://www.info.gov.hk/gia/general/201711/28/P2017112700800.htm.

3   Pratapaditya Pal and Julia Meech-Pekarik, *Buddhist Book Illuminations* (New York: Ravi Kumar, 1988), p. 31.

4   Online at https://www.thebuddhistsociety.org/page/scriptures-texts, with a clear outline of the sequence of translation projects.

From the Translator's Workshop

Sam van Schaik

The act of translation has been key to the spread of Buddhism across Asia and now the world. Even within India, Buddhist scriptures were translated into Sanskrit and Pali. After that, as Buddhism moved beyond India, major translation efforts allowed its assimilation into China, Tibet and beyond. Some of the most important routes for the transmission of Buddhism were the ancient trade routes popularly known as the Silk Road. The town of Dunhuang, situated at a confluence of trade routes that cross the Taklamakan Desert, was a trade hub and an important Buddhist site. Along with many Buddhist monasteries, the town boasted a magnificent complex of cave temples nearby. It was in one of these temples that a cache of ancient manuscripts was discovered at the beginning of the twentieth century, some of which are now at the British Library.

Among the manuscripts from Dunhuang, we find evidence of a translation workshop, where monks translated Chinese Buddhist scriptures into the Tibetan language. Buddhists had been translating texts into Chinese since the second century CE, and Tibet only fully embraced Buddhism in the eighth century, so it was natural that Tibetans would look to China, as well as India, for the Buddhist scriptures. Ultimately it was India, the original home of Buddhism, that became the source of the vast majority of Tibetan Buddhist scriptures. But some scriptures were translated from Chinese as well, and Dunhuang was one of the major sources of these translations.

Much of the translation activity at Dunhuang was down to a single monk called Facheng who worked there during the early ninth century. Facheng began as a scribe and was later the head of a scriptorium producing *sutras* for the Tibetan emperor. The translation work for which he is famous came at the end of the Tibetan Empire, commissioned by the final emperors. Some of Facheng's translations can still be found in the Tibetan Buddhist Canon, including his translation of the *Lankavatara Sutra* from Chinese. This text is found in the Canon immediately after the translation of the *Lankavatara Sutra* from Sanskrit.

Since Facheng lived and worked in Dunhuang, it is not surprising that we find manuscripts from here that shed light on his work. Along with his translations, Facheng wrote several short introductions to key concepts in Buddhism, in both Chinese and Tibetan, one of which was requested by the Tibetan emperor. Thus, he seems to have been well respected as a teacher as well as a translator. One of the most interesting manuscripts, which sheds light on the process of translation itself, is shown here. This is a concertina-format manuscript, containing a Chinese commentary on the *Lankavatara Sutra*. In the usual format of Buddhist commentaries, the text includes the full *sutra* with line-by-line explanations. In between the vertical lines of Chinese characters, somebody has written the Tibetan translation of the *sutra*.

This is a truly hybrid manuscript. The concertina format can be seen as a combination of the scroll with the *pothi*, the oblong loose-leaf format derived from Indian palm leaf manuscripts. When the Chinese characters are read in vertical format, it works like a scroll; when the Tibetan letters are read in the horizontal direction, it reads like a *pothi*. There is even a string hole through each page, a feature of *pothi* manuscripts that is entirely unnecessary in a concertina, and seems to be here purely as a signifier of the *pothi* format.

This manuscript was probably not originally meant to be bilingual, however, as there is little space for the Tibetan writing, which is squeezed in between the lines of Chinese. Whoever wrote the Tibetan did so carefully, with marks to show exactly what part of the Chinese text it corresponded to. In a very light red/yellow ink, difficult to see at first glance, the first few Tibetan letters of the alphabet denote each sentence in a paragraph, with each new paragraph beginning with *ka*, the first letter of the Tibetan alphabet.

Who would have annotated the manuscript in this way, and for what purpose? It is likely that this manuscript was used as an aid to Facheng's translation of the *Lankavatara Sutra* into Chinese. This is supported by the colophon to the canonical translation, which says, 'At the order of the divine emperor [of Tibet], and in coordination with the commentary by Wenhui, the translator monk Facheng made and edited this translation.' The commentary by Wenhui mentioned here was lost before the discovery of the Dunhuang manuscripts, and it is none other than the one found in this British Library manuscript.

So, someone carefully wrote the existing Tibetan translation of the *Lankavatara Sutra* (from Sanskrit) between the lines of Wenhui's commentary. It could be a study aid, and it would also have been very useful to a translator who was working on a new translation of the *Lankavatara Sutra* from the Chinese. Add to this the fact that Facheng worked at Dunhuang, and we have other manuscripts associated with him, and it seems likely that he could have used this very manuscript to make his own translation of the *sutra*.

This is a rare example of a manuscript from a Buddhist translation workshop and it is a small part of one of the biggest translation projects ever undertaken:

the translation of the whole of the Buddhist Canon into Tibetan. Yet it is also a very personal book, annotated for a translator's work. It also shows us how Buddhism forged connections across Asia. The city of Dunhuang stands on the Silk Road, which ran east–west from China to Europe, also south through Tibet and India. Buddhism travelled these routes and became established in new cultures through the process of translation. Each act of translation, including the one preserved in this manuscript, was also an act of connection.

Bilingual copy of the *Lankavatara Sutra* in Chinese and Tibetan. Dunhuang, China, 9th or 10th century.

British Library, Or.8210/S.5603, ff. 90–95

Bhutan's Sacred Texts

Karma Phuntsho

Ananda! just as you have given affection, faith and respect to me now in this incarnation, just so, Ananda, should you act after my decease toward the Perfection of Wisdom. One should know that those beings live in the presence of the Buddha who hear this Perfection of Wisdom, take this up, study, spread, repeat and write this, and who honour, revere, adore and worship this.

The Buddha

When MIT's Michael Hawley created the world's largest book, *Bhutan: A Visual Odyssey Across the Last Himalayan Kingdom*, in 2003, he perhaps did not know that there was already a tome in a remote temple in Bhutan that weighed more than his colossal 60-kilogram opus. Gangteng Monastery's volume is an illuminated manuscript of *The Eight Thousand Verses of the Perfection of Wisdom*, weighing about 80 kilograms and no less beautiful than Hawley's monumental work. Like hundreds of other texts, it was probably produced locally during the heyday of Gangteng under the second Gangteng Tulku Tenzin Legpai Dhondup (1645–1726).

The scripture, called *Gyatongpa* in short, is one of the popular religious texts in the Tibetan Buddhist world. The Bhutanese tradition traces the origin of the *Gyatongpa*, like the rest of the *Perfection of Wisdom* corpus of teachings to which it belongs, to the historical Buddha. After the Buddha's death, the text is believed to have been taken to the subterranean world of serpents (*naga*) until Nagarjuna, the second-century Indian master, brought it back to the human world. Modern scholars, however, argue that the text may actually have been composed between 100 BCE and 100 CE in southern India. Whatever its beginning, the *Gyatongpa* has ever since spread across the globe, from Mongolia to Indonesia and from Korea to the Americas. It has been translated into many dozen languages and commented on by scores of Buddhist scholars and meditation masters.

The *Gyatongpa* is a philosophical classic on the ways of perfecting wisdom, a central Mahayana practice of refining and transforming our perception of life and the world. Its main messages deal with emptiness, exploring how everything, from one's own body to the enlightenment of the Buddha, is utterly empty of real existence, and how we can eliminate the assumptions and conceptual constructions we have about people, things, life and existence. For these essential themes of wisdom and compassion, the *Gyatongpa* and other scriptures on the *Perfection of Wisdom* came to be ranked as the central doctrine of Mahayana Buddhism and hold immense religious significance.

It is thus no surprise that the *Gyatongpa* in Gangteng is produced in exquisite calligraphy, written partially in gold and silver, adorned with intricate art, embellished in extravagant silk and wood covers, and accorded a highly venerable status. 'The Gyatongpa is the most commonly decorated Buddhist scripture,' claims Karma Delek, a Tibetan manuscript specialist. Veneration of *Gyatongpa* and other *Perfection of Wisdom* texts appears also in other forms of practice. 'In the old days, only families with a complete set of *Perfection of Wisdom* scriptures can hoist a tall flag in front of their house to honour the presence of holy books. Nowadays, people hoist tall flags in front of their houses with no significance,' laments Tshewang Dargey, an Ura village elder.

But it is not just the *Gyatongpa* that deserves veneration and worship. 'Since all scriptures embody the precious teachings of the Buddha and the paths and practices which lead a person to enlightenment, the respectful treatment should be extended to all scriptures,' advises Khenpo Tshewang Sonam, an eminent Bhutanese scholar. As in the cult of the books in ancient India and China, Bhutanese people view the books as holy objects in their own right. Just as a *stupa* represents the enlightened mind of the Buddha, the books are the representation of the Buddha's speech. The books are cherished not merely as reading materials but as powerful relics. Thus, they are produced with great care to very high artistic and scribal standards and are carefully wrapped and stored in the upper sanctums of the temple space, from where they radiate blessings upon the whole environment. They are worshipped, circumambulated and prostrated to. Occasionally, they are paraded through the valley to bless the environment and protect it from natural calamities.

Books like the *Gyatongpa* are also read for both ritual and academic purposes. During the ritual readings, the monks or lay priests loudly read through the book without any attempt to understand the text. Many *Gyatongpa* editions are specifically designed and produced for this purpose and are read very frequently. Such ritual reading is usually done to accumulate merit, remedy illnesses, dispel obstacles or as a funerary rite.

In addition to the profuse ritual use, books such as the *Gyatongpa* are also seriously studied by scholars, and many are included in the monastic curriculum or used as references. To the Buddhist virtuosi, the scriptural corpuses constitute the words of the Buddha and their proper use lies in the scholarly study and practical application of the content. Reading and reflection are chief components of the Buddhist spiritual training. Rituals are merely skill methods to lead the world to the higher goal of enlightenment. Thus, the books are viewed as profound scriptures to be read and understood, and as sources of inspiration and wisdom.

The role of books, such as the *Gyatongpa*, is thus multifarious and considerable. The use of text permeates all facets of the Himalayan Buddhist life, although no single volume represents Buddhism, as the Bible and Quran do for Christianity and Islam. 'The Himalayan Buddhist culture', says Professor David Germano of Virginia University, 'is culture of the Text'. It is a culture where books are respected for more than their utilitarian and educational value as reading materials. The book, to sum up the Bhutanese 'book-view', is the Buddha (author) in written form. Some of the Buddha's last words were: 'In the last of the five hundred cycles, I shall return in the body of letters. Think of them as me; respect and honour them.' They instil a positive attitude towards books.

A monk assessing a volume of the *Gyatongpa* before digitization in the Endangered Archives Programme project at Gangteng Monastery, Bhutan, 2005.
British Library, EAP039

Searching for Surviving Buddhist Manuscripts in Siberia

Nikolai Tsyrempilov

A Russian UAZ-452, an off-road vehicle often simply nicknamed a 'tablet', stands on the icy surface of a frozen mountain river. The locals say that this is the only car that can be used in the conditions of the Eastern Sayan ridge. Off-road here means not just poor road but no road whatsoever. March is the only month when it is possible to reach far-away Soyot settlements, albeit along unsafe, half-frozen riverbeds.

The aim of this field trip to one of the most remote districts of the Republic of Buryatia (Russian Federation), taken by myself and colleagues from the Buryat State University in Ulan-Ude, was to discover a treasury of Buddhist manuscripts hidden by locals in the 1930s. The mountainous areas of Okinskii district are the home of the Soyots, an ancient Siberian people of Samoyedic stock that first experienced Turkification and then from the eighteenth century was subject to assimilation into Buryat–Mongol culture. In the nineteenth century some Soyots converted to Tibetan Buddhism and thenceforth followed this religion. Although their Buddhism blended with shamanist beliefs, they venerate Buddhist books and manuscripts in Tibetan and Mongolian.

We had learnt about the library of Buddhist manuscripts concealed in a small *obo*, or artificial stone pyramid the locals traditionally construct on top of hills and mountains, from a local school headmaster. Our previous trip to Okinskii district was fantastically fruitful: we discovered many manuscript leaves in a small cave in the Eastern Sayans. The leaves were placed in a cardboard box and covered with an old newspaper. The findings were very valuable: although most of the leaves were severely damaged by moisture, fungus and insects, some surviving manuscripts contained unique knowledge of the history of local monasteries, folk medicine, Buddhist astrology, fragments of sermons, ritual texts, Tantra manuals and canonical writings. We managed to attribute and restore twenty-five manuscripts that are now deposited in the library of the Buryat State University. Thus, as soon as we heard about another book cache, we immediately made another expedition to Okinskii district.

The establishment of Soviet power in East Siberia in 1921 did not much change the lives of common Buddhists. Just as before, they sent their children to study in the local monasteries, attended Buddhist services, received medical treatment from lamas and participated in communal rituals in order to protect their health, wellbeing and property. However, in 1927, the Soviets launched a resolute anti-religious campaign throughout the whole country. The Soviet project of a new socialist nation was incompatible with religion, which was proclaimed a harmful phenomena in full accordance with Marxist theory. Buddhism in the Soviet Union was the only organized religion that virtually ceased to exist for a few years as an institutionalized community. Thousands of lamas were arrested, imprisoned in gulags or executed. Young monks and nuns were forcefully laicized, and monasteries were demolished, shut down or adjusted to economic needs. Squads of militant atheists, with the support of local party and Komsomol cells, participated in demonstrative pogroms of the monasteries. During these pogroms, statues of Buddhas and deities were thrown outside and crushed with hammers; books were heaped and burnt to ashes. Laypeople managed to save a part of the book heritage by hiding manuscripts at home before the officials began to raid private residences. Heads of households, where they revealed religious books, were arrested and punished. People started to conceal books in the nearby forests, in the holes of trees, in caves and at far-away camps. Villagers kept a book's whereabouts secret, but over the years more people came to know about the book sites. In all cases, these sites became the objects of special veneration. Villagers still believe that each book treasury is under protection of local spirits who gave oath to guard the books for better times. But who can say when these better times will come? Even today, when Buddhism in Russia is reviving rapidly and the state is much more tolerant of religious feelings, the faithful still do not trust researchers and refuse to collaborate, fearing that the manuscripts will be relocated if their whereabouts are revealed. Being aware of this, the headmaster asked us not to tell others about the purpose of our trip.

In early March we set out from the village of Orlik, administrative centre of the Okinskii district. We were heading to a far-away Soyot camp where local herders keep their yaks and horses. The *obo* with manuscripts was located in the vicinity of the camp. After two days of travelling across desolate forest tundra and two nights' sleep in a hunters' hut we finally reached the site. Having climbed the hill and found the *obo*, we experienced great disappointment: no manuscripts and nothing except for a few religious utensils were inside. Most likely the villagers had moved the cache before our arrival. We faced the same problem before and after that case. Seventy years of the Soviet regime's opposition to religion and confiscation of Buddhist literature have not passed unnoticed. Meanwhile, thousands of manuscripts are silently kept in monastic libraries and hiding places throughout the whole of Buryatia. These manuscripts had been created by local Buddhists and keep alive memories of the unique Buddhist culture that flourished here in the eighteenth and nineteenth centuries.

In the framework of the project EAP813, 'Preserving the Book Heritage of Siberian Buddhists', our research team managed to digitize some 250 manuscripts. These books are partially in vertical Mongolian script and partially in Tibetan. In some cases, books can be bilingual. The collections contain both printed and handwritten books. The latter are especially valuable since they usually exist only in one copy. In the private collection of a simple village lama in Kizhinga village we found travel notes of a Buddhist monk who undertook a trip to Moscow and Saint Petersburg to participate in the ceremony of coronation of Tsar Nicholas II. In his notes, the monk did not simply describe the ceremony, but did it with use of ancient Indian allegories and symbols. The young Tsar is seen by him as an epic Rama, the river Neva resembles the Ganges and Saint Petersburg is portrayed as a Buddhist paradise, *Sukhavati*. In the library of Tsongol Monastery, which is situated at the Russia–Mongolia border, we discovered a rare reference book written in a Tibetan calligraphic style. The book is a calendar of Buddhist festivals with correspondences to the Russian Orthodox Christian calendar. In the rich library of Aga Monastery we uncovered a number of prophetic manuscripts. The prophecies ascribed to various Buddhist gurus and deities predicted the advent of the era of decline of religion.

In the bulk of various Buddhist philosophical treatises, *Prajnaparamita* texts, medical and astrological manuals, guidebooks for meditation and collections of Tantric *dharanis* we paid special attention to the manuscripts that can be found only in this part of the Buddhist world. We were successful in finding such books. One can only guess how many unique manuscripts still await discovery, gradually decaying in hidden places under summer heat or winter frost. How many lie in piles in maladjusted monastic treasuries?

Thanks to generous support of the British Library, a part of this book heritage of Siberian Buddhists has been digitized and made accessible for a wide circle of researchers and believers. Yet the work is far from being finished. On the contrary: it has only just begun.

Tracing the disappearing book heritage of Siberian Buddhists, Buryatia, Russian Federation, 2016.

The Qianlong Emperor's Anthology of *Dharanis* in Manchu, Chinese, Mongolian and Tibetan

Eleanor Cooper

The Qianlong emperor who commissioned this work was the fourth Qing emperor to rule over China (1735–1796) at a time of great prosperity as well as imperial expansion.

Ethnically Manchu, with their homeland to the northwest, the Qing rose to power in 1636, succeeding the Han Chinese Ming dynasty in 1644 and ruling China until 1912. They had long-established relationships with Buddhist leaders in Tibet and Mongolia and a belief in their divine right to rule as Buddhist monarchs. Under the Qianlong emperor, the territory of China reached its maximum extent, encompassing the lands of Mongolia and Tibet and reaching west into Central Asia. Some have seen Qianlong's patronage of Buddhism as a cynical move to maintain control over his Mongolian and Tibetan subjects, but he was also a devout man, receiving Buddhist instruction and performing Buddhist rituals throughout his long life.

Qianlong was a cultured and learned ruler, a prolific poet and a polyglot. Manchu was the language of the imperial court and Qianlong's native tongue but from his early childhood he received tuition in Chinese, Mongolian and Sanskrit, and as his empire took in more territories he learned Tibetan, Chagatai and Tangut.

In 1758, Qianlong ordered work to begin on an ambitious project: the compilation of an anthology of all the *dharanis* in Sanskrit from the Tibetan Buddhist Canon. These were then to be transliterated in Manchu[1], Chinese, Mongolian and Tibetan by vast numbers of translators and scholars, and presented together. Completed in 1773, the resulting work, in 82 volumes, contains more than 10,000 *dharanis* and several hundred *sutras*. Each volume, with a yellow silk cover indicating its imperial status, is around 35 centimetres in height, but stretches to several metres in width when fully extended. The paper is folded like a concertina, but not bound at the spine, allowing the reader to view two or more pages at a time. Six volumes are housed together in a firm case (*tao*) and together the sixteen cases take up around 3 metres of shelf space. As the entire work is woodblock-printed, what you see are imprints from a staggeringly large number of wooden blocks, each individually carved with the full contents of a page – in reverse.

Dharani is a contested term and difficult to define, but can be thought of as a code or mnemonic device that condenses and encapsulates the meaning of part of a *sutra*; a grasp of the *dharani* helps the practitioner to understand and remember the essence of the *sutra*. *Dharanis* may be used in written form, sometimes enclosed in Buddhist prayer wheels, which, when spun, 'recite' the written words. As effective utterances, the *dharani* must be pronounced correctly. However, some Sanskrit sounds are difficult for speakers of other languages to reproduce orally, and the same is true on the

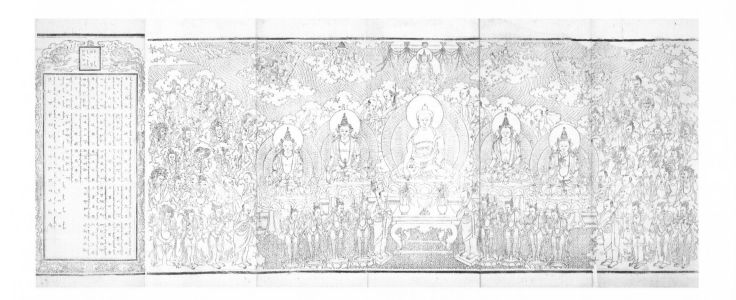

page. In order to convey the desired phonetic rendering of the Sanskrit *dharanis* in print, the Manchu and Mongolian scripts were enhanced with supplementary sets of letters and diacritics. Philological explanations and essays concerning the correct pronunciation of Sanskrit terms in the various languages are found within this vast work alongside the religious texts.

Befitting such an important religious work, the first volume begins with a large, auspicious image and a poem composed by Qianlong himself, shown here.

At the centre of the main image, the Buddha sits in *bhumisparsa mudra* (the earth-touching pose) surrounded by a large retinue of devotees, *arhats* (one who has achieved *nirvana* in Theravada Buddhism) and worshippers. The larger figures are the *pancatathagata*, a grouping of five Buddhas important in Tibetan Vajrayana Buddhism: Amitabha and Aksobhya on the left, Ratnasambhava and Amogasiddhi on the right, and Vairocana above the central Buddha. They are identified by their poses (*asanas*), hand gestures (*mudras*) and the ritual accoutrements they hold, all of which act as visual cues to their nature and power.

The poem on the left is bordered by five-toed dragons, reserved for imperial uses, chasing the flaming pearl of Buddhist wisdom. Its eighteen short verses run in parallel vertical columns from right to left, appearing in Manchu, Chinese, Mongolian and Tibetan. It is a remarkable feat of translation; despite the grammatical and structural constraints of these very different languages, the same ideas are mirrored in all four, with each exhibiting its own internal poetic devices, such as metre, rhyme and alliteration.

The harmony of yin and yang principles, mentioned in the poem, perhaps also alludes to Qianlong's desire for unity amongst the disparate peoples within his imperial realm. The propagation of Buddhist teachings is a civilizing mission, bringing light to the remotest regions. Correct recitation of the *dharanis* presented here, Qianlong assures us, will benefit all those who hear these 'heavenly', divine syllables, and bring prosperity to all. The poem expresses the more benevolent sentiments behind Qianlong's huge translation project: to bring peace, contentment, wisdom and Buddhist enlightenment to all sentient beings within his ever-expanding, multi-ethnic empire.

1   Manchu title: *Han-i araha Manju Nikan Monggo Tanggut hergen-i kamciha amba g'anjur nomun-i uheri tarni*

Anthology of *dharanis* in Manchu, Chinese, Mongolian and Tibetan. China, 1773.

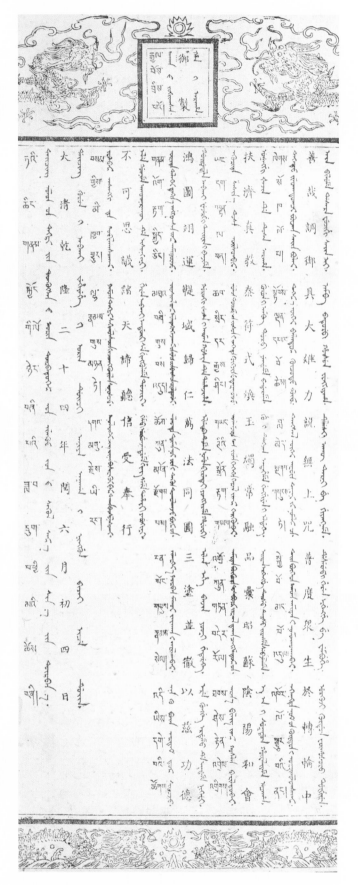

BUDDHIST PRACTICE: MINDFULNESS AND COMPASSION

Dion Peoples

The historical Buddha was born near Lumbini, situated in today's Nepal, over 2,500 years ago. The doctrines of Siddhattha Gotama, a former prince from a warrior-caste clan, would later comprise various forms of Buddhism that would spread across India and into other neighbouring regions. Buddhism has three main branches, or vehicles, for disseminating doctrine: the Theravada vehicle is the methods of the elders who have kept the tradition the same since its original days and now primarily exists in Sri Lanka, Myanmar (Burma), Thailand, Cambodia and Laos; the greater vehicle, known as the Mahayana, is present in Japan, Korea, China and other areas under Chinese influence; Vajrayana, the final vehicle, is found in and around the Tibetan Autonomous Region of modern China, just north of India. The Theravada tradition is often a simpler way of following suggested ways of living; the Mahayana path is often derivative of or an advancement on traditional ideas; Vajrayana is sometimes referred to as a quick way towards advancement in Buddhist doctrine.

The merchant class was likely the group to have spread Buddhism via the development of the ancient Silk Road; the beneficiaries of trade along this route were rich traders who also funded Buddhist monasteries. Commentary for the *Sangiti Sutta* (*Sutta Pitaka*) mentions that cloth brought into the region came from China and Sumer (Iraq). Greeks also ventured into these areas near India and interacted with Buddhist monks. There is a famous Buddhist text composed of question-and-answer-style conversations between a Greek king and a Buddhist novice monk preserved in the non-canonical Milindapanha text; the Buddha also used this format when discussing doctrinal aspects with leading Brahmins. In the years before writing was more popularized, knowledge and information was often transmitted orally, either in conversations or debates. Buddhists often debated, and the results were disseminated to students. The Vajrayana tradition is known to carry on the debate spirit, but, in Theravada lands, learning the Buddhist texts and being able to recite them is determined to be of more importance. In fact, most of the discourses of the Buddha are in the format of questions from someone, followed by the remarks of the Buddha, and a teaching usually concludes with conversion into the Buddha's dispensation.

As Buddhism took hold on the Indian subcontinent, emperors and kings would adhere to certain aspects of Buddhist doctrine and urge their populations to follow these selected principles from the numerous ideas that Buddhists propagated. Emperor Ashoka erected pillar-edicts in distant places, urging people within his extensive empire to follow his own selection of teachings that he determined to be of importance. At this stage in history, Buddhism was turning from a monastic institution towards an ideology for civilizing and controlling the masses. Buddhism, presented as a compassionate ideology, was used for social control, important in consolidating an empire and colonizing distant people. Regulating society through a system of knowledge highlighting Three Worlds – the bad, the current and the good – was advocated, painted on temple walls and drawn in palm leaf manuscripts. The Three Worlds comprise: the world of desire, which humans inhabit; the world of form, that of lesser deities; and the world of formlessness, that of higher deities. The first book recognized as being in the Thai language is a manual depicting these Three Worlds (the *Traibhumikatha*), which collects ideas from various places in the Buddhist canonical texts, the *Tipitaka* (the *Suttanta Pitaka*, *Vinaya Pitaka* and *Abhidhamma Pitaka*). The main principle for governing or controlling people's behaviour is to emphasize *kamma* (*karma*) as a method of civilizing populations. Do good, speak good and think good, and good results should accrue for the practitioner; perform with greed, hatred or delusion, and states of loss are to be expected. To practise Buddhism means one should be more mindful of one's personal behaviour and more compassionate towards others.

The Spread of Buddhist Doctrine

In order to understand the development of Buddhist practice, one must first consider the spread of Buddhist doctrine, as mindfulness of the doctrine is integral for practising Buddhists. Buddhist doctrine, in a more technical sense, was often spread through missionary trips abroad or within the large universities that received thousands of students in ancient times. Buddhists from overseas often aimed to attend these centres for Buddhist learning. Many travelling Chinese monk-pilgrims chronicled their experiences in Takkasila, Nalanda and other Indian areas of importance for institutional learning. They wrote in-depth accounts of their encounters within these monastic universities as well as the land of the Buddha's birth, enlightenment and death, and any areas honoured with relic-housing *stupas*. The accounts included ceremonies, rituals, chants and other Buddhist practices, and authors brought these ideas and sacred texts back into China to better develop traditions more holistically. It is from these translated accounts that we can trace changes in what has been chanted by Buddhists over the years or what has comprised the system of doctrinal learning within Buddhist centres.

Doctrinal learning, following the demise of the sermon-giving Buddha, occurred orally until three baskets of literature were formulated into the *Tipitaka*. Most of the Buddha's teachings, the actual dialogue sermons, are found in the volumes of the *Suttanta Pitaka*, most of the monastic regulations are found in the *Vinaya Pitaka*, and the higher philosophical ideas on how the mind works are found in the *Abhidhamma Pitaka*. One lesson highlighting the Buddha's summarized teachings can be found within the *Sangiti Sutta*; a sermon sanctioned by the Buddha is found in the *Digha Nikaya* of the *Suttanta Pitaka*. While most other global religions usually just have a single holy book, Buddhism has a set of scriptures, and there has been no official 'Common Buddhist Text' consisting of guidance and insight from the Buddha until recently. In the Theravada Buddhist tradition within Thailand there are forty-five volumes of texts for Buddhists to consider; other Buddhist traditions have a collection of texts that is even more voluminous. Part of Buddhist practice involves mindfully knowing the Buddhist texts and actualizing Buddhist principles compassionately in daily life.

Getting back to the importance of the *Sangiti Sutta*, the text narrates that one day the Buddha was feeling tired and asked his most prominent disciple, Sariputta, to give the evening's teaching. After agreeing, Sariputta delivered the *Sangiti Sutta*, which was sanctioned by the Buddha at the end of the lesson as the teaching for monks to learn and recite. Essentially, it was numerically formulated as a text for Buddhist education, since it contains 230 important doctrinal aspects that need to be recollected by monastics. Buddhism at this stage was a very important intellectual tradition and the political elite also found a multitude of Buddhist doctrines to be important. Kings issued edicts on doctrine, yet these compromised Buddhist tradition by picking one idea over another instead of comprehending everything, seemingly so that common people could feel better about themselves or acquire a summarized or condensed, easy-to-learn knowledge. Buddhism shifted from being a system of learning to a system of mainstream culture.

Doctrinally important discourses such as the *Sangiti Sutta* were contemplated by the disciples of the Buddha and later formulated into matrices, which classify *dhamma* (*dharma*; one's duty, the right way of living), included in the *Abhidhamma Pitaka*. The *Sangiti Sutta* was of specialized importance because once these disciples learnt doctrine they could create skeleton matrices for the many Buddhist texts that emerged over the next few centuries. This had an influence over the *Abhidhamma* material, which comprises higher doctrinal principles that often pertain to the inner workings of the mind. When the discourse is closely examined and it is conceived how it can be utilized and applied, meditation schemes can be contrived and practised. Buddhism has been able to evolve and maintain its orthodoxy. People continue to travel into Theravada Buddhist regions and India to discover more original forms of Buddhism and make continued enquiries into Buddhist wisdom. In this way, Buddhist practice has changed from a culture of intellectual monastics, centred around mindfulness, to a culture of compassion for society.

I-Tsing (Yijing) was one traveller who made a pilgrimage from China. In his meanderings to acquire higher knowledge, he visited many important learning centres to discover authentic Buddhist practices from places close to the source of the original teachings. I-Tsing, when looking into monastic affairs and

Bilingual edict by the 6th Panchen Lama Lobsang Palden Yeshe (Tibetan: Blo-bzang Gpal-Idan Ye-shes, 1738–1780) in Tibetan with interlinear translation in Manchu. It is a document authorizing the travels of a monk within and beyond Tibet. Tibet, 18th century.

British Library, Or.14067

ceremonies, noted that there was a common reading of a *sutta* followed by praise for the Buddha, the *dhamma* and the *sangha* (the monastic community) – all together known as the Triple Gem – and then another short discourse after which some prayers for merit were performed. Already, the *Sangiti Sutta*, once recollected and used for the skeleton of *Abhidhamma* texts, was no longer being utilized for the intended original purpose due to the urging of the political elite who promoted their vision for society distinctly from how the textual tradition designs itself. The *Mahavamsa* of Sri Lanka (an epic poem in Pali) promotes only a short selection of discourses, and modern temples only use a short chant edited as recently as the middle of the nineteenth century in Thailand. Used in morning and evening chanting ceremonies, as heard in Buddhist temples in Theravada nations, this is known as Tam Wat Chao or Tam Wat Yen. Buddhist disciples in monastic training only learn basic principles to prepare them for living a life in monastic robes, some basic ideas to learn while they remain in the robes and, later, more ideas to prepare them for re-entry into common lay society after being ordained for one rainy season (Vassa), usually before getting married. Here again we see Buddhist practice as a transformation from mindfulness into compassion.

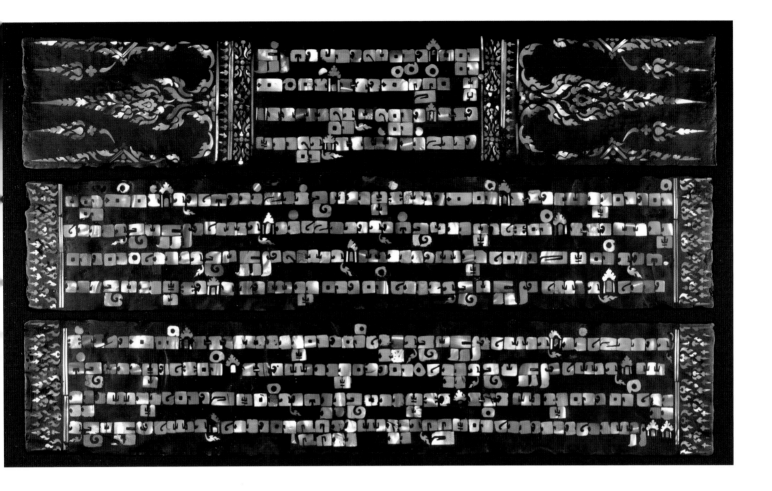

OPPOSITE: Copy of the *Yojana-pathama-samantapasadika*, Nanakitti's commentary on Buddhaghosa's commentary on the *Vinaya Pitaka*, thought to have been commissioned by a queen of Siam as a royal gift. Bangkok, Central Thailand, *c.* 1824–1910.
British Library, Or.5107

ABOVE: Fragment of an ordination text for monks (Pali: *Kammavaca*) in mother-of-pearl inlay, which is recited at the ordination ceremony of monks. Burma, 18th century.
British Library, Add. MS 23939

Buddhism, when used as a form of social control, is in danger of losing its original characteristics because of the manipulation of sponsors advocating for principles that they themselves urge to be important rather than what the tradition asserts as key elements. There are new sects of Buddhism guaranteeing people a place in heaven if their donations are high enough to benefit the temple. Buddhism, formerly, was a system set up to support those who renunciated the world; now the commercialization of temple activities often appears to support capitalist ambitions. Buddhism today emphasizes doing good, refraining from speaking negatively, and trying to be happy while dealing with the forces of globalization and expansion of one's temple propaganda. It is rare to find any emphasis on Buddhist teachings, probably because many people no longer follow the texts; rather, people follow the divergent methods of temple leaders who sometimes act in their own self-interest. Buddhist practice, though, is supposed to be about mindfulness and compassion; while people are encouraged to acquire Buddhist knowledge for themselves, they should also show compassion by donating to temple projects that benefit the entire community.

Monasticism

Originally, Buddhism was an intellectually powerful system that turned some monasteries into important centres for learning wherever Buddhism took root, as we can see throughout Asia. Today, monastics, male and female, can be seen in modern universities studying secular subjects that are useful to bring back into the monastery: advertising, marketing, business, management or religious studies. They learn other subjects useful for their careers inside the monastery and possibly also for later life, in the event they decide to disrobe and utilize their acquired skills in a salaried position for civil society. Buddhism has transformed from a system for world renouncers into another social sphere controlled by governments. In some Buddhist cultures, entry into the monkhood is for life; for others, it is a personal decision and the ordained can come and go as they please.

Today, Buddhism continues to be globally important. It is a fulfilling lifestyle for millions of people. Within Buddhist cultures many people wake up early and prepare a fresh meal to offer to monks wandering the city streets and rural paths in the early morning in search of almsfood. A family member may go to the market and buy a prepared meal to offer to monks conveniently venturing into these public areas.

Monks themselves may wake up around 4:00am or 4:30am, shower and re-robe themselves, and walk into the temple for morning chanting with the *sangha*. The time for communal chanting can differ from temple to temple, rural or urban. Afterwards, in Theravada Buddhist culture, some will go into the residential areas in search of their almsfood for the day; others may await transportation to an offered meal at a business or other sanctioned function. If going on almsround independently, a monk can eat what he acquires alone, or partake in a common meal, during which almsfood individually acquired is shared collectively among the other members of the *sangha*, perhaps around 8:00am. Usually, small groups of monks will eat together. Monastic life is not so regulated in terms of doing what, when and where, but doing activities with mindfulness, discipline and compassion is needed among all individual monastics yearning for *nibbana* (*nirvana*), the mental liberation or final release from the cycle of suffering. Monks must yield to others compassionately, in the spirit of teamwork. In this sense, we can see how the mindful Buddhist practice of eating together involves compassion; the spirit of being a team member is beneficial to anyone participating for the benefit of the collective.

In Buddhist discourses from the *Tipitaka*, in the Theravada tradition and particularly in Thailand there is often a distinction between forest monks and monastery monks. Both are told to respect each other's differences because each monk has a different nature. Modern city life makes traditional means of acquiring food more difficult since many or most regular people no longer actively give daily alms because of the demands of career employment. People with time on their hands are often more available to offer alms, or they offer alms on special holidays. Housewives or retirees are generally those participating in Buddhist events, while working people often do not have time, so merit-sharing activities are determined to be culturally important. In a common household, the working family member's salary often provides for the food that the alms donor offers to the ordained Buddhist seeking almsfood. Some monks never go on almsround: instead

Procession at the opening of the Manuscript Preservation Centre at Vat Sainyaphum, Savannakhet, 2004. Manuscripts are carried on silver offering bowls that are also used to make offerings to the Buddhist temple.

they accept food offered by lay followers within daily temple merit-making activities.

Monetary donations can also cover temple construction projects and repairs, gas and maintenance fees for vehicles along with a salary for the driver, seminars and meditation retreats, and other sanctioned and sponsored social activities. In pre-modern times, temples were the centre of village life; monks were considered the wise and intellectual elite. Modern societies have become secularized and evolved away from traditional activities; modern Buddhists struggle to maintain the links between temple importance and household life. To practise Buddhism involves mindfulness of what is occurring in society and to compassionately react to the experiences of others.

Monks now employ themselves within the temple since modern culture condemns slavery, while lay-people have always volunteered to do certain works in the monastery. Families also sent boys to live there as attendants and helpers of the monks, though this is far from slavery: they were not owned by the monastery. The relationship was more like that found in a children's home, where the young were looked after, fed and educated in return for doing some work. Following the meal and cleaning of the almsbowl, monks can either engage in meditation or cleaning of the temple, unless the abbot has some duty for the monks to perform, such as a construction project or travelling in a vehicle to perform in a chanting ceremony, or teaching courses in schoolrooms and universities. Most monks are one-meal-per-day eaters; others decide to eat twice, but before noon. Monastic discipline suggests that monks eat only once before noon, and only something like tea is consumed in the afternoon to ease light-headedness after a day of cleaning or sweeping. Most contemporary people cannot adjust to this regime, and many new monks lose a lot of weight after they undertake this rigorous diet of eating once a day while performing labour chores. Sometimes medical advice urges laypeople to follow such a diet, along with the exercises of walking, cleaning and meditation. Again, after the meal, monks clean their utensils and almsbowl, and later clean common areas. Monks dwelling in forests or caves can then perform meditation; monks in the cities may attend to their doctrinal studies. Many temples in the forest or rural areas have paths suitable for walking meditation. Sitting meditations can be performed alone in one's cell room or in group settings in the temple or meditation pavilion. As we can see, being a Buddhist practitioner involves a higher level of both mindfulness and compassion towards each other, because everyone is suffering equally while trying to attain liberation from defiling characteristics – greed, hatred and delusion – that spoil the purity of the mind.

Meditation

There is much to contemplate for the practising Buddhist. Strictly pertaining to types of meditation, there are those focused on colours, on attributes of the Buddha, on conditions of bodily disgust, on the breath, on feelings within the body, on thoughts occurring in the mind, on aspects of a deity's radiance, and on other ways to generate positive attributes conducive towards purification of the mind. The aim is to lead a person towards enlightenment, the final liberation known as *nibbana*. In the Visuddhimagga, a famous Buddhist text and commentary on the *Tipitaka* by Buddhaghosa, some of the above meditations are within the forty types of meditation explained. Zen meditation is said to be a derivative of Chan meditation, which in turn is a derivative of Theravada *jhana* meditation, a system within traditional Buddhism that cultivates calm and is used to experience the temporary liberation of the mind. Different sects of Buddhism have varying meditation techniques due to how they have interpreted meditation material over the centuries through their cultural expressions.

Monastics can spend their free moments in the meditation technique and positions of their preference. Of the forty sanctioned types of Theravada Buddhist meditations, most monastics now only participate in calming meditations or insight meditations because finding a skilled elder to teach other methods is nearly impossible. In the evenings, monks may be called upon to chant in ceremonies over the dead bodies of villagers – the idea here is that merits that the monks acquire can transfer to the dead person and aid in a chance at a better future rebirth. Sometimes the monks receive money for their performances, although Buddhist doctrine suggests that monks should never handle money, gold or silver; however, contemporary society sees things differently because every transaction mandates a price. Money is offered by the laity as a form of charity, but also towards acquiring merit in their lives.

The urban and rural poor in Buddhist communities often perceive monkhood to be an avenue for upward social mobility. If the monks are trained in Buddhist doctrine, these ideas can be implemented into the regular society, and people hope that the society will improve and become filled with the traits of mindfulness and compassion. People continue to visit Buddhist monks for employment and business advice, discussions on health, economic wellbeing, children, care for the elderly, food, money, influence and even socio-political legitimacy – when people are photographed with Buddhist monks, the perception is that they must be good people seeking ancient and morally beneficial advice.

ម្ចាស់អាស្រោវុ ...
ភា ម្ប្លា បក្ក ...
ផ្ទៃកា កុជ្ជ័ត ...
សាំ សេន អំប្ប្រ ...

ក៏ម្ប្លា ១ សឞា ផ្ណ ...
ទុំ មជ្ឈ ឈេ ចេរ ...
ឫ ក្លួា ៕ ✤ ។
ញ្ញា សេម្ប្រ ...

នៅ ក្ងេនោ ៗ

ៗ ស្មរណាទស្ងៈ

ណិរសា៤សោ ៤

នៅ នន្ទុក្ខា

កាហេ្គៗឆ្លឆុំវិ

ំស្ញាបំលក្ហាភ្

ត្សម្ញ្ញាណាអា

 ស្ញ្ញាណាអាញ្ញន៖

Illustration in a funeral or commemoration book showing four monks chanting blessings at a wake for a deceased person in order to pass on merit for a fortunate rebirth, a practice that is alive today. Central Thailand, 19th century.

British Library, Or.13703, f. 40

Temples are also often places where the poorest people in society can come to eat after the monks have finished their meals. In this sense, temples serve as a place of wealth redistribution. Wealthy people can donate funds and foods to temples and abbots can redistribute the food or wealth towards those receiving the charity. Temples can also be havens for stray animals or animals in ill health. Some temples take in old cattle, for instance, so that the bovine can live out life without the fear of being slaughtered. Buddhism teaches that every being aims to have happiness, to live without fear.

Buddhist Art and Monasteries

The Buddhist monkhood was originally designed for people who wanted to renounce the problems of regular worldly society and follow a more righteous way of living, void of greed, hatred and delusion, conditions that inhibit mental liberation and make *nibbana* impossible. An alternative use of the monkhood is as a way to personal development, employment and even reputation. Buddhist nations often have very elaborate temple complexes that need to be maintained, and many Buddhist monks are skilled artists because maintaining their abodes and temples is a duty. Artists often paint interior temple walls with images of the Three Worlds or tales from the Buddha's life or past lives. Temple walls can often depict modern events or psychedelic images, depending on the commission, although these are usually found as sub-elements behind or to the side of the main point of the depicted scene.

Buddhist art, or statue-images of the Buddha, can be seen in many forms of media. There are sacred and obscene utilizations of the Buddha's image. Away from temples, Buddha images are marketed as souvenirs in amulet shops and Buddha statue shops; Buddhas can be

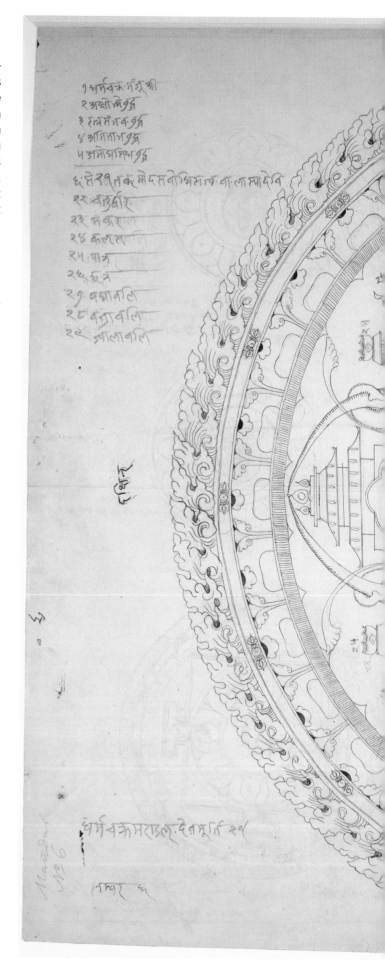

Mandala drawing on paper by Rajbir Citrakar, a Nepalese artist of the early 19th century. A mandala is a circular diagram representing the entire idealized universe of a deity, entourage, palace and surroundings. Mandalas can be used as tools for meditation or in the performance of sacred rites. Nepal, *c.* 1820–1844.
British Library, Add.Or.5334

Mandal No 6.
The Dharmachakra mandal.
copied
from a picture
on cloth
(Manjusri in the midst)
(Exoteric)

seen on clothing, in displays inside alcohol-serving bars, as objects in settings for pornography or music videos, and on shoes; 'Buddha' is also used as a colloquial term for marijuana and some people even tattoo depictions of the Buddha onto their body. There is a thriving trade of Buddhist amulets for people who practise black magic and other mystical arts, which are frowned upon doctrinally, but are socially acceptable in modern society. Additionally, a project does not qualify as 'Buddhist art' simply because it was created by a Buddhist. Some contemporary artists cheaply interpret their understanding of doctrinal issues, without actually studying or understanding the doctrine represented in their work.

However, there are instances and places where respect for the Buddha truly drives artists and talent actually illustrates what we see on temple walls: in colourful sand mandalas, in cabinet inlays with mother-of-pearl, and in the fine ancient book art we can see in the museums and libraries that preserve nationally important works and examples. Museum exhibitions are important reminders of these works, displaying statues, illustrated palm leaves, paper scrolls, silk cloth, almsbowls, temple architecture, recordings of chants, wooden print-blocks, items for altars, photographs, traditional illustrations and other related media used for expressing devotion towards Buddhism, or its potential for preserving items for the sake of generating revenue.

Some musicians also attempt to capitalize on Buddhism by using Buddhist ideas in their music. The modern era has seen several genres of music exploring Buddhist content, while popular forms of music – hip-hop, metal, punk rock and others – sometimes employ Buddhist wisdom in their song lyrics. Buddhist ideas are conveyed in film, on television, in live performances, in novels, in poetry and in other forms of disseminated information.

Buddhist temples often have elaborate altars where a Buddha statue resides along with flowers, candles, incense, fragrant woods and images of the nation's political leader. The Buddha image can be inlaid with jewels and covered in gold. When making a Buddha image, donors can offer their old jewellery or add other heavier elements into a cauldron containing melted-down metals, which will be poured into the cast for the image. In areas with ancient temples, gold Buddha statues appear headless because invading armies have retrieved the valuable metals for treasure and wealth. Today, art collectors often just have Buddha heads in their private collections; some of these are said to be stolen artefacts from the precolonial era. In the homes of Buddhist families, smaller Buddha images are found on top of altars. Some cultures dedicate an entire room of the house to the Buddha image and altar. Buddhist

families or dedicated family members will chant and perform meditation in front of the image nightly, or on important Buddhist lunar calendar observation days, when people are sanctified by observing five, eight, or ten precepts, or moral rules, according to their traditional preference. Most Buddhist families try to attend a temple on these important Buddhist holidays, which are not on single prescribed days of the week, but appear on the calendar at seemingly random intervals due to the lunar cycle. If donors are caught up in the contemporary rush of life, then temple visits are made on weekends instead of the important lunar day. Many temples are run independently, but have common chants or routines that cater to the needs of the lay society in which they serve. Some temples have unique features, so visitors may have minor adjustments to make before becoming familiar with the routine of that temple. There are only a few sects within Theravada Buddhism, so usually most activities are the same across South and Southeast Asia. In Mahayana areas, some services are more in demand than other areas of monastic life. Some cultures prefer temple visitations to only pertain to funeral services and grave shrines to ancestors. Some temples in Mahayana Buddhism are kept within biological families where the tradition of monks comes from the paternal line of the family maintaining the temple as their occupation. In some communal Mahayana cultures there is not enough income for the temple, so monks seek outside employment and maintain temples from their civil-sector salary since governments may not be interested in supporting Buddhism.

In traditional Buddhist cultures, young people (male and sometimes female, depending on the country) are afforded the opportunity to become ordained as either a novice or a monk at least once in life and they can stay in the robes for as long as they desire unless they commit some major violation of monastic discipline (killing someone, having sex, lying or stealing). Depending on the severity of other breaches, the *sangha* will meet and issue an injunction for rehabilitation. Women are not commonly afforded the opportunity to ordain fully in some modern Buddhist nations, although there are new forces, besides globalization and the ease of international travel, which can provide a chance. Many nations in Southeast Asia prohibit females from being ordained into the Buddhist 'monkhood'; being a nun is nearly impossible, yet women and their allies are doing their best to resurrect the lost tradition and make it more socially acceptable and sanctioned officially by monastic authorities. In the modern world the monastic assembly of *bhikkhuni* (the Theravada Pali word for a Buddhist nun) is lacking in Theravada Buddhist cultures. Fully ordained nuns exist as *bhiksunis* (the Mayahana Sanskrit word for a Buddhist

Painting by a native artist showing a horse-racing contest at the Kamigamo shrine at Kyoto which was founded in 678. Today the Shinto shrine is a UNESCO World Heritage Site and a destination for pilgrimage. Japan, *c.* 1690. From Engelbert Kaempfer's collection.

British Library, Add. MS 5252, no. 49

nun) in several Mahayana and Vajrayana cultures, and they are sometimes imported into Theravada nations to reintroduce the lost lineage of nuns and to assist in the move towards resurrecting this valuable asset.

Women can choose to dwell near temples and accept ten training rules in an attempt at purifying themselves towards the attainment of enlightenment, but many monks still frown upon totally accepting women as equal beings in monasticism. In Thailand, it is popular to see 'Buddhist nuns' who are not fully ordained – or, as they are called, Mae Chee: they wear white robes and follow ten rules, similar to a Buddhist male novice. However, in the broader Buddhist world, many leading figures in popular Buddhism in various cultures are indeed fully ordained Buddhist women who undertake 311 training rules. The number of rules someone undertakes does not expedite *nibbana*: it is the Buddhist practice of mindfulness and compassion, rather than social status, which is of importance towards one's final attainment. Gender identity and

Manuscript painting depicting a scene from the *Life of Buddha*
when he received a food offering from a courtesan. The scene
illustrates the importance of making merit by supporting the
monastic communities with food, which continues to be one of
the most important activities of lay Buddhists in the Theravada
tradition. Burma, 19th century.

British Library, Or.13534, ff. 18–19

sexual orientation are not issues with which Buddhist doctrine is concerned; male and female monastics are permitted eight requisites as stated in the *Patimokkha*, and they are expected not to display any features of gender identity or sexual orientation. Ordination into the *sangha* for monks or nuns is determined by biological gender. In most Buddhist traditions membership of the *sangha* is also bound to practising celibacy.

Buddhist Practice in Daily Life

Many people ponder how Buddhism is applicable to daily life, away from the monastery. To be born a human is considered a rare and fortunate circumstance due to the beneficial volitions committed in a previous life circumstance. As a young person develops and becomes more aware of consciousness, volitions become more influential upon their life. Children can be conditioned to attain high meditative results, entering into stages of calmness that lead towards the realization of the existence of *nibbana*, the highest stage of the path of purification: in other words, the extinction of one's defiling characteristics.

According to general Theravada Buddhism, when the Buddha was a ten-year-old prince, he attained a meditative one-pointedness of mind, a concentration level known as the first *jhana*, which is often categorized as the yearning to seek solitude away from sensual pleasures. The mind within the first *jhana* has the characteristic of being totally absorbed or attentively immersed in the object of focus for the meditation. A stock formula for the first *jhana* reads: 'quite secluded from sense-pleasures, secluded from unwholesome states of mind, [the Buddhist] enters and dwells in the first *jhana*, which is accompanied by applied thought and sustained thought with rapture and happiness born of seclusion'. This, from Henepola Gunaratana's book *The Path of Serenity and Insight*, reads as if someone becomes basically happy by finally being alone for enough time to contemplate something in a meditation. While the first *jhana* is not considered a difficult attainment, and Buddhist practice often involves mindfulness and compassion, it is very hard to be alone in today's world.

With diligent effort, the highest stage of attainment can occur in this very lifetime, but some alternative teachings suggest that it can occur in the next life if one decides to make a resolute decision to delay progress. Therefore it comes to be important to teach schoolchildren to learn the ways of adults and open up the possibility of a better life to enable them to create a world that empowers success. All of our actions, our volitions of body, speech and mind are fundamentally rooted in greed, hatred or delusion, but should be of non-greed, non-hatred, non-delusion. Our volitions of the past and future, as well as the present, transition from the arising, presence and fading away of thoughts. As beings, we are comprised of our form, our feelings, perceptions, mental formations and consciousness – body and mind. We are not a self, identifiable, because we are constantly evolving and are subjected to suffering. We have a conventional temporarily existing selfness, but ultimately we are comprised of various and changing aggregates. Buddhism has many teachings on how our brain and thought processes operate and advocates for an introspection that aims to better comprehend our own minds. The *Abhidhamma* texts largely depict how the mind operates and are quite accurate for premodern science.

Buddhism teaches that since we have yet to be enlightened then we must be ignorant; being born without complete knowledge, clearly we are ignorant, lacking in knowledge. Our ignorance can affect our volitions and the formation of our *kamma*; because of the volitional engagements of body, speech and mind, our consciousness arises. From our consciousness arises mind and matter. From our minds or matter arise the six Buddhist sense bases: sight, hearing, taste, touch, smell and thought. These are affected by contact with some sense-affecting object, from which feelings arise as a reaction. If the reaction is pleasurable, craving or repulsion arises. From craving, clinging arises; from clinging arises the process of transferring into an existence. From dependence on this transference arises birth; after birth, dependence on birth gives rise to aspects of suffering such as decay, sorrow, lamentation, pain, grief, despair and death. When mindfully considering these concepts our compassion for others can develop.

Buddhism advocates for and reminds everyone, wisely, that there are Four Noble Truths. There is the truth of suffering: we all experience this. There is the truth of the cause of the suffering that afflicts us, and we know that eventually our suffering will cease. Buddhism teaches that there is a path that will lead us away from our suffering. This is a major attraction for converts to Buddhism – we

Painting of Garuda, a bird-like deity in Indian mythology. In the Vajrayana tradition, it protects against diseases and poisoning. It is also one of the four dignities associated with the 'wind horse'; the other dignities are dragon, snow lion and tiger. Tibet, *c.* 1800.
British Library, Add. MS. 3050

can terminate this miserable condition. Buddhism, as we know it, is a system that was designed for people who have renounced the world. To free us from suffering there is a path that is composed of proper understanding, proper thoughts, proper speech, proper action, proper livelihood, proper effort, proper mindfulness and proper concentration: the Noble Eightfold Path (see pages 94–101). When we engage in proper modes of volitions we can improve our life circumstances and our future. Whatever we do, think or say can change our future existence.

Refraining from killing, refraining from stealing, refraining from lying, refraining from sexual misconduct and refraining from consuming intoxicants are basic Buddhist principles that can improve the condition of one's life. Following these prescriptions for ethical behaviour is said to be more effective for change in one's individual life than praying for a miracle to happen or waiting for a deity to intercede. Rather than the latter, humans are taught to think critically, through

methodologies. The Buddha offered and encouraged critical-thinking skills, for example in the famous *Kalama Sutta* of the *Anguttara Nikaya*. The extra-canonical commentary by Buddhaghosa, the *Visuddhimagga*, is written in a way that defines the characteristic, function, manifestation and proximate cause of moral virtue, mental concentrations and wisdom. In this way, important topics are examined critically through such criteria. Another Buddhist text, the *Nettippakaranam* (*Sutta Pitaka*), advocates for sixteen steps that aid in critically examining any topic, but chooses the Four Noble Truths for scrutiny. Other methods ask practitioners to learn, grasp, attend, reflect, penetrate, represent and explain the criteria they aim to interpret. Buddhism was one of the earliest and most credible mental sciences. What we cannot learn from wise monks and professors of the tradition, we can learn from translations of the original Pali texts, a few volumes of the *Tipitaka* and the various commentaries that have yet to be completely translated.

Some volumes of the Tibetan *Tanjur* (the collected translated Buddhist commentaries), which consists of 225 volumes altogether. The printing blocks were made at Narthang, Tibet, between 1741 and 1742, but the actual prints may be of a later date. The block-printed volumes were bound in Western book format at the British Museum before their transfer to the British Library in the 1970s.
British Library, 14310.a

Scriptural Texts Relevant for the Practising Buddhist

Recently, volumes from the *Tipitaka* have been published in Western languages. Maurice Walshe has translated the *Digha Nikaya*, which features thirty-four long lessons on various topics. Some of these discourses are very important for Buddhist studies. The first lesson in the text deals with sixty-two wrong views of sectarians and contains a section on discipline; the second lesson deals with the benefits of ordaining into the monkhood; the ninth lesson discusses states of consciousness; the thirteenth, three types of knowledge; and the fifteenth, dependent origination. The sixteenth lesson is a major cultural phenomenon used throughout Buddhist regions in ceremonies, as it discusses the passing away of the Buddha, detailing important things for Buddhists to consider and how to behave in the future after his demise. The twenty-second lesson is considered important for meditations for establishing mindfulness, and the twenty-seventh illustrates the creation of the world as we know it, including our societies, and is used as the reference for Buddhist forms of good governance. The thirty-first lesson deals with aspects of life established to be important for lay followers of Buddhism. The thirty-third discourse is the often-cited *Sangiti Sutta*. This offers 230 aspects of *dhamma* that need to be recollected by students of Buddhism working towards becoming learned teachers, so serving as an early and fundamental educational tool. Efforts are being made to have this discourse's commentary and sub-commentary completely translated into English, along with a fresh translation of the discourse itself. The last discourse in the text, the thirty-fourth lesson, is an alternative device for learning doctrine, but contains only a hundred points arranged into ten categories. Overall, there is no apparent method for the arrangement of these teachings in the collection of long discourses.

The *Anguttara Nikaya* has recently been translated by Bhikkhu Bodhi. The contents of this large text are arranged numerically. There are more than 9,000 discourses, but many teachings are replications or short variations on important ideas, divided by their numerical content. The text is like a magnified version of the *Sangiti Sutta*. It contains several notable discourses from the thousands available: the types of people that are considered to be fools; the *Kalama Sutta*, which is often cited for its ideology of scrutinizing everything before undertaking it as a practice; and further discourses on morality, consciousness and how to manage wealth. The *Yodhajiva Sutta* touches on nationalism as an ideology, raising the question of whether soldiers should fight for a leader who has only speculative motives while suggesting that great results occur if someone dies for their nation. Discourse on how to engage with others on friendly terms is the main theme in the *Saraniya Sutta*. There are many discourses throughout the *Tipitaka* that discuss the importance of *jhana* meditation as well as other forms of beneficial advice to put the Buddha's teachings into practice.

The *Majjhima Nikaya* is a very valuable text for comprehending Buddhist doctrines. Although these discourses are of middle length, there are 152 lessons to contemplate, making this volume perhaps the best choice if selecting just a single *Tipitaka* volume from which to learn. Many of the teachings within this volume are conducive towards learning Buddhist critical-thinking skills. The discourses discuss several aspects of the Buddha's doctrines, so describing specific lessons here would be too lengthy. Many comment on proper meditation techniques, like contemplation of breathing, contemplation of the body, lessons on the various elements of the natural world, distinctions between the wise man and the fool, analytical questioning and answering by major disciples, voidness, discerning suffering and much more. This text is invaluable and could be considered the major stand-alone volume for Buddhist principles.

The *Samyutta Nikaya* was formerly published by Wisdom Publications in two volumes but has made an appearance as a single volume with no apparent distinction. This volume makes an excellent addition to the library of Buddhist texts, but it is unlikely to be completely read due to the thousands of small discussions contained within; this is despite the importance of the criteria, touching on every aspect of the Buddha's *dhamma*. It is an invaluable reference tool and a mechanism for researching important ideas, but is probably more important for a scholar than a practitioner.

The recently published *Sutta Nipata* incorporates some commentaries and external material brought in to defend certain positions and to supplement the text. The main text itself is relatively concise, at about seventy short lessons, but the addition of the commentaries on the work is an invaluable and major contribution for Buddhist studies, providing glimpses of historical perspectives on how ancient people used to think. If twenty-first-century people see ancient life as distant, in black and white, this text provides colour to the rigidity within other texts; for example, while the main discourse might mention something that is bad, the commentary will discuss the rationality of why it is bad, alongside other examples of wrongness.

Another recently translated major work is the *Abhidhammattha Sangaha*. There is an original translation by Mahathera Narada and a modern, updated variation

Sathou Khamchan Virachitto (1920–2007), the Abbot of Vat Saen Sukharam in Luang Prabang, at the age of about thirty, practising forest meditation. From the archive at Vat Saen Sukharam, Luang Prabang, Laos, c. 1950. A film documentation is available at www.buddhist-archive.org.

Endangered Archives Programme, EAP 177/1/1, image no. 213

by Bhikkhu Bodhi, but an alternative variation was also published by the scholars R.P. Wijeratne and Rupert Gethin. This means that three variations of this general compendium of material of higher philosophical insights now exist in bookstores. Indeed, the translation is a major work for the learning of Buddhism. It discusses how the mind works and even places the reader within Buddhist cosmology issues. It suggests how some mind states are equated with heavenly or hellish cosmological realms. Although this book is not a canonical text from the *Tipitaka*, it is an excellent summary of the higher insights derived from Buddhist consciousness. Any respectable Buddhist teacher should have deep comprehension of the ideas inside the book. Two other proper *Abhidhamma* books, the *Vibhanga* and the *Dhammasangani*, deserve mention for the uniqueness of the material.

Many of the other major works in the Buddhist *Tipitaka* can be summarized here, briefly. The *Vinaya Pitaka* is a vitally important work for acquiring knowledge of Buddhist monastic discipline. Its volumes also contain the stories behind the creation of the monastic regulations. Sometimes these stories are very graphic in nature, but it is necessary to discuss ideas related to female menstrual cycles, how to engage in maintaining bodily hygiene, what to eat and when, how to build a meditation hut, whether an orgasm emission in a dream equates to having sex, whether male and female monastics should sit together when alone and much more. There are 227 rules for Buddhist monks and 311 for female nuns, the *bhikkhuni*, and there are stories about all of these regulations, many of which were formulated after laypeople confronted the Buddha over questionable behaviours observed in social settings. These six volumes are major components of a researcher's library of Buddhist texts. There are alternative volumes of just the regulations, known as the *Patimokkha*, where the regulation is noted along with a basic explanation organized by a ranking of punishment for any violation.

Buddhists believe the Buddha had 547 past lives before he became this Buddha for our era. These old-world stories are found in the *jataka* tales (see page 16). Scholars have analysed these past-life stories for decades; many are considered worthy for reading to children and are often used in temple celebrations in Buddhist cultures. Apart from the interesting narratives are the actual settings of and introductions and conclusions to these mythical past-life stories, as these highlight the attainment level of the listener (indeed, research has been done on the effectiveness of these old-world stories, taken from information the *jatakas* provide). Did the listener care about the story or not? Sometimes a listener was unaffected; many times a listener became converted to the Buddhist teachings as someone entering a stream (*sotopanna*). Other listeners could become someone who might become an enlightened being in the next life, or may never return in some future rebirth. If the listener became one of the *arahants* – someone who has seen the true nature of being and achieved *nibbana* – this is, of course, a great achievement.

There is perhaps only one additional work from a modern scholar that deserves mentioning: the *Buddhadhamma*. The recently translated edition of this text is over 1,500 pages long including the index, glossary and other endmatter. P.A. Payutto's text, translated by Robin Moore, is a feat of epic proportions. Although it took seventeen years to complete, it shows depth and maturity through expressing the Thai interpretation of the Buddha's teachings. Some scholars who can read Thai will, often in the university setting, use this original work as the only reference for their academic work. Moore received permission to reorganize his translation, so it differs a bit from Payutto's original work, but its contents pertain to human life, components of our being, our senses, life's attributes, dependent origination, *kamma*, life's goals, *nibbana*, awakened beings, calm and insight, the supernatural and the divine, desire and happiness, the Middle Way, friendship, faith and confidence, factors of wisdom, the Four Noble Truths and other important criteria of *Buddhadhamma*. It is an ambitious undertaking that will take a reader many months to consider.

Many Buddhists are content with just a few slogans from their respected guru-teacher and never pick up any volume to read; they do not study the authentic teachings of the Buddha but live life through these guru slogans and simply engage in daily life, hoping futilely for important changes in a future life while burning away their suffering in the current one. This situation is not helped by the fact that, too often, people take shortcuts in Buddhist scholarship. While most people give financial donations to monks for their private expenses or for temple expenses, bills and construction projects, even Buddhist institutions refrain from funding translation projects that are not in their native language. They will only translate texts that are already translated. A case in point is the *Dhammapada* – hundreds of editions of this work exist, yet translations of commentaries into English do not. Scholars who are able to work in the English language and use Pali are numerous in South and Southeast Asia, yet progress has not been made in making these editions available for the English-speaking world. There are new online editions of variations of discourses from the *Digha Nikaya*, *Majjhima Nikaya*, *Anguttara Nikaya*, *Samyutta Nikaya* and the *Sutta Nipata*, but translations of the *Niddesa* or updated translations of the *Vinaya*, and of all the commentaries and sub-commentaries, are still lacking. This work is not being done. The author of this chapter is currently the only scholar working on *Digha Nikaya* commentaries – the aspiration is to retranslate certain important discourses, for instance the *Sangiti Sutta*, and then its commentary and sub-commentary relative to the discourse. If sufficient funding existed, scholars could undertake translations of commentaries and sub-commentaries for all *Nikaya* collections of literature; due to the lack of benevolent patrons to support such a project, however, comprehension of Buddhism in its entirety is impossible for the English-speaking world. Members of the political elite in Southeast Asia have often sponsored textual translations and are given credit through their merit once the project has been completed. Many inscriptions exist on statues and in texts noting the generosity of the benefactor. However, in the English-speaking world support is very limited. Global Buddhist scholarship is really in need of adequate funding and busy benefactors could achieve merit from sponsoring a translation project so that scholars could improve worldwide knowledge of Buddhism. Global knowledge of Buddhism cannot improve without financial offerings and time sacrificed by scholars.

(overleaf)
Illustration of royal donations made in 1856 at Amarapura to the Buddhist order of monks. These included gifts of decorated bedsteads, gilded manuscript chests, and sets of *Tipitaka* texts. Burma, 19th century.
British Library, Or.13681, f. 10–11

ကျွာ ။ခ်ိုဂ ရ ာ ပ ည္မ ္ အ လ်ည ္ ရ ။အ န ပု ရ ္ ္ မ် အ ရ ္ ေ ္ ာ ္ အ ပ္ ္ ္မ ္ ္ မ် ္ ရ ္ ္ ္ ္ ္ ္ ္
ရ ္ ္ ္ မ ္ ္ ္ ္ ္ ္ ္ ္ ္ ္ ္ ္ ္
ရ ္

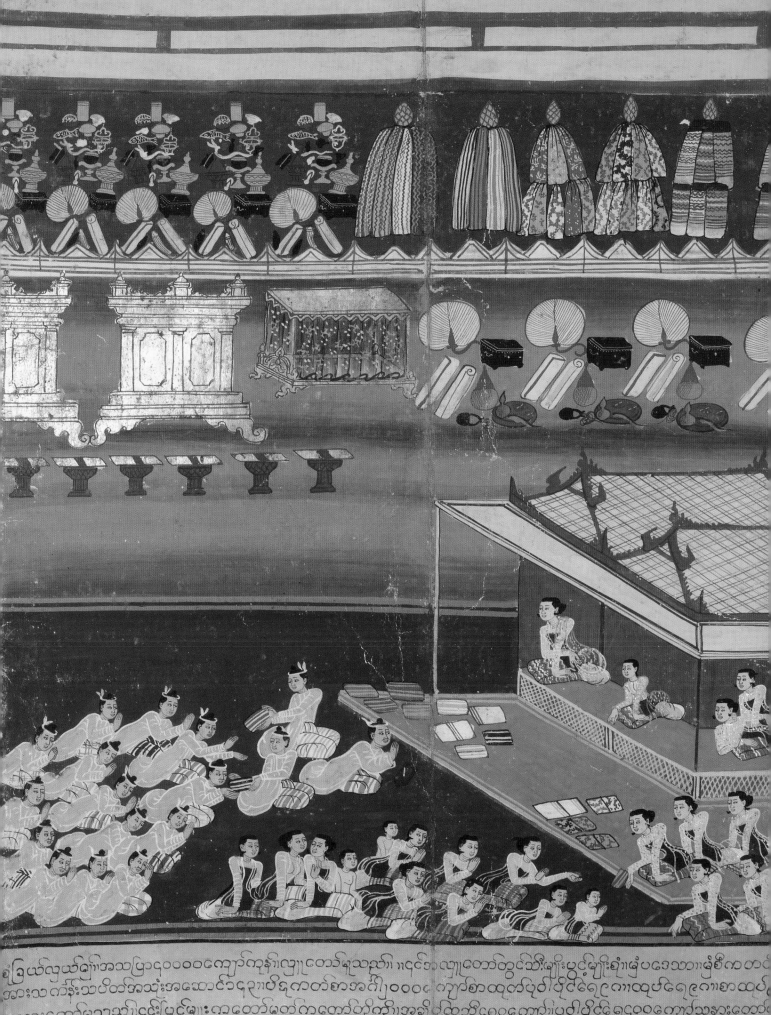

ရုံငြိုယ်လှ္ယယ်ချ္ုကြာအသဖြ္ာ္ုဝ္ဝဝဝ္ဝေကျ္ောကုန္ုဂ္ုလှ္ုူရုတ္ုဝ္ုရုသညြ္ာ္ုဂ္ု ရင္ုငြ္ုအလှ္ုူရုုတ္ုတ္ုဂ္ုငြ္ုသ္ုီး္ုျမိဳး္ုပင္ုငြ္ုမဲ်ႆ္ုရ္ုံဖ္ုုံ္ုပဒ္ုေသ္ုာ္ုာမြ္ုဖ္ုစ္ုကုတုုဝ္ုရ္ု
ဘ္ုား္ုဝ္ုသ္ုကာန္ုးသ္ု္ုပ္ုိတ္ုအသ္ုံု္ုးအသ္ုေားဝ္ု္ု ၄ုုဝ္ုါ္ု ္ုဝ္ုုံ္ုရ္ုကတ္ုစ္ုအ္ုက္ုုံ္ုျာ္ု္ုဝ္ုဝ္ုဝ္ုကျ္ုုာက္ုစ္ုာထ္ုုတ္ုဖ္ုုံု္ုဖ္ုုိုင္ုငြ္ုရ္ုေ္ုဝ္ုာ္ုက္ုာထ္ုုံုတ္ုဖ္ုုံ္ုရ္ုဝ္ုေ္ုဝ္ုက္ုာ္ုဏ္ုးထ္ုုတ္ု
သ္ုနား္ုေ္ုတ္ုတ္ုဝ္ုရ္ုုသညြ္ာ္ုဂ္ုင္ုးုပင္ုငြ္ုမ္ုျိုး္ုက္ုာ္ုေတ္ုတ္ုမ္ုတ္ုက္ုေတ္ုတ္ုဖ္ုုံု္ုကြ္ုုာ္ုအဏ္ုု္ုဝ္ုစ္ုတ္ုဏ္ုတ္ုဝ္ုဝ္ုကျ္ုုာ္ုဂ္ုပ္ုဝ္ု္ုဖ္ုုံ္ုဝ္ုဝ္ုကျ္ုုာ္ုသနားေ္ုတ္ုတ္ု
္ုရ္ုုာ္ုဝ္ုဝ္ု ္ုကျ္ုုာ္ုတ္ုဖ္ုုံ္ု္ုက္ုကြ္ုုင္ုးကြ္ုုပ္ုးေ္ုက္ုမ္ုးေ္ုတ္ုဖ္ုုံ္ုုသညြ္ာ္ုဂ္ုငြ္ုအလှ္ုူရုု္ုဝ္ုကိ္ုုထ္ုုက္ုေ္ုတ္ုတ္ုဖ္ုုံ္ုျေ္ု္ုေဝ္ုက္ုသ္ုုန္ုြ္ုးခ္ုျ္ုအ္ုသ္ုုံ္ု်ာ္ုပးေ္ု

Buddhism and Society

There are other dilemmas in Buddhist societies. Most countries where Buddhism is practised face challenges, and one issue receiving considerable media attention is that of forced conversions away from Buddhism due to intermarriage. However, an increased number of people are converting to Buddhism due to the ongoing caste oppression and growth of religious nationalism in India. Although there is a vision for national consolidation (of Hinduism), Buddhism has validity on Indian soil as a native tradition; within India, Buddhism should be well respected and supported. Evidence of state-sponsored support is ongoing through the recognition and preservation of sacred or historical sites and more universities are opening programmes that offer degrees or certificates in Buddhism or related fields. More ancient archaeological sites are being discovered with the help of better imaging technologies; people are becoming more familiar with places that non-natives seldom hear about, such as in Bhutan, Sikkim, Assam, Arunajal Pradesh and other places where Buddhism is a national minority religion but is important for certain ethnic groups that rejected Hinduism and the imposition of Christianity by European missionaries. Tai peoples are spread from Northeast India in the west to Vietnam in the east, and from South China to Malaysia: all embrace Buddhist culture to various extents.

In Sri Lanka, a civil war that arose from the post-colonial ethnic tensions between mainly Buddhist Sinhalese and non-Buddhist Tamils lasted more than two decades and finally ended in 2009. In some nations with a large Islamic presence, groups of people have destroyed Buddhist temples and cliff statues, killed Buddhist monks and forced tribal Buddhists away from their ancient lands. The Republic of the Union of Myanmar, a collection of various ethnic states comprised of historically Buddhist lands before European colonization, which is now recovering from decades of military nationalism, is seeking to strengthen Buddhism as the legitimate national ideology used to regulate the daily affairs of its citizens. Ethnic minority groups who adhere to alternative religions struggle to maintain their unique identities because of pressure from the majority to learn its language and history and to adopt Burmese national culture and tradition.

Thailand is a relatively stable country with the majority of people professing Buddhism as their religion. As an entire nation state, it has unique ways to manage any conflicts arising from the small Muslim separatist population in the southern region near Malaysia. The Kingdom of Thailand is more concerned with regulating politics within the nation, which is now subservient to a military government espousing loyalty to the Kingdom, at the expense of democracy – a personal religion is not a factor for keeping the integrity of the national borders. Even Buddhist nations are relegating Buddhism and other religions to the private sphere. Laos and Cambodia are unique cases because they are still recovering from war during which they had been reduced to impoverished conditions by American bombings, phases of communism or the trauma and depopulation created by Khmer Rouge units. Life within these nations is still difficult, but there are stories and evidence of happiness, which are often found and rooted in traditional activities. Many historical sites in Laos and Cambodia, as well as Thailand, have become UNESCO World Heritage Sites.

The presence of Buddhism within Vietnam had diminished due to a period of French and American antagonism against the national effort towards communism and subsequent socialist policies, but it has recently begun to increase again and Buddhism has become more socially acceptable. Many Vietnamese monastic students live abroad to study in degree programmes in Buddhism.

Buddhism is nearly 2,600 years old and many modern Buddhist cultures have been advocating for the original Indian Buddhist tradition ever since Buddhism became established within their nations many centuries years ago. However, there are processes of people becoming Buddhists in other ways, such as by direct contact not with Indian or South Asian Buddhists but with other Buddhist cultures like those in China or Tibet. This was the case for Mongolian or Siberian Buddhists, and perhaps what their ancestors might have brought back to their lands when they dominated much of Asia under Kublai Khan, leaving their influence in some parts of Eastern Europe and Central Asia such as Kazakhstan, Kyrgyzstan, Turkmenistan, Tajikistan and so on. One can also cite the development of the first Buddhist European nation of the Kalmyks, who live near the Volga River and Caspian Sea. The Kalmyk Khanate, established by

Rubbing of a stone inscription found near Kengtung, Shan State. The inscription in Tai Khuen script records a donation of a Buddha statue and a *vihara* (assembly hall) that was made in honour of the king of Chiang Saen (Thailand) and his queen, by Nang (Ms) Kham Daeng and her family. The Tai Khuen people are one of the ethnic groups that live in various Southeast Asian countries as a result of colonial border demarcation. Shan State, Burma, 1921.
British Library, Or.16993

Kalmyk Buddhist migrants from northwest China in the early seventeenth century, became an Autonomous Socialist Soviet Republic, Kalmykia, in 1935, under Stalin.

Countries with Buddhist majorities are among the less economically developed nations, and many Asian nations have been governed by some militarized nationalistic or communist regime, displacing freedoms because of a desire to rebuild and enforce order following periods of European colonialism. When different nations were clamouring for power or democracy, a military effort was put into action to unify these individual nations; through some form or another, citizens lived in fear. In the *Yodhajiva Sutta* a mercenary cries to the Buddha because he is misled into thinking he is going to heaven for fighting for nationalism, but since his mind is in a low state when killing, only low animal–hellish realms are the destination for his rebirth. A nation's attempt to unify internally to consolidate power is shown here as distinct from unifying as an act of compassion.

Compassion

Compassion, as we can see, has a broad meaning, more so than conventional perceptions of the term. Synonyms for the term inside the *Tipitaka* are numerous. The word is mentioned at least 87 times in the *Vinaya*, 83 times in the *Digha Nikaya*, 76 times in the *Majjhima Nikaya*, 66 times in the *Samyutta Nikaya*, 78 times in the *Anguttara Nikaya*, 253 times in the *Khuddaka Nikaya*, 71 times in the *Abhidhamma*, 55 times in the *Visuddhimagga* and numerous times in other texts. The Pali word that is used to mean compassion, *karuna*, is also tied closely to pity and even mercy; *metta* is the Pali word for loving-kindness. *Karuna* and *metta* can be seen as aspects of friendship and teamwork, again generalized as 'compassion'. Characteristic of compassion is a heartfelt sensitivity towards someone's suffering with some aspiration that the problem can terminate and everyone will be happy. Compassion comprehends suffering. The function of compassion is the activation of the volition towards assisting the being in that distressed state.

OPPOSITE: Painting of Padmasambhava (the 'Lotus-Born'), an 8th-century Buddhist master originally from the Indian subcontinent, who is associated with the foundation of the first monastery at Samye in central Tibet. According to legend, he used his great yogic powers to subdue all local demonic forces, thus enabling Buddhism to take hold in Tibet. Tibet, *c.* 1800.

British Library, Or.3048

BELOW: *Pancaraksa*, ritual texts in Sanskrit on the Five Protections with illustrations of the five protective and healing Bodhisattvas called Mahapratisara, Mahasahasra-pramardani, Mahamayuri, Mahamantranudharani and Mahasitavati, who are invoked for protection against diseases, serpents, demons, wild animals and dangerous insects. Nepal, 1676.

British Library, Or.13946, covers and ff. 61v–62r

Understanding the origin of suffering is beneficial towards the removal of that suffering. Compassion, for example, can result from witnessing an act of violence. We know that we, ourselves, would not like to be a victim, and it is within our human nature to assist others. When we know that suffering has an origin we can act from our compassion to uproot and eliminate the problematic circumstance, ideally, or do our best to manage in another way, or find alternative coping mechanisms. Compassion does not arise from social ethics, from others telling us what to do, but from our own intuition. Intuition can, of course, be trained, but Buddhism teaches that humans instinctively know what is right and wrong. Compassion's proximate cause comes from our wholesome consciousness. The consciousness tells us that there is a way out of suffering, so we embark on the proper path towards having a more compassionate and peaceful society.

Inherent within Buddhism is the compassion to welcome foreigners into Buddhist tradition and communities through the loving-kindness developed within individual practitioners. The early days of Buddhism had a missionary spirit. Buddhism would venture off where the Silk Road took travelling monastics, who probably sought shelter in caves in areas where building from wood was not really possible. Caves are areas where some religious leaders received revelation from divine spirits or learned monks shared wisdom and emphasized recitation of oral texts before the widespread development of writing – others could not learn if the noble texts were not recited. Chants for revering the Buddha run parallel to the structure other traditions use in calls to prayer. Buddhist laity wear white clothing when going on pilgrimages and during their temple visits for the sake of listening to sermons and practising meditation; other traditions also urge the wearing of white robes during holy pilgrimages. Buddhism now advocates for the principle of 'come and see' rather than monks going door to door seeking converts. When monks do go door to door, it is usually to acquire almsfood from members of society who have the compassion to support their religious leaders with requisite materials rather than mega-complexes, private jets, the newest technical gadgets and other excesses. The Buddha and the original monks travelled on foot. Merchants probably allowed monks to travel with them on large animal-pulled caravans (usually oxen if Indian merchants, or camels if coming from elsewhere) and some made their way overseas on boats.

Compassion is seen through monks desiring to benefit humans who listen to the Buddhist teachings. Even deities are believed to be able to listen to the messages of the Buddha, thus acquiring knowledge of

the *dhamma*. This would enable them to be reborn as humans and subsequently offer them the opportunity to become enlightened, which is nearly impossible in a rebirth as a deity. The Buddha was known as the teacher of gods and humanity, therefore Buddhist monastics endeavour to develop and demonstrate similar compassion by providing advice and reassurance to lay disciples or various audiences when people face difficult decisions. Buddhist temples are also a means of protection for people facing challenges and hardship in their lives.

Buddhist compassion can be further demonstrated through the recognition that women have equal potential to men in attaining doctrinal goals. This would suggest that men possessing gender biases should reconsider women as equals on the path to developing mental purity and final attainment of the Buddhist ideal, *nibbana*. Some aspects of women's lives are beyond male comprehension – menstruation, pregnancy and childbirth are obvious examples – so it is always best if women have the opportunity to obtain advice from a fully ordained *bhikkhuni*. Buddhism was established to have monks, nuns, laymen and laywomen, four assemblies of practitioners, and compassion requires a fully operating *sangha*.

To learn more about compassion, texts should be read and lessons taught; students can repeat the lessons and

Miniature brush-painted protective amulets with basic Buddhist teachings and images of Buddhas and Bodhisattvas, preserved by a British collector in a custom-made folding book with silk covers and silk-covered paper folds. China, 19th century.
British Library, ORB.Misc.111

further recite and even ponder upon compassion, and they can additionally ask seniors about aspects of compassion. Buddhist critical-thinking skills further allow us to know the consequence of compassion: that is, knowing all beings desire happiness and should have basic human security afforded to them under the umbrella of universal human rights. Again, understanding the origin of compassion, how it is used in language and society, and having the knowledge to properly engage with compassion are all basic hallmarks of Buddhist compassion. A Buddhist would see a situation and determine whether an act is unprofitable or blameworthy, whether it conduces to loss or sorrow. Compassion, then, is worthy to be practised by Buddhists, but it is both a practice that knowingly engages with a suffering being and a form of compassion that can be pre-emptive and protect citizens from any measure of harm.

Compassion today, in a wider sense, can be seen in acting for the public good. Compassion is not necessarily volunteerism and neither is it slavery. Employers have a duty to their employees and employees also have a duty towards their employers, but compassion is necessary to have better working conditions, fair pay and a good work ethic. In our modern societies, even office work can be done in the home, so there is no need to have an office that is many kilometres away; traffic jams can be reduced, the air can be cleaner, energy can be saved, work–life balance can be improved, stress and violence can be reduced and lives can even be saved. Compassion means listening to grievances, adjusting policies and providing relief. Compassion is educating children equally, protecting them from violence, abuse and exploitation, and raising them to know what compassion is and to cultivate compassion. Compassion centres on behaving better and having thoughts that are not rooted in hatred, greed or delusion. Compassion for others allows us to manoeuvre and sense knowns and unknowns; it allows us to think about the effects of our actions; it allows for critical thinking, towards ensuring we protect the environment and leave a lasting positive legacy upon the Earth, our local societies and our families. Compassion brings us all together and allows us to experience life, colour, variety and diversity in positive ways, ensuring we progress collectively and equally. A greater amount of compassion will create a better world for all of us.

When we consider what the Buddhist world has offered us throughout its development we can learn more about our past, present and future, and we can see from such experimentation that better ways are possible for humanity to be civilized and content. Despite being known as less economically developed nations, many Buddhist countries are rich in happiness, or, as recent financial reports have stated, among the least miserable. Buddhists can better comprehend how to escape from suffering because compassion is an integral unit in daily information processing. If more people around the world knew about these basic truths we, in our daily lives, could transform not only ourselves but others as well.

Sacred wall hanging (Thai: *phrabot*) depicting thirteen key scenes from the *Vessantara jataka*, visualizing the Buddhist virtue of generosity. Acrylic and gold leaf on canvas. Painting by Irving Chan Johnson, Lim Su Qi and Rungnapa Kitiarsa, National University of Singapore. Singapore, 2019.

Illustrated Manuscript of the *Guanyin Sutra*

Mélodie Doumy

Avalokitesvara, the Bodhisattva of Infinite Compassion, was introduced to China from India. His name was translated as Guanyin, short for Guanshiyin, which means 'Perceiver of the World's Sounds'. This refers to his ability to hear the prayers for help of anyone calling upon him with a sincere and faithful heart. He notably appears in the *Lotus Sutra*, one of the most important scriptures of the Mahayana branch of Buddhism. Chapter 25, 'The Universal Gate of Bodhisattva Guanyin', is entirely devoted to the deity. It details, through a series of episodes, how he assumes thirty-three different emanations to succour people facing challenging life situations and to bring them to spiritual salvation. This chapter became increasingly popular and was often singled out for copying, sometimes to the point of being regarded as an independent text known as the *Guanyin Sutra*.

Besides the fine scrolls produced by scribal circles for monastic libraries, a wide range of manuscripts was also copied for personal use. Booklets started to develop as an alternative form to scrolls between the end of the eighth century and the beginning of the ninth century. Because of their design and diminutive size, they were both portable and easy to consult. The 'Universal Gate' chapter is the main subject of the one shown here. Roughly dated to the tenth century, this small book was reassembled from scattered pages in the 1950s and 1960s and was arranged in the order of the *Sutra*. It is made from forty-two folios in a thick cream paper (18 cm x 9 cm), now bound together by a thread passing through one of its top corners.

All pages are vividly illustrated, except for the last few that contain the short *Dizang Sutra* (a scripture about the Bodhisattva Ksitigarbha or Dizang). While the drawings at the start are coloured in with bright red and yellow pigments, towards the end of the booklet quite a few are merely outlined in black ink, providing further evidence that the item was left unfinished. The pictures are placed on the upper half, complementing the text below. This layout later came to be standard for narrative block-printed Buddhist and secular books. By bringing the scripture to life and conveying the sense of the Buddhist teachings written below, illustrations were especially useful to those who were illiterate or had a limited command of Chinese. They represent Guanyin rescuing people from all sorts of dangerous circumstances, such as fire, drowning, shipwreck, theft and imprisonment, and even helping with infertility.

The depictions on the verso of folio 9 and the recto of folio 10, shown here, are particularly insightful. Their signification unfolds when reading them from right to left. On the right, the deity is materialized in the form of a bejewelled male Bodhisattva sitting cross-legged on a lotus flower. He looks benevolently at a couple kneeling before him, their hands gathered in a supplicatory gesture. They are urging him to give them a child. On the left, we can see that their wish has been fulfilled: a woman is giving birth to a healthy-looking baby, whose head and arms emerge from underneath the drapes of her robe. A female attendant, seemingly acting as a midwife and perhaps a manifestation of Guanyin, is positioned behind her. She has laid out two water vessels and a large jar to assist with labour. Both scenes are displayed as a set of pictorial parallels, working together as a single composition and echoing the before-and-after structure of the text:

> If a woman wishes to give birth to a male child, she should offer obeisance and alms to Bodhisattva Perceiver of the World's Sounds and then she will bear a son blessed with merit, virtue, and wisdom. And if she wishes to bear a daughter, she will bear one with all the marks of comeliness, one who in the past planted the roots of virtue and is loved and respected by many persons.[1]

Originally, Avalokitesvara was represented as a male Bodhisattva. However, in modern Chinese society, Guanyin is portrayed as a female deity. It is from the promise to grant heirs described in the episode above that the belief in a child-bestowing Guanyin, later depicted in this role as a feminine figure, gradually emerged in China from the eleventh century onwards. Buddhist miracle stories also began to be compiled from the fourth century, emphasizing the deity's power to answer the prayers of those with an ardent desire for offspring. In *Records of Signs from the Unseen Realm* (*Mingxiang ji*), written by Wang Yan at the end of the fifth century, a tale recounts how a childless man, who was already fifty years old, confessed his predicament to a monk and was instructed by the latter to recite the *Guanyin Sutra* devoutly. He followed this advice and had a revelation in a dream, waking up to the news that his wife was pregnant. She later gave birth to a male infant.

The British Library's booklet was recovered from cave 17 of the Mogao Caves complex, a Buddhist site located near Dunhuang.[2] This small room, whose existence remained secret until 1900, was possibly walled up in the early eleventh century, after being filled with tens of thousands of manuscript and printed books, paintings,

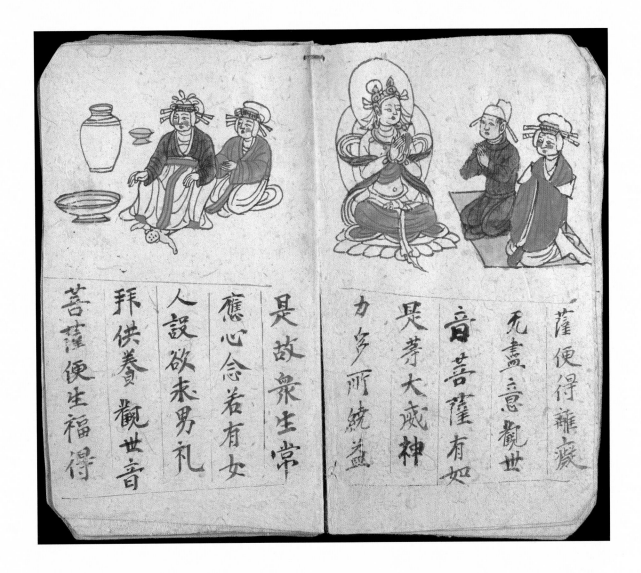

菩薩便生福得　拜供養觀世音　人說欲求男礼　應心念若有女　是故眾生常

力多所饒益　是菩薩大威神　音菩薩有如　无盡意觀世　薩便得離癡

Illustrated copy of the *Guanyin Sutra* in the form of a small booklet. Cave 17, Mogao Caves near Dunhuang, China, Gansu Province, c. 10th century.
British Library, Or.8210/S.6983 ff. 9v–10r

textiles and other artefacts. Numerous copies of chapter 25 of the *Lotus Sutra* and portable paintings on the same theme were also found in it. Moreover, the wall paintings adorning the Mogao Caves themselves frequently show Guanyin as a saviour from perils. This testifies to the deity's well-established cult across all levels of society. Local clerics and laypeople, noblemen and civilians, men and women: many worshipped Guanyin, a Bodhisattva willing to aid any person in distress and concerned even with the worldly matters of fertility, pregnancy and childbirth.

The reason why the so-called 'Library Cave' was sealed up is still a mystery, but we know that a significant part of its precious contents came from nearby monas-teries and nunneries. Could the booklet have belonged to a monk or a nun? Could it have been made for a non-monastic? Would it have been used to help perform rituals or as some kind of protective talisman? In any case, it gives us a glimpse into some of the Buddhist practices of medieval China and points to a religious system perfectly attuned to the needs of the laity.

1   Burton Watson, trans., *The Lotus Sutra* (New York: Columbia University Press, 1993), p. 300.
2   For more information on Dunhuang, please see Sam van Schaik's essay 'From the Translator's Workshop' on pages 156–157, which focuses on another one of the manuscripts discovered in cave 17.

The Bhaja Stupas: Henry Cousens' View

Gethin Rees

Stupas at the caves of Bhaja, Pune district, India, taken by Henry Cousens *c*. 1880.
British Library, Photo1000/5(593)

Dating from the early 1880s, this photograph of a group of Buddhist *stupas* was taken under the direction of Henry Cousens (1854–1933) as part of his work for the Archaeological Survey of Western India. It forms part of the detailed photographic documentation of the Buddhist monastery at Bhaja made by Cousens during one of his early archaeological tours. The fourteen small *stupas* are often described as 'votive', being monuments to revered monks and nuns. They are housed both within and outside a rock-cut cave, one of twenty-six that form the Bhaja monastery situated in the Pune dis-

trict of modern Maharashtra. Bhaja is located within the Western Ghats mountain range in a dramatic yet peaceful location high in the hills overlooking the river valley below. The intricate architecture was cut between the third century BCE and the third century CE and features a pillared *chaitya* hall containing a *stupa* for worship and exquisite sculptures, including the only depiction of a narrative in stone found in the Western Ghats.[1]

Rock-cut architecture can be found throughout the Indian subcontinent and results from the activities of several faiths. Some well-known examples include the Hindu caves at Badami, those cut by Jains at Ellora and the painted Buddhist monastery at Ajanta. The Western Ghats mountains have the greatest concentration of Buddhist rock-cut activity in India, despite being more than 1,300 kilometres from Bihar, where the religion originated. Rock-cut caves are not natural but human-made spaces hewn entirely from cliff faces: the monastery at Bhaja and the *stupas* depicted were cut from basalt and offered a cool and shady retreat. An existence isolated from life in the valleys was suitable for contemplative devotion and the pursuit of *nirvana* that characterized monastic life. Over time, the design of caves became adapted to specific purposes such as the *vihara* for habitation, *chaitya* for worship and *mandapa* for meals and gatherings.[2]

A *stupa* was originally a mound of earth containing the cremated remains of the Buddha. As time passed, the remains and relics of prominent monks and nuns came to be interred within *stupas*. *Stupas* grew in size and came to be made from stone, incorporating elaborate carvings and areas for worship and circumambulation (moving around a sacred object or idol). Large *mahastupas* like Sanchi, Bharhut and Amaravati became foci of pilgrimage for the laity and monastics alike. Placement within monasteries suggests that the monastic community or *sangha* were actively engaged in *stupa* veneration. The small *stupas* from Bhaja cave 20, depicted in this photo, are located within a monastery and although usually described as 'votive', a more appropriate description might be 'funerary'.[3] Inscribed with the names and status of monks, nuns and possibly members of the laity, the monuments often contain cremated human remains. Such inscriptions are just legible on the bases of the *stupas* in the photograph. Funerary *stupas* were often clustered around larger ones, but it appears 'that those interred within them were not intended to be venerated, but rather that their placement around a *mahastupa* was itself an act of veneration of another'.[4] Interment in these locations was auspicious, allowing the accumulation of merit through perpetual association with prominent individuals or even 'rebirth in heaven'.[5] The pattern exists at monasteries across India, such as Bodhgaya, Ratnagiri and Kanheri, as well as further afield.

Large areas of the subcontinent were under British rule when this photograph was taken. The growth of interest in the heritage of India over the course of the nineteenth century led to the formation of the Archaeological Survey of India (ASI) in 1871 and the documentation of the northern and central regions of the subcontinent by the ASI's director general Alexander Cunningham and others.[6] In western India, European scholars had been investigating rock-cut Buddhist architecture with official encouragement since the 1840s and their research led to the formation of the Archaeological

Survey of Western India (ASWI) in 1873, under the directorship of James Burgess (1832–1916). Burgess wrote extensively on rock-cut architecture, his outstanding work being *Cave Temples of India*.[7]

This photograph was taken by Burgess's assistant Henry Cousens as part of the ASWI and he has placed himself in the composition as an indication of scale. Cousens had a distinguished career in the ASWI between 1875 and 1910, conducting significant fieldwork and writing prolifically on the architecture and archaeology of the west and south. He also surveyed and excavated in Sindh (present-day Pakistan), where a series of *stupas* similar to those depicted in the photograph were later found surrounding the main *stupa* at Mirpur Khas.[8] After archaeological investigation came under local government control in 1890, Cousens was appointed archaeological surveyor, based in Bombay,[9] and remained in charge of the western survey until his retirement in 1910.

The growth of interest in Indian heritage and the publication of research by the Archaeological Survey of India and Asiatic Societies fed into a growing understanding of the history and significance of Buddhism. By the mid-nineteenth century and certainly by the time this photograph was taken, the basic facts of Buddhism were known to scholarship. The religion had been identified as separate from Brahminism and was recognized to be Indian in origin whilst the existence and antiquity of the historical Buddha were understood. Furthermore, it was generally acknowledged that heterogeneous regional Buddhist traditions were, in fact, manifestations of the same pan-Asian religion.[10] This understanding and the wider Victorian, middle-class interest in the religion was fuelled by the documentation and publication of Buddhist archaeological sites by the ASI.

1   George Michell and Gethin Rees, *Buddhist Rock-cut Monasteries of the Western Ghats* (Mumbai: Jaico, 2017), p. 80.
2   S. Nagaraju, *Buddhist Architecture of Western India* (Delhi: Agam Kala Prakashan, 1981).
3   Gregory Schopen, 'Burial "ad sanctos" and the Physical Presence of the Buddha in Early Indian Buddhism: A Study in the Archeology of Religions', *Religion 17* (1987), p. 199.
4   Lars Fogelin, 'The Place of Veneration in Early South Asian Buddhism' in Sarah Tarlow and Liv Nilsson Stutz, eds, *The Oxford Handbook of the Archaeology of Death and Burial* (Oxford: Oxford University Press, 2013), p. 233.
5   Ibid., p. 236; Schopen, 'Burial "ad sanctos"', p. 196.
6   Upinder Singh, *The Discovery of Ancient India* (Delhi: Permanent Black, 2004), p. 82.
7   James Burgess and James Fergusson, *Cave Temples of India* (London: W.H. Allen, 1880).
8   Henry Cousens, 'The Antiquities of Sind: With Historical Outline', *Archaeological Survey of India, Imperial Series*, vol. 46 (Calcutta: Government of India, 1929), p. 97.
9   Dilip K. Chakrabarti, *A History of Indian Archaeology from the Beginning to 1947* (New Delhi: Munshiram Manoharlal, 1988), p. 105.
10 Philip C. Almond, *The British Discovery of Buddhism* (Cambridge: Cambridge University Press, 1988), p. 32.

A Khmer Meditation Manual

Jana Igunma

Meditation is an essential part of Buddhism. It aims to develop mental discipline and to cultivate a wholesome, awakened state of mind, which eventually results in the practice of Buddha's teachings in everyday life. Meditation is regarded as a world-renouncing activity, sometimes combined with chanting and visualization methods, and helps one to reach a mental state of happiness (*piti*), one of the Seven Factors of Enlightenment (*satta bojjhanga*). Apart from happiness, these Factors comprise mindfulness, investigation, effort, tranquillity, concentration and equanimity.

Happiness in the Buddhist sense, however, should not be misinterpreted as a state of individual happiness or temporary contentment. It cannot be self-centred or selfish but is rather a state of mind that has overcome all attachment and desire (*tanha*) – the principal cause of suffering (*dukkha*). *Dukkha* is often simply described as suffering or pain, but it also refers to impermanence and change as well as to conditioned states of mind, that is, being dependent on or affected by something/someone. Meditation is a powerful tool that can help to overcome such states of mind by focusing in different ways on the body, on emotion and on the conscious or subconscious mind. Common methods of contemplation can be by breath and body movements, by means of a meditational device – an image of the Buddha or a Bodhisattva, or several of these; a candle flame; a meditation disc; beads; mandalas; an empty space between two objects; etc. – and through sounds and smells, which help with reflection on one's own senses and emotions.

To advance meditation skills, an unfavourable or polluted environment can be chosen in which to practise meditation, for example where the meditation practitioner is exposed to unpleasant temperatures, darkness, harmful animals, as well as disturbing smells and noises. Such places could be (tropical) forests, caves, mortuaries or cemeteries (historically charnel grounds). Texts on meditation form a small but important fraction of Canonical as well as post-canonical literature. 'Meditation on the foul' is described in the Buddha's discourse on the practice of mindfulness (*Maha Satipatthana Sutta*), one of the earliest Buddhist teachings. It is possibly the most efficient of all meditation practices aiming to overcome conditioned states of the mind and emotion. According to Buddhaghosa, a fifth-century Buddhist scholar who compiled numerous commentaries on the Buddha's teachings, meditation on the foul is explained as follows:

As though he were to see a corpse thrown aside in a charnel ground – one, two, three days dead, bloated, livid, and oozing matter ... being devoured by crows, hawks, vultures, jackals, or worms ... a skeleton with flesh and blood, held together with sinews ... disconnected bones scattered in all directions, bones bleached white, the colour of shells ... bones, heaped up, more than a year old ... bones rotten and crumbling to dust – a monk compares his own body, 'this body too is of the same nature, it will end up like that, it is not exempt from that fate'. In this way, he abides contemplating the body as body ... and he abides independent, not clinging to anything in the world.[1]

The highest state of meditation is reached when both attraction and repulsion cease to exist:

In the arahant, there is neither liking nor disliking: he regards all things with perfect equanimity, as did Thera Maha Moggallana when he accepted a handful of rice from a leper.[2]

A rare manuscript in Khmer script dealing with meditation in the Yogavacara tradition is a fragment of a folding book dating back to the early eighteenth century or before. Written in Pali, the sacred language of the Theravada school, the text explains various states of insight. Yogavacara practices are open to lay and monastic practitioners and aim at incorporating qualities of the Buddha into the self.

The paintings in this manuscript fragment illustrate six stages of meditation; four other illustrations survive only partially. Folio 4 depicts a Buddhist monk contemplating the unavoidable exposure of the human body to suffering, here shown as illness and death. The latter is symbolized by the bloated corpse by the riverside.

Buddhadasa Indapanno explains this scene as follows: 'At this stage of knowledge one has the insight that all forms of being are the cause of suffering, which one should fear as if one met a lion. The corpse on the ground reminds the practising person to what extent life is subject to suffering.'[3] This illustration also refers to the first of the nine charnel-ground meditations according to the *Maha Satipatthana Sutta*, describing the observation of the bloated, blue-black or festering corpse. By touching the corpse with his walking stick while meditating the monk transfers merit to the deceased person so that their suffering will not continue in a future existence. This is seen as an act of unparalleled compassion that can be reached through meditation.

The method of meditation on the foul is very well documented in Southeast Asian Buddhist manuscript painting. Many manuscripts containing the legend of the monk Phra Malai (see page 128), which is based on the Ksitigarbha Bodhisattva, include one or more scenes of meditation on the foul. These manuscripts, which are often lavishly illustrated with scenes of Phra Malai's encounters in the Buddhist heavens and hells, were commissioned by families of deceased persons as funeral offering books or commemorative volumes.

1   Peter Skilling, 'The Aesthetics of Devotion: Buddhist Arts of Thailand' in Heidi Tan, ed., *Enlightened Ways: The Many Streams of Buddhist Art in Thailand* (Singapore: Asian Civilisations Museum, 2012), p. 30.
2   Francis Story, *Dimensions of Buddhist Thought: Collected Essays* (Kandy: Buddhist Publication Society, 2011), vol. 3, pp. 278–279.
3   Buddhadāsa Bhikkhu, *Siamesische Illustrationen der Buddhalehre* (Tübingen/Basel: Horst Erdmann Verlag, 1969), p. 75; translation by author.

Fragment of a manual of a Buddhist mystic on meditation practices in the Yogavacara tradition in the Pali language in Khmer script. Thailand or Cambodia, 18th century.

British Library, Or.14447, f. 4

CONTRIBUTORS TO THIS BOOK

Jana Igunma is Henry Ginsburg Curator for Thai, Lao and Cambodian Collections at the British Library. She was lead curator of the exhibition *Buddhism* and co-authored the book *Buddhism Illuminated: Manuscript Art from Southeast Asia* (British Library, 2018). Her research interests focus on Thai and Lao manuscript art and literatures.

San San May is Curator for Burmese Collections at the British Library. She has co-curated the exhibition *Buddhism* and was co-author of the book *Buddhism Illuminated: Manuscript Art from Southeast Asia* (British Library, 2018).

Angela S. Chiu is an independent researcher with a focus on Thai Buddhist art and literature. She is the author of *The Buddha in Lanna: Art, Lineage, Power, and Place in Northern Thailand* (University of Hawai'i Press, 2017).

Pasquale Manzo is Curator for Sanskrit Collections at the British Library. His research interests include archaeology and history of art in India with a focus on early Buddhist and Gandharan art. He is currently involved in a project for the online publishing of a collection of India Office Library Sanskrit manuscripts on microfilm.

Hamish Todd is head of East Asian Collections at the British Library. His research interests include the history of printing and the culture of the book in Japan and Korea, the history of the British Library's Japanese and Korean collections, and early Anglo-Japanese relations.

Venerable Khammai Dhammasami is a Theravada Buddhist monk based in Oxford. Originally from Shan State, Myanmar, he has lived and studied in Thailand, Sri Lanka and Britain, where he obtained his doctorate degree at Oxford University. He is secretary general of the International Association of Buddhist Universities, trustee and research fellow at the Oxford Centre for Buddhist Studies, Buddhist chaplain to Oxford University and founder–rector of Shan State Buddhist University. His thesis, *Buddhism, Politics and Education*, was published by Bloomsbury in 2018.

Yasuyo Ohtsuka is Curator for Japanese Collections at the British Library. She has a background in librarianship both in Japan and the UK. Her main interests include Japanese studies, the history of printing and publishing, museum studies and library automation.

Chachuen Khamdaengyodtai is lecturer at the Arts and Culture Centre, Rajabhat University in Chiang Mai. He is executive member of Wat Papao Foundation Shan monastery and co-ordinator of the Tai Literary and Cultural Centre, both in Chiang Mai. Books he has co-authored include *Shan Manuscripts, Part One* (Franz Steiner, 2003) and *The Words of the Buddha in the Languages of the World* (Bavarian State Library, 2005).

Beth McKillop is a senior research fellow at the Victoria and Albert Museum in London. She lectures on Korean and Chinese subjects at SOAS, University of London, and at the Rare Book School, University of Virginia.

Sam Van Schaik is head of the Endangered Archives Programme (EAP) at the British Library. He has previously worked for the International Dunhuang Project and has been a principal investigator on the projects 'Beyond Boundaries: Religion, Region, Language and the State' (ERC), 'Tibetan Zen' (British Academy), and 'Tibetan and Chinese Paleography' (Leverhulme Trust). His publications include *Tibet: A History* and *The Spirit of Tibetan Buddhism* (Yale University Press, 2011 and 2016).

Lopen Karma Phuntsho is a Buddhist thought leader, writer and social worker in Bhutan. He is a research associate at Clare Hall, Cambridge University, and SOAS, and founder and president of the Loden Foundation.

Nikolay Tsyrempilov is associate professor at the School of Humanities and Social Sciences at Nazarbayev University, Astana. His PhD thesis analysed the interrelations between Buryat Buddhist communities and the eighteenth- to early twentieth-century Russian state. He is an explorer of Mongolian and Tibetan written heritage and led an Endangered Archives Programme (EAP) project, 'Preservation of the Disappearing Book Heritage of Siberian Buddhists'.

Eleanor Cooper currently works in the Library's digital scholarship team and was Curator of the Mongolian and Manchu collections at the British Library from 2014 to 2018. Her research focuses on the relationships between Mongolian religious and secular art, historiography and nationalism.

Dion Peoples is a foreign expert working with the College of Religious Studies at Mahidol University, Bangkok. He wrote his PhD thesis on the *Sangiti Sutta*, and his current project is a translation of the *Sangiti Sutta* and its commentary and sub-commentary from Pali and Thai into English.

Mélodie Doumy is Curator for Chinese Collections at the British Library. She joined the Library in 2015 to work as a curator and researcher for the International Dunhuang Project (IDP). Her research focuses on the Stein Collection, and her interests include the material cultures of China and the Eastern Silk Road, Buddhism, history of collections and cultural diplomacy.

Gethin Rees is Lead Curator for Digital Mapping at the British Library. He wrote his PhD thesis on the Buddhist rock-cut monasteries of the Western Ghats at the Department of Archaeology, University of Cambridge.

မြတ်စွာဘုရားသာဝင်သည်။ ဉာဏ်တော်အာနန္ဒာ မေးသည်ကို၊

�’’ဘုရား၊’’   ’’ဖြတ်စွာဘုရားသခင်၊’’သည်၊’’သရ၊

REFERENCES AND FURTHER READING

Introduction

App, Urs, *The Cult of Emptiness: The Western Discovery of Buddhist Thought and the Invention of Oriental Philosophy* (Rorschach/Kyoto: University Media, 2012)

Berkwitz, Stephen C., *Buddhist Manuscript Cultures: Knowledge, Ritual and Art* (London: Routledge, 2009)

Cordoni, Constanza and Matthias Meyer, eds, with Nina Hable, *Barlaam und Josaphat: Neue Perspektiven auf ein europäisches Phänomen* (Berlin and Boston: De Gruyter, 2015)

Darlington, Susan M., 'The Ordination of a Tree: The Buddhist Ecology Movement in Thailand', *Ethnology* 37/1 (1998), pp. 1–15

Field, Graham, 'Market Stalinism: Burma, China, Laos, North Korea and Vietnam' in *Economic Growth and Political Change in Asia* (London: Palgrave Macmillan, 1995), pp. 127–151. Online at https://link.springer.com/chapter/10.1007/978-1-349-24189-7_6

Hsing Yun, *Ecology from a Buddhist Perspective* (Los Angeles: Buddha's Light, 2016)

Imhof, Arthur E., *Geschichte sehen. Fünf Erzählungen nach historischen Bildern* (Munich: Beck, 1990)

Mahinda Deegalle, 'Norms of War in Theravada Buddhism' in Vesselin Popovski, Gregory M. Reichberg and Nicholas Turner, eds, *World Religions and Norms of War* (Tokyo, New York and Paris: United Nations University Press, 2009), pp. 60–86

Ozeray, Michel-Jean-François and Urs App, *The First Western Book on Buddhism and Buddha: Ozeray's Recherches sur Buddou of 1817* (Wil/Paris: University Media, 2017)

Radchenko, Sergey, *The Soviet Union and Asia, 1940s–1960s*. Online at http://src-h.slav.hokudai.ac.jp/rp/publications/no09/09_08_Radchenko.pdf

Sulak Sivaraksa, *Conflict, Culture, Change: Engaged Buddhism in a Globalizing World* (Somerville: Wisdom, 2005)

Thich Nhat Hanh, *Interbeing: Fourteen Guidelines for Engaged Buddhism* (Berkeley: Parallax Press, 1993)

Tikhonov, Vladimir and Torkel Brekke, eds, *Buddhism and Violence. Militarisation and Buddhism in Modern Asia* (New York/London: Routledge, 2013)

Wallis, Glenn, *A Critique of Western Buddhism: Ruins of the Buddhist Real* (London: Bloomsbury, 2019)

Chapter 1

Appleton, Naomi K., *Jataka Stories in Theravada Buddhism: Narrating the Bodhisatta Path* (Burlington: Ashgate, 2010)

Appleton, Naomi and Sarah Shaw, *The Ten Great Birth Stories of the Buddha: The Mahanipata of the Jatakatthavannana*, vol. 2 (Chiang Mai: Silkworm Books and Chulalongkorn University Press, 2015)

Beal, Samuel S., trans., *Si-Yu-Ki: Buddhist Records of the Western World, Translated from the Chinese of Hiuen Tsiang (A.D. 629)* (London: Kegan Paul, Trench, Trübner, 1906)

Bowie, Kathryn A., *Of Beggars and Buddhas: The Politics of Humor in the Vessantara Jataka in Thailand* (Madison: University of Wisconsin Press, 2017)

Brown, Robert L., 'Narrative as Icon: The Jataka Stories in Ancient Indian and Southeast Asian Architecture' in Juliane Schober, ed., *Sacred Biography in the Buddhist Traditions of South and Southeast Asia* (Honolulu: University of Hawai'i Press, 1997)

Chiu, Angela S., *The Buddha in Lanna: Art, Lineage, Power, and Place in Northern Thailand* (Honolulu: University of Hawai'i Press, 2017)

Chutiwongs, Nandana, *The Iconography of Avalokitesvara in Mainland South East Asia* (New Delhi: Indira Gandhi National Centre for the Arts and Aryan Books International, 2002)

Cowell, E.B., ed., *The Jataka or Stories of the Buddha's Former Lives*, vol. 1, Robert Chalmers, trans. (Bristol: Pali Text Society, 2013 [1895])

Crosby, Kate, 'Devotion to the Buddha in Theravada and its Role in Meditation' in Anna S. King and John Brockington, eds, *The Intimate Other: Love Divine in Indic Religions* (New Delhi: Orient Longman, 2005), pp. 244–77

Crosby, Kate, *Theravada Buddhism: Continuity, Diversity, and Identity* (Chichester: Wiley Blackwell, 2014)

Dehejia, Vidya, 'Aniconism and the Multivalence of Emblems', *Ars Orientalis* 21 (1991), pp. 45–66

Dehejia, Vidya, 'On Modes of Visual Narration in Early Buddhist Art', *Art Bulletin* 72/3 (Sept. 1992), pp. 374–392

Geiger, Wilhelm, *Culture of Ceylon in Mediaeval Times*, Heinz Bechert, ed. (Wiesbaden: Harrassowitz, 1960)

Geiger, Wilhelm, trans., *The Mahavamsa or The Great Chronicle of Ceylon* (Colombo: Ceylon Government Information Department, 1960)

Gombrich, Richard, 'The Significance of Former Buddhas in the Theravadin Tradition' in Somaratna Balasooriya et al., eds, *Buddhist Studies in Honour of Walpola Rahula* (London: Gordon Fraser, 1980)

Green, Alexandra, *Buddhist Visual Cultures, Rhetoric, and Narrative in Late Burmese Wall Paintings* (Hong Kong: Hong Kong University Press, 2018)

Horner, I.B., trans., *The Minor Anthologies of the Pali Canon, vol. III: Chronicle of Buddhas (Buddhavamsa) and Basket of Conduct (Cariya Pitaka)* (Bristol: Pali Text Society, 2013 [1975])

Huntington, Susan L., 'Aniconism and the Multivalence of Emblems: Another Look', *Ars Orientalis* 22 (1992), pp. 111–156

Inchoetchai, Charuni and Khwanchit Loetsiri, *Phra Bot* [*Buddhist Paintings on Cloth*] (Krung Thep: Samnak Boranakadi lae Phiphitiphan Sathan haeng Chat, 2545 [2002])

Jayawickrama, N.A., trans., *The Story of Gotama Buddha: The Nidana-katha of the Jatakatthakatha* (Oxford: Pali Text Society, 1990)

Kieschnick, John, *The Impact of Buddhism on Chinese Material Culture* (Princeton: Princeton University Press, 2003)

Kinnard, Jacob N., 'Buddhist Iconography' in Lindsay Jones, ed., *Encyclopedia of Religion* (Detroit: Macmillan Reference USA, 2005, 2nd ed.), pp. 4327–4331

Lefferts, Leedom and Sandra Cate, *Buddhist Storytelling in Thailand and Laos: The Vessantara Jataka Scroll at the Asian Civilisations Museum* (Singapore: Asian Civilisations Museum, 2012)

Leidy, Denise Patry, *The Art of Buddhism: An Introduction to Its History and Meaning* (Boston: Shambhala, 2008)

Luce, G.H., 'The 550 Jatakas in Old Burma', *Artibus Asiae* 19 (1956), pp. 291–307

May, San San and Jana Igunma, *Buddhism Illuminated: Manuscript Art from Southeast Asia* (London: British Library, 2018)

McGill, Forrest, 'Jatakas, Universal Monarchs, and the Year 2000', *Artibus Asiae* 53.3/4 (1993), pp. 412–448

Monwithun, Saeng, trans., *Ratanaphimphawong: Tamnan Phra Kaeo Morakot* [*Chronicle of the Emerald Buddha Image*] (Bangkok: Krom Sinlapakon, 2510 [1967])

Reynolds, Frank E. and Charles Hallisey, 'Buddha' in Lindsay Jones, ed., *Encyclopedia of Religion*, 2nd ed. (Detroit: Macmillan Reference USA, 2005), pp. 1059–1071

Schopen, Gregory, 'On Monks, Nuns and "Vulgar" Practices: The Introduction of the Image Cult into Indian Buddhism', *Artibus Asiae* 49 (1988/89), pp. 153–168

Shorto, H. L., 'The Dewatau Sotapan: A Mon Prototype of the 37 Nats', *Bulletin of the School of Oriental and African Studies* 30/1 (1967), pp. 127–141

Skilling, Peter, ed., *Past Lives of the Buddha: Wat Si Chum – Art, Architecture and Inscriptions* (Bangkok: River Books, 2008)

Skilton, Andrew, *A Concise History of Buddhism* (New York: Barnes & Noble Books, 1994)

Strong, John S., 'Buddha Bhakti and the Absence of the Blessed One' in Jacques Ryckmans, ed., *Premier Colloque Etienne Lamotte* (Louvain-la-Neuve: Université Catholique de Louvain, Institut Orientaliste, 1993), pp. 131–140

Strong, John S., *The Buddha: A Short Biography* (Oxford: Oneworld, 2001)

Strong, John S., *Relics of the Buddha* (Princeton: Princeton University Press, 2004)

Strong, John S., *Buddhisms: An Introduction* (London: Oneworld, 2015)

Strong, John S., *The Legend of King Asoka: A Study and Translation of the Asokavadana* (Delhi: Motilal Banarsidass, 2016 [1983])

Tan, Heidi, 'Art, Power, and Merit: The Veneration of Buddha Images in Myanmar Museums' in Sylvia Fraser-Lu and Donald M. Stadtner, eds, *Buddhist Art of Myanmar* (New York: Asia Society, 2015), pp. 81–87

Walshe, Maurice, trans., *The Long Discourses of the Buddha: A Translation of the Digha Nikaya* (Boston: Wisdom, 1987)

Walters, Jonathan S., 'The Buddha's Bad Karma: A Problem in the History of Theravada Buddhism', *Numen* 37/1 (June 1990), pp. 70–95

Walters, Jonathan S., 'Communal Karma and Karmic Community in Theravada Buddhist History' in John Clifford Holt, Jacob N. Kinnard and Jonathan S. Walters, eds, *Constituting Communities: Theravada Buddhism and the Religious Cultures of South and Southeast Asia* (Albany: State University of New York Press, 2003), pp. 9–39

Wang, Eugene Y., *Shaping the Lotus Sutra: Buddhist Visual Culture in Medieval China* (Seattle: University of Washington Press, 2005)

Wang, Quanyu and Sascha Priewe, 'Scientific Analysis of a Buddha Attributed to the Yongle Period of the Ming Dynasty', *British Museum Technical Research Bulletin* 7 (2013), pp. 61–68

Watt, James C.Y. and Denise Patry Leidy, *Defining Yongle: Imperial Art in Early Fifteenth-Century China* (New York: Metropolitan Museum of Art, 2005)

Knox *Lalitavistara*

Catalogue of the Sanskrit and Prakrit Manuscripts of the Library of the India Office, vol. 2, part II (London: 1935)

De Jong, J.W., 'Recent Japanese Studies on the Lalitavistara', *Indologica Taurinensia* XXIII–XXIV, 23–24 (1997–1998), pp. 247–255

Foucaux, Philippe Edouard, *Histoire du Bouddha Sakya Mouni* (Paris, 1860)

O'Keefe, M.J.C., 'Sakyamuni Buddha' in Annabel Teh Gallop, ed., *A Cabinet of Oriental Curiosities: An Album for Graham Shaw from his Colleagues* (London: British Library, 2006)

Losty, J.P., entry 45 in W. Zwalf, ed., *Buddhism: Art and Faith* (London: British Museum, 1985)

The *Lotus Sutra*

Watson, Burton, trans., *The Lotus Sutra* (New York: Columbia University Press, 1993)

Teiser, Stephen F. and Jacqueline I. Stone, eds, *Readings of the Lotus Sutra* (New York: Columbia University Press, 2009)

Tanabe, George J. and Willa Jane Tanabe, *The Lotus Sutra in Japanese Culture* (Honolulu: University of Hawai'i Press, 1989)

Chapter 2

Bhikkhu Analayo, *Dirgha-agama Studies* (Taipei: Dharma Drum, 2017)

Bhikkhu Analayo, *Rebirth in Early Buddhism and Current Research* (Somerville: Wisdom, 2018)

Buswell Jr, Robert E. and Donald S. Lopez Jr, *The Princeton Dictionary of Buddhism* (Princeton and Oxford: Princeton University Press, 2014)

Bogle, James Emanuel, *Buddhist Cosmology: The Study of a Burmese Manuscript* (Chiang Mai: Silkworm, 2016)

Gethin, Rupert, *The Foundations of Buddhism* (Oxford: Oxford University Press, 1998)

Hamar, Imre, 'Buddhavatamsakasutra', in *Brill's Encyclopaedia of Buddhism* (Leiden: Brill, 2015)

Harvey, Peter, 'Buddhas, Past and Future' in Damien Keown and Charles S. Prebish, eds, *Encyclopedia of Buddhism* (London: Routledge, 2007)

Harvey, Peter, *Introduction to Buddhism: Teachings, History and Practices* (Cambridge: Cambridge University Press, 2013, 2nd ed.)

Isaacson, Harunaga and Francesco Sferra, 'Tantric Literature: Overview South Asia' in *Brill's Encyclopaedia of Buddhism* (Leiden: Brill, 2015).

Kabat-Zinn, Jon, *Full Catastrophe Living* (New York: Penguin, 2013)

Kabat-Zinn, Jon, *The Healing Power of Mindfulness* (London: Piatkus, 2018)

Kabat-Zinn, Jon, *Wherever You Go, There You Are: Mindfulness Meditation in Everyday Life* (New York: Hyperion, 2004)

Kloetzli, W. Randolph, *Buddhist Cosmology: Science and Theology in the Images of Motion and Light*, Delhi, 1989)

May, San San and Jana Igunma, *Buddhism Illuminated: Manuscript Art from Southeast Asia* (London: British Library, 2018)

Nyanaponika Thera, *The Heart of Buddhist Meditation: The Buddha's Way of Mindfulness* (San Francisco: Weiser Books, 2014)

Radich, Michael, 'Thathagatagarbha Sutras' in *Brill's*

Encyclopaedia of Buddhism (Leiden: Brill, 2015)

Sadakata, Akira, *Buddhist Cosmology: Philosophy and Origins* (Tokyo: Kosei, 2009, 5th ed.)

Singh, N.K., *Buddhist Cosmology* (Delhi: Global Vision, 2004)

Skilton, Andrew, 'Samadhiraja Sutra' in *Brill's Encyclopaedia of Buddhism* (Leiden: Brill, 2015)

Solomon, Richard, *Ancient Buddhist Scrolls from Gandhara: The British Library Kharosthi Fragments* (Washington: University of Washington Press, 1999)

Spiro, Melford E., *Buddhism and Society: A Great Tradition and its Burmese Vicissitudes* (London: George Allen and Unwin Ltd., 1971)

Zacchetti, Stefano, 'Prajnaparamita Sutra' in *Brill's Encyclopaedia of Buddhism* (Leiden: Brill, 2015)

Tengu no dairi

Kimbrough, R.K., Haruo Shirane, David Atherton, Paul S. Atkins and William Bryant, *Monsters, Animals, and Other Worlds: A Collection of Short Medieval Japanese Tales* (New York: Columbia University Press, 2018)

The *Patimokkha* of the *Bhikku* and *Bhikkhuni*

Kabilsingh, Chatsumarn, *The Bhikkhuni Patimokkha of the Six Schools* (Delhi: Sri Satguru, 1998)

Karma Lekshe Tsomo, *Eminent Buddhist Women* (Albany: State University of New York Press, 2014)

Pruit, William, ed., and K.R. Norman, trans., *The Pratimokkha* (Oxford: Pali Text Society, 2001)

An *Abhidhamma* Commentary in Shan Language

Terwiel, B.J. and Chaichuen Khamdaengyodtai, *Shan Manuscripts, Part One* (Stuttgart: Franz Steiner, 2003)

Grönbold, Günter, *Die Worte des Buddha in den Sprachen der Welt* (Munich: Bavarian State Library, 2005)

Chapter 3

Buswell Jr, Robert E. and Donald S. Lopez Jr, *The Princeton Dictionary of Buddhism* (Princeton: Princeton University Press, 2014)

Cleary, Thomas, trans., *The Flower Ornament Scripture: A Translation of the Avatamsaka Sutra* (Boston and London: Shambhala, 1993)

Edgren, Sören, *Chinese Rare Books in American Collections* (New York: China House Gallery, 1984)

Elliott, Mark and James Canary, *Buddha's Word: The Life of Books in Tibet and Beyond* (Cambridge: Cambridge University Museum of Anthropology and Archaeology, 2014)

Gombrich, Richard, *How Buddhism Began: The Conditioned Genesis of the Early Teachings* (London: Routledge, 2006, 2nd ed.)

Guy, John, *Palm Leaf and Paper: Illustrated Manuscripts of India and Southeast Asia* (Melbourne: National Gallery of Victoria, 1982)

Helman-Wazny, Agnieszka, *The Archaeology of Tibetan Books, Tibetan Studies Library* vol. 36 (Leiden: Brill, 2013)

Legge, James, trans., *A Record of Buddhistic Kingdoms: Being an Account by the Chinese Monk Fa-Hien of his Travels in India and Ceylon* (Oxford: Clarendon Press, 1886). Online at http://onlinebooks.library.upenn.edu/webbin/gutbook/lookup?-num=2124

Pal, Pratapaditya and Julia Meech-Pekarik, *Buddhist Book Illuminations* (New York: Ravi Kumar, 1988)

Skilton, Andrew, *A Concise History of Buddhism* (Birmingham: Windhorse, 1994)

Suarez, Michael F. and H.R. Woudhuysen, *The Book: A Global History* (Oxford: Oxford University Press, 2013)

Takakusu, Junjirō and Kaigyoku Watanabe, eds, *The Taisho shinshu daizokyo*, 100 vols (first ed.; Tokyo: Taisho shinshu daizokyo kanko kai, 1924, repr. 1962)

Van Schaik, Sam and Imre Galambos, *Manuscripts and Travellers: The Sino-Tibetan Documents of a Tenth-Century Pilgrim* (Berlin: De Gruyter, 2011)

Watson, Burton, trans., *The Lotus Sutra* (New York: Columbia University Press, 1993)

Wu, Jiang and Greg Wilkinson, eds, *Reinventing the Tripitaka: Transformation of the Buddhist Canon in Modern East Asia* (Lanham: Lexington, 2017)

Zwalf, W., ed., *Buddhism: Art and Faith* (exhibition catalogue; London: The British Museum, 1985)

From the Translator's Workshop

Takasaki, Jikido, 'Some Problems of the Tibetan Translations from Chinese Material' in Louis Ligeti, ed., *Proceedings of the Csoma de Koros Memorial Symposium* (Budapest: Akademiai Kiado, 1978), pp. 459–467

Ueyama, Daishun, *Tonko bukkyo no kenkyu* (Kyoto: Hozokan, 1990)

Searching for Surviving Buddhist Manuscripts in Siberia

Kara, Gyorgy, *Books of the Mongolian Nomads: More than Eight Centuries of Writing Mongolian* (Bloomington, IN: Indiana University Press, 2005)

Bernstein, Anna, 'Buddhist Revival in Buriatia: Recent Perspectives' in *Mongolian Studies* 25, pp. 1–11

Zhukovskaia, Nataliia L., 'The Revival of Buddhism in Buryatia' in Marjorie Mandelstam Balzer, ed., *Religion and Politics in Russia: A Reader* (Abingdon: Routledge, 2015), pp. 197–215

The Qianlong Emperor's Anthology of *Dharanis* in Manchu, Chinese, Mongolian and Tibetan

Berger, Patricia Ann, *Empire of Emptiness: Buddhist Art and Political Authority in Qing China* (Honolulu: University of Hawai'i Press, 2003)

Elverskog, Johan, *Our Great Qing: The Mongols, Buddhism and the State in Late Imperial China* (Honolulu: University of Hawai'i Press, 2006)

Farquhar, David M., 'Emperor as Bodhisattva in the Governance of the Ch'ing Empire', *Harvard Journal of Asiatic Studies* 38(1), pp. 5–34

Grupper, Samuel Martin, 'Manchu Patronage and Tibetan Buddhism During the First Half of the Ch'ing Dynasty: A Review Article', *Journal of the Tibet Society* 4, pp. 41–75

Perdue, Peter C., *China Marches West: The Qing Conquest of Central Eurasia* (Cambridge, MA: Belknap Press of Harvard University Press, 2005)

Chapter 4

Bhikkhu Bodhi, *The Connected Discourses of the Buddha: A Translation of the Samyutta Nikaya* (Somerville: Wisdom, 2003)

Bhikkhu Bodhi, *The Numerical Discourses of the Buddha: A Translation of the Anguttara Nikaya* (Boston: Wisdom, 2012)

Gunaratana, Henepola, *The Path of Serenity and Insight: An Explanation of Buddhist Jhanas* (Delhi: Motilal Banarsidass, 2016)

Narada, Mahathera, *A Manual of Sbhidhamma: Being Abhidhammattha Sangaha of Bhadanta Anuruddhacariya. Edited in the Original Pali Text with English Translation and Explanatory Notes* (Kandy: Buddhist Publication Society, 1968)

Peoples, Dion Oliver, *Chanting the Sangiti Sutta* (Bangkok: Mahachulalongkornrajavidyalaya University, 2012)

Peoples, Dion Oliver, *Advanced Analytical Assessment of Buddhist Critical Thinking Skills and Additional Philosophical Concerns or Perspectives for the Field of Critical Thinking* (Bangkok: Mahachulalongkornrajavidyalaya University, 2014)

Payutto, Prayudh and Robin P. Moore, *Buddhadhamma: The Laws of Nature and Their Benefits to Life* (Bangkok: Buddhadhamma Foundation, 2017)

Takakusu, Junjiro, trans., *A Record of the Buddhist Religion as Practised in India and the Malay Archipelago (AD 671–695) by I-Tsing* (Delhi: Munshiram Manoharlal, 1966)

Walshe, Maurice, *The Long Discourses of the Buddha: A Translation of the Digha Nikaya* (Boston: Wisdom, 2012)

Illustrated Manuscript of the *Guanyin Sutra*

Chang, Cornelius P., 'Kuan-Yin Paintings from Tunhuang: Water-Moon Kuan-Yin', *JOOS*, vol. 15 (1977), pp. 141–160

Watson, Burton, trans., *The Lotus Sutra* (New York: Columbia University Press, 1993)

Whitfield, Susan and Ursula Sims-Williams, eds, *The Silk Road: Trade, Travel, War and Faith* (London: British Library, 2004), pp. 244–245

Yü, Chün-fang, *Kuan-yin: The Chinese Transformation of Avalokitesvara* (New York: Columbia University Press, 2001)

The Bhaja Stupas: Henry Cousens' View

Almond, Philip C., *The British Discovery of Buddhism* (Cambridge: Cambridge University Press, 1988)

Burgess, James and James Fergusson, *Cave Temples of India* (London: W.H. Allen, 1880)

Chakrabarti, Dilip K., *A History of Indian Archaeology from the Beginning to 1947* (New Delhi: Munshiram Manoharlal, 1988)

Cousens, Henry, 'The Antiquities of Sind: With Historical Outline', *Archaeological Survey of India, Imperial Series*, vol. 46 (Calcutta: Government of India, 1929)

Fogelin, Lars, 'The Place of Veneration in Early South Asian Buddhism' in Sarah Tarlow and Liv Nilsson Stutz, eds, *The Oxford Handbook of the Archaeology of Death and Burial* (Oxford: Oxford University Press, 2013), pp. 227–241

Michell, George and Gethin Rees, *Buddhist Rock-cut Monasteries of the Western Ghats* (Mumbai: Jaico, 2017)

Nagaraju, S., *Buddhist Architecture of Western India* (Delhi: Agam Kala Prakashan, 1981)

Schopen, Gregory, 'Burial "ad sanctos" and the Physical Presence of the Buddha in Early Indian Buddhism: A Study in the Archeology of Religions', *Religion* 17 (1987), pp. 193–225

Singh, Upinder, *The Discovery of Ancient India* (Delhi: Permanent Black, 2004)

A Khmer Meditation Manual

Buddhadāsa Bhikkhu, *Siamesische Illustrationen der Buddhalehre* (Tübingen/Basel: Horst Erdmann Verlag, 1969)

Mahasatipatthana Sutta (Pali–English version), online at http://www.tipitaka.org/stp-pali-eng-parallel

Rhys Davids, T.W., *The Yogavacara's Manual of Indian Mysticism as Practiced by Buddhists* (London: Pali Text Society, 1896)

Skilling, Peter, 'The Aesthetics of Devotion: Buddhist Arts of Thailand' in Heidi Tan, ed., *Enlightened Ways: The Many Streams of Buddhist Art in Thailand* (Singapore: Asian Civilisations Museum, 2012), pp. 18–31

Soma Thera, *The Way of Mindfulness: The Satipatthana Sutta and its Commentary*, 30 November 2013, online at http://www.access-toinsight.org/lib/authors/soma/wayof.html

Story, Francis, *Dimensions of Buddhist Thought: Collected Essays* (Kandy: Buddhist Publication Society, 2011), 3 vols.

Story, Francis, 'Buddhist Meditation' (from *The Anagarika Sugatananda*), 24 November 2013, online at http://www.accesstoinsight.org/lib/authors/story/bl015.html

။အပွမ်လိက်မသည်။လှ္ယ်ကဆင်းၾၖျ၊။မြတ်စွား။

Illustration Credits

PAGES 204–205, 212–213, 222–223:
Scenes depicting the later years of the Buddha's life during his long ministry of forty years. Burma, 19th century.
British Library, Or.13534, ff. 3, 7, 15.

INDEX

Page references in *italic* are to illustrations

မြတ်စွာသုရားသခင်သည်။လိ

ဝင်း...င်္ဂိုရာဝတ်ိုကိုတရားတော်ဝေါဟာဟံ။ ၊